The
Synoptic
Problem

The Synoptic Problem

FOUR VIEWS

Edited by
Stanley E. Porter
and Bryan R. Dyer

Baker Academic
a division of Baker Publishing Group
Grand Rapids, Michigan

Published by Baker Academic
a division of Baker Publishing Group
P.O. Box 6287, Grand Rapids, MI 49516-6287
www.bakeracademic.com

Printed in the United States of America

Library of Congress Cataloging-in-Publication Data
Names: Porter, Stanley E., 1956– editor.
Title: The synoptic problem : four views / edited by Stanley E. Porter and Bryan R. Dyer.
Description: Grand Rapids : Baker Academic, 2016. | Includes bibliographical references and index.
Identifiers: LCCN 2016013302 | ISBN 9780801049507 (pbk.)
Subjects: LCSH: Synoptic problem. | Bible. Gospels—Criticism, interpretation, etc.
Classification: LCC BS2555.52 .S96 2016 | DDC 226/.066—dc23
LC record available at http://lccn.loc.gov/2016013302

Unless indicated otherwise, Scripture translations are those of the authors.

16 17 18 19 20 21 22   7 6 5 4 3 2 1

Contents

Preface

The Synoptic Problem continues to fascinate biblical scholars and students of the New Testament, with no end in sight so far as arriving at a final solution or even a truce in the ongoing debate. This is the environment in which we offer this volume as a contribution to the continuing discussion. The current form of the discussion presents four major views of the Synoptic Problem. These are the Two Source Hypothesis, the Farrer Hypothesis, the Two Gospel Hypothesis, and the Orality and Memory Hypothesis. Each hypothesis has points of overlap with the others, but each one also has a distinct viewpoint on resolution of the major questions. As a result, it is our privilege to publish this introduction to the topic, with fresh articulations and interactions by leading proponents of each of the major views. We are grateful to each of the four scholars—Craig A. Evans, Mark Goodacre, David Barrett Peabody, and Rainer Riesner—for their excellent essays and constructive responses. We have enjoyed working with each of these scholars and hope that the model that they provide in this volume—one of respect despite differing viewpoints—will encourage future discussion on this topic.

The opening chapter of this volume sets the stage for the discussion of the Synoptic Problem. Students new to the issue will find a presentation of the critical issues, the key terms, a brief history of scholarship, and an introduction to the four views that follow. We then offer the major proposals by each of the proponents of their viewpoints. These four positive proposals are followed by a response to the other three by each of the major proponents. A concluding chapter offers an assessment of the discussion and lays out ways forward in scholarship on the Synoptic Problem. These opening and concluding chapters frame the discussion of the multiple views by placing it within a historical context and assisting in finding agreements and points of departure among the four proponents. We trust that readers will find value in these summative chapters.

This is the second collaborative work that we as the editors have engaged in together. We have found it a rewarding experience to be able to work together on a project of such importance to the field of New Testament studies that we value so highly. We are grateful for the opportunity to collaborate.

We also offer sincere thanks to James Ernest, our editor at Baker Academic, and to the entire team there, including Jim Kinney and Tim West. Finally, we wish to extend our deepest appreciation to our wives, Wendy Porter and Anna Dyer, for their ongoing support and encouragement.

Abbreviations

1QS	1QRule of the Community	CCS	Classical Culture and Society
1QSa	1QRule of the Congregation	CD	Cairo Genizah copy of the Damascus Document
11QPs^a	11QPsalms^a		
AB	Anchor Bible	ConBNT	Coniectanea Biblica: New Testament Series
ABD	*Anchor Bible Dictionary*. Edited by D. N. Freedman. 6 vols. New York, 1992.		
		Cont. Life	Philo, *On the Contemplative Life*
		COQG	Christian Origins and the Question of God
Ag. Ap.	Josephus, *Against Apion*		
Ant.	Josephus, *Jewish Antiquities*	*Dreams*	Philo, *On Dreams*
ASBT	Acadia Studies in Bible and Theology	ÉB	Études bibliques
		EChr	*Early Christianity*
AT	author's translation	*Embassy*	Philo, *On the Embassy to Gaius*
BAG	Bauer, W., W. F. Arndt, and F. W. Gingrich. *Greek-English Lexicon of the New Testament and Other Early Christian Literature*. Chicago, 1957.	*1 En.*	*1 Enoch (Ethiopic Apocalypse)*
		ET	English translation
		ExpTim	*Expository Times*
		FAT	Forschungen zum Alten Testament
BECNT	Baker Exegetical Commentary on the New Testament	HermSup	Hermeneia Supplements
		HSCL	Harvard Studies in Comparative Literature
BETL	Bibliotheca ephemeridum theologicarum lovaniensium		
		JBL	*Journal of Biblical Literature*
b. Hag.	Babylonian Talmud, tractate Hagigah	*JECS*	*Journal of Early Christian Studies*
BibSem	Biblical Seminar	*Jos. Asen.*	*Joseph and Aseneth*
BNTC	Black's New Testament Commentaries	*JSHJ*	*Journal for the Study of the Historical Jesus*
BRS	Biblical Resource Series	JSNTSup	Journal for the Study of the New Testament: Supplement Series
BZNW	Beihefte zur Zeitschrift für die neutestamentliche Wissenschaft		
		Jub.	*Jubilees*
CamCS	Cambridge Classical Studies	*J.W.*	Josephus, *Jewish War*

KEK	Kritisch-exegetischer Kommentar über das Neue Testament (Meyer-Kommentar)	SAC	Studies in Antiquity and Christianity
KTAH	Key Themes in Ancient History	SBLECL	Society of Biblical Literature Early Christianity and Its Literature
LCL	Loeb Classical Library		
LD	Lectio Divina	SemeiaSt	Semeia Studies
Life	Josephus, *The Life*	SJSJ	Supplements to the Journal for the Study of Judaism
LNTS	The Library of New Testament Studies		
		SLFCS	Studies in Literacy, Family, Culture, and the State
LXX	Septuagint		
m. Abot	Mishnah, tractate *Abot*	SNTSMS	Society for New Testament Studies Monograph Series
MNTS	McMaster New Testament Studies		
		SNTW	Studies of the New Testament and Its World
MP	Myth and Poetics		
m. Shab.	Mishnah, tractate *Shabbat*	*T. Abr.*	*Testament of Abraham*
NA	New Accents	TANZ	Texte und Arbeiten zum neutestamentlichen Zeitalter
NA²⁸	Nestle-Aland, *Novum Testamentum Graece*. 28th ed. Stuttgart: Deutsche Bibelgesellschaft, 2012.		
		TD	*Theology Digest*
		T. Dan	*Testament of Dan*
NGS	New Gospel Studies	TI	Theological Inquiries
NovT	*Novum Testamentum*	*T. Levi*	*Testament of Levi*
NovTSup	Supplements to Novum Testamentum	TSAJ	Texte und Studien zum antiken Judentum
NPNF²	*Nicene and Post-Nicene Fathers*, Series 2	TSJTSA	Texts and Studies of the Jewish Theological Seminary of America
NTS	*New Testament Studies*		
PL	Patrologia Latina [= Patrologiae Cursus Completus: Series Latina]. Edited by J.-P. Migne. 217 vols. Paris, 1844–64.	*TSK*	*Theologische Studien und Kritiken*
		TTKi	*Tidsskrift for Teologi og Kirke*
		WBC	Word Biblical Commentary
RBL	*Review of Biblical Literature*	WUNT	Wissenschaftliche Untersuchungen zum Neuen Testament
RBS	Resources for Biblical Study		
RSV	Revised Standard Version		

1

The Synoptic Problem

An Introduction to Its Key Terms, Concepts, Figures, and Hypotheses

Stanley E. Porter and Bryan R. Dyer

The Unity and Diversity of the Four Gospels

The New Testament begins with four accounts of the life, teaching, and death of Jesus of Nazareth. These accounts, or Gospels, are formally anonymous but throughout the history of the Christian Church have been attributed to four writers: Matthew, Mark, Luke, and John. All four Gospels tell a similar story about Jesus: he came from Nazareth; he was announced by John the Baptist; he had twelve disciples, taught them many things, and performed a variety of healings; his disciple Judas betrayed him; he was crucified and raised from the dead. Numerous events are told in all four Gospels: the baptism of Jesus, the miraculous feeding of five thousand people, Jesus's triumphal entry into Jerusalem, Peter's confession, and many events surrounding Jesus's death (his arrest, trial, and burial). There is strong agreement among the four Gospels regarding who Jesus was, his historical context, and the theological significance of his life. Broadly speaking, each Gospel writer paints a similar portrait of Jesus.

Yet, while these Gospels provide similar accounts, they are also four separate and distinct Gospels. This may seem obvious, but it is not uncommon for the four Gospels to be conflated into one narrative. The most common example of this is the imagery and retelling of the nativity scene surrounding the birth of Jesus, reenacted every Christmas season.[1] Almost any person sitting in a pew during a Christmas service can describe the scene: Mary and Joseph travel to Bethlehem, where Jesus is born and placed in a manger in the presence of farm animals, angels, shepherds, magi offering gifts, and a bright star above. It is a familiar scene, but one that takes bits and pieces found in different Gospel retellings. In fact, only two Gospels—Matthew and Luke—contain accounts of Jesus's birth; Mark's Gospel begins with Jesus's baptism, and John's Gospel begins on a cosmic scale, describing the divine *logos*. Luke's is the only Gospel to situate the newborn Jesus in a manger and the only one to include shepherds. While Matthew's Gospel similarly places Jesus's birth in Bethlehem, it is the only Gospel to give the account of magi following a star and presenting gifts of frankincense, gold, and myrrh.

This illustrates the great benefit of having four Gospel accounts. Mark's Gospel, for whatever reason, does not include a description of the birth of Jesus. If it were the only Gospel we had, we would know little of the various traditions surrounding Jesus's birth. Fortunately, Matthew and Luke, while sharing several details, both offer unique descriptions that represent differing traditions of Jesus's birth.[2] However, it is not always the case that each Gospel either shares the exact information with the other Gospels or provides brand-new information not otherwise accounted for. It is often the case that these Gospels provide the same account but offer differing viewpoints or provide specific information unique to the Gospel. All four Gospels, for example, describe the person Barabbas, the prisoner whom the crowd chooses to receive freedom instead of Jesus at his trial (Matt. 27:15–23; Mark 15:6–14; Luke 23:17–23; John 18:39–40). In his Gospel, Matthew describes Barabbas as a notorious prisoner (Matt. 27:16); Mark and Luke describe him as a murderer who started an insurrection (Mark 15:7; Luke 23:19); John simply notes that he was a robber (John 18:40). These descriptions of Barabbas need not conflict with one another; he may have been a notorious prisoner who started an insurrection and was guilty of murder and theft. But it is curious that each

---

1. This illustration is also provided in the opening of Mark Goodacre's introduction to the Synoptic Problem: *The Synoptic Problem: A Way through the Maze*, BibSem 80 (London: Sheffield Academic Press, 2001), 13.

2. The relationship between these two accounts has been the subject of much speculation and, in some circles, major controversy. The theories that have been proposed variously argue for independence or various types of dependence.

Gospel writer chose the description that he did. If Barabbas were a known murderer, why would Matthew and John not mention this?

The differences between the Gospels regarding Barabbas may seem insignificant, but what are we to do with even greater differences that we encounter in the four accounts? Each of the Gospel writers describes Jesus's cleansing of the temple, but should we understand that it happened right at the beginning of Jesus's public ministry (John 2:14–22) or at the end of his ministry while in Jerusalem (Matt. 21:12–13; Mark 11:15–17; Luke 19:45–46)? Did Jesus cleanse the temple on two occasions? Or, when Jesus miraculously fed five thousand people, should we understand it as occurring in the city of Bethsaida (Luke 9:10), on a mountain near the Sea of Galilee (John 6:1–3), or in an uninhabited, deserted place (Matt. 14:13; Mark 6:32)? Most readers who have spent significant time with the four Gospels have asked these or similar questions. What is the relationship of the Gospels to one another? Why do some stories appear in multiple Gospels and others in only one? What are we to do with the differences between accounts, whether minor points or more significant variations?

Harmony and Harmonization

In the middle of the second century, within a hundred years of the Gospels' compositions, a Syrian Christian by the name of Tatian created the earliest known attempt to smooth out the differences of the four Gospels into one single narrative. Titled *Diatessaron* (meaning "through the four"), Tatian's work is the first of what has become known as a **harmony** of the Gospels.[3] Tatian's harmony wove together main sections from all four Gospels into one continuous story and essentially became the Gospel manuscript used throughout Syria into the fifth century. No full copies of the *Diatessaron* exist today (Theodoret, bishop of Cyrrhus in the fifth century, destroyed over two hundred copies out of orthodox zeal), but various later versions and commentaries on it remain, and numerous early Christian writers refer to it.

The *Diatessaron* was probably not the first and certainly not the last attempt to harmonize the Gospels.[4] In fact, it is a popular approach to addressing the

3. On Tatian's *Diatessaron*, see Bruce M. Metzger, *The Text of the New Testament: Its Transmission, Corruption, and Restoration*, 2nd ed. (New York: Oxford University Press, 1968), 89–92; Robert H. Stein, *Studying the Synoptic Gospels: Origin and Interpretation*, 2nd ed. (Grand Rapids: Baker Academic, 2001), 18; Stanley E. Porter, *How We Got the New Testament: Text, Transmission, Translation*, ASBT (Grand Rapids: Baker Academic, 2013), 88–93.

4. Justin Martyr (100–165 CE) may have been the first to construct a harmony of the Synoptic Gospels.

differences that appear within the Gospel accounts. Another famous example is Andreas Osiander's *Harmoniae Evangelicae*, published in 1537, which similarly combined the four Gospel accounts into one seamless narrative. Unlike Tatian's harmony, however, it was common for Osiander to interpret differing accounts of a similar incident as indications of two (or more) separate occasions. So, for example, Jesus is presented as raising Jairus's daughter twice, and Peter is portrayed as denying Jesus nine times instead of three.

Today few follow Osiander to the extent that he went to disprove any potential contradictory elements in the Gospels, but harmonization remains an approach to explaining at least some of the differences encountered when surveying the Gospels. **Harmonization,** then, refers to *the attempt to reconcile seeming contradictions in the Gospels by arguing that the Gospel writers are describing separate events or different aspects of a single event.*[5] The opening example of combining the birth narratives of Jesus into one story is an illustration of harmonization. In the last two centuries harmonization has been approached with skepticism, although it is often pointed out that any re-creation of any historical event involves some level of harmonization of sources.

A Synopsis and the Synoptics

In order to compare the Gospels and assess their similarities and differences, a tool called a **synopsis** is often utilized. A synopsis (from the Greek *syn,* "with," + *opsis,* "seeing") presents parallel texts from each of the Gospels side by side in vertical columns in order to compare and contrast the individual accounts. Table 1.1 indicates what a synopsis might look like for the passages describing the confrontation at Jesus's arrest.

Table 1.1. Jesus Arrested

Matthew 26:51–52	Mark 14:47	Luke 22:49–51	John 18:10–11
		And when those who were about him saw what would follow, they said, "Lord shall we strike with the sword?"	
And behold, one of those who were with	But one of those who stood by	And one of them	Then Simon Peter, having a sword,

5. See Craig L. Blomberg, "The Legitimacy and Limits of Harmonization," in *Hermeneutics, Authority, and Canon,* ed. D. A. Carson and John D. Woodbridge (Grand Rapids: Academie, 1986), 144.

Matthew 26:51–52	Mark 14:47	Luke 22:49–51	John 18:10–11
Jesus stretched out his hand and drew his sword, and struck the slave of the high priest, and cut off his ear.	drew his sword, and struck the slave of the high priest and cut off his ear.	struck the slave of the high priest and cut off his right ear.	drew it and struck the high priest's slave and cut off his right ear. The slave's name was Malchus.
Then Jesus said to him, "Put your sword back into its place; for all who take the sword will perish by the sword."		But Jesus said, "No more of this!" And he touched his ear and healed him.	Jesus said to Peter, "Put your sword into its sheath; shall I not drink the cup which the Father has given me?"

A synopsis is set up so that similar material appears horizontally; in this way, it aids in seeing where and how the Gospel writers include both similar and different materials in their discourses. So in the example above, it becomes obvious that while all four accounts mention the high priest's slave's ear being cut off, only two (Luke and John) specify that it was his right ear. Similarly, all four Gospels make clear that the person with the sword was standing by Jesus, but only John's Gospel attributes the act to Simon Peter. Only Matthew's Gospel contains the famous saying that those who "take the sword will perish by the sword." Only Luke's Gospel mentions that Jesus heals the slave, while John is the only Gospel writer to identify the slave's name.

In many ways, synopses developed out of the popularity of harmonies as scholars attempted to analyze and make sense of the variation found within the Gospel accounts. The first synopsis proper—that is, one that was not created for the intent of harmonizing the Gospels—was composed by Johann Jakob Griesbach in 1776. Numerous synopses have appeared since the eighteenth century (many of them still called harmonies), many of them by some of the best-known New Testament scholars. Some of the most notable are from Wilhelm de Wette and Friedrich Lücke, Constantine Tischendorf, Ernest De Witt Burton and Edgar J. Goodspeed, Albert Huck, H. F. D. Sparks, Burton H. Throckmorton, John Bernard Orchard, and Robert W. Funk.[6] The

6. See John S. Kloppenborg, "Synopses and the Synoptic Problem," in *New Studies in the Synoptic Problem: Oxford Conference, April 2008; Essays in Honour of Christopher M. Tuckett*, ed. Paul Foster et al., BETL 239 (Leuven: Peeters, 2011), 51–85; J. K. Elliott, "Which Is the Best Synopsis?," *ExpTim* 102 (1991): 200–204.

most widely used synopsis today is *Synopsis of the Four Gospels* by Kurt Aland (also available in Greek).[7]

One thing that becomes immediately apparent when looking at a synopsis of all four Gospels is that Matthew, Mark, and Luke contain a good deal of similar material. These three Gospels share many of the same stories, often in similar order and utilizing the same wording. They are so alike that they have been given the name "Synoptic Gospels" to emphasize their similarities. Furthermore, the term **Synoptic Gospels** differentiates Matthew, Mark, and Luke from John's Gospel, which has numerous unique accounts and often uses different wording when telling a similar story. Relatively few pages in a synopsis of the Gospels contain material from all four Gospels. The bulk of material is shared by the Synoptic Gospels, while the material found in John's Gospel is often by itself.

The Similarities of the Synoptic Gospels

The Gospels of Matthew, Mark, and Luke have been identified as having such strong similarities that they are often grouped together and understood as related to one another in some special way other than the way they relate to John's Gospel. But what are these similarities, and what do they tell us of the relationships between the Synoptic Gospels? At least four types of similarities in the Synoptic Gospels point to some kind of relationship. First, there is the sheer amount of material shared by these Gospels. While it is not always apparent what constitutes "shared material," it is abundantly clear that the Synoptic Gospel writers shared the same stories, sayings, and accounts of Jesus and his followers. Second, the wording found within this shared material is often so alike that some type of relationship between Gospels seems to be evident. Third, the order of each Gospel, along with how each author presents his material, is so similar that some form of influence between Gospels is often suggested. Fourth, there are editorial or parenthetical comments found in multiple Gospels at exactly the same place, which is difficult to account for if the Gospel writers wrote independently of one another. Each of these types of material warrants further comment.

Shared Material

If one looks closely at a synopsis of the Gospels, it is clear that many of the same stories are told in the Synoptic Gospels. In fact, numerous scholars

7. Kurt Aland, ed., *Synopsis of the Four Gospels*, 10th ed. (New York: United Bible Societies, 1993); Aland, ed., *Synopsis Quattuor Evangeliorum* (Stuttgart: Deutsche Bibelgesellschaft, 2005).

have estimated that over 90 percent of Mark's Gospel is shared with either Matthew or Luke or with both. In fact, nearly all of that 90 percent of Mark is found in Matthew's Gospel, while roughly 50 percent of Mark's Gospel is found in Luke. Nearly 60 percent of Matthew is shared with the other two Gospels; around 40 percent of Luke is shared.[8] Of the roughly 665 verses in Mark's Gospel, over 600 appear in some form in Matthew or Luke. Additionally, Matthew and Luke share over 230 verses not found in Mark. Often it is useful to look not only at verses but also at the different stories or sayings found in the Gospels. The term **pericope** (pl. pericopae) refers to a collection of verses that form a contained unit in the text—a speech of Jesus, miracle account, or other episode in the narrative. Mark's Gospel can be divided into eighty-eight pericopae; of those eighty-eight, only five do not appear in either the Gospel of Matthew or the Gospel of Luke.

Material that appears in all three Synoptic Gospels is called the **triple tradition**. The bulk of this material is narrative, but it does contain some sayings of Jesus as well.

Table 1.2. The Triple Tradition

Pericope*	Matthew	Mark	Luke
John's Messianic Preaching	3:11–12	1:7–8	3:15–18
The Baptism of Jesus	3:13–17	1:9–11	3:21–22
The Temptation	4:1–11	1:12–13	4:1–13
Peter's Confession	16:13–20	8:27–30	9:18–21
Jesus Heals a Boy Possessed by a Spirit	17:14–21	9:14–29	9:37–43a
Jesus Blesses the Children	19:13–15	10:13–16	18:15–17
The Rich Young Man	19:16–22	10:17–22	18:18–23
The Triumphal Entry	21:1–9	11:1–10	19:28–40
The Parable of the Wicked Husbandmen	21:33–46	12:1–12	20:9–19
The Betrayal by Judas	26:14–16	14:10–11	22:3–6
The Trial before Pilate	27:11–14	15:2–5	23:2–5

*The names of pericopae are taken from Aland, *Synopsis of the Four Gospels.*

Since 90 percent of Mark is found in Matthew and 50 percent is found in Luke, some material shared by Matthew and Mark is not in Luke. A good

8. The statistics in this section are taken from Bruce M. Metzger, *The New Testament: Its Background, Growth, and Content* (Nashville: Abingdon, 1965), 80–81; Brooke Foss Westcott, *An Introduction to the Study of the Gospels*, 8th ed. (London: Macmillan, 1895), 195–97; Donald A. Hagner, *The New Testament: A Historical and Theological Introduction* (Grand Rapids: Baker Academic, 2012), 132.

chunk of this material (Matt. 14:22–16:12//Mark 6:45–8:26)[9] has been titled Luke's "great omission." Some material that Mark and Luke share is not present in Matthew's Gospel, including the account of the chief priests conspiring against Jesus (Mark 11:18–19//Luke 19:47–48).

Over 230 verses found in Matthew and Luke are absent from Mark's Gospel. This material is often called the **double tradition** and has a high percentage of sayings of Jesus (including Matthew's Sermon on the Mount and Luke's Sermon on the Plain) but some narrative elements as well. As we will see, the double tradition is a key issue in how scholars have understood the relationships between the Synoptic Gospels. There is, of course, material found in either Luke or Matthew that has no parallel in the other Synoptics. This is often called **Special Matthew** (or **M**) and **Special Luke** (or **L**) and includes each Gospel's unique birth narrative, resurrection account, numerous parables, and narrative material.

Close Wording in Shared Material

Not only do the Synoptic Gospels share an abundant amount of material, but also in many places the wording in each Gospel is so similar as to suggest some type of close relationship. As an example, consider the account of Jesus being questioned about his authority. In the synopsis below, underlining marks identical wording in all three Gospels, broken underlining refers to identical wording in two Gospels, and squiggly underlining refers to very similar wording in two or more Gospels.

Table 1.3. Jesus Questioned about His Authority

Matthew 21:23–27	Mark 11:27–33	Luke 20:1–8
	Again they came to Jerusalem.	One day, as
When he entered	As he was walking	he was teaching the people
the temple,	in the temple,	in the temple
		and telling the good news,
the chief priests	the chief priests,	the chief priests and
	the scribes,	the scribes came with
and the elders of the people	and the elders came to him	the elders
came to him as he was		
teaching,		
and said,	and said,	and said to him, "Tell us,
"By what authority are you	"By what authority are you	by what authority are you
doing these things, and	doing these things?	doing these things? Who is it
who gave you this authority?"	Who gave you this authority to	who gave you this authority?"
	do them?"	

9. The two virgules, //, identify parallel material found in the indicated Gospels.

Matthew 21:23–27	Mark 11:27–33	Luke 20:1–8
Jesus said to them, "I will also ask you one question; if you tell me the answer, then I will also tell you by what authority I do these things.	Jesus said to them, "I will ask you one question; answer me, and I will tell you by what authority I do these things.	He answered them, "I will also ask you a question, and you tell me:
Did the baptism of John come from heaven, or was it of human origin?"	Did the baptism of John come from heaven, or was it of human origin? Answer me."	Did the baptism of John come from heaven, or was it of human origin?"
And they argued with one another,	They argued with one another,	They discussed it with one another, saying,
"If we say, 'From heaven,' he will say to us, 'Why then did you not believe him?'	"If we say, 'From heaven,' he will say, 'Why then did you not believe him?'	"If we say, 'From heaven,' he will say, 'Why did you not believe him?'
But if we say, 'Of human origin,' we are afraid of the crowd; for all regard John as a prophet."	But shall we say, 'Of human origin'?" —they were afraid of the crowd, for all regarded John as truly a prophet.	But if we say, 'Of human origin,' all the people will stone us; for they are convinced that John was a prophet."
So they answered Jesus, "We do not know."	So they answered Jesus, "We do not know."	So they answered that they did not know where it came from.
And he said to them, "Neither will I tell you by what authority I am doing these things.	And Jesus said to them, "Neither will I tell you by what authority I am doing these things."	Then Jesus said to them, "Neither will I tell you by what authority I am doing these things."

In this example we see how often the three Gospel writers use exactly or nearly the same wording in their accounts. In this particular example what jumps out is how often quotations from both Jesus and his opponents are the parts that are so close in wording across the three Gospels.

As another example, consider the calling of Levi:

Table 1.4. The Calling of Levi

Matthew 9:9–10	Mark 2:13–15	Luke 5:27–32
As Jesus passed on from there, he saw a man called Matthew sitting at the tax office; and he said to him, "Follow me."	And as he passed on, he saw Levi the son of Alphaeus sitting at the tax office, and he said to him, "Follow me."	After this he went out, and saw a tax collector, named Levi, sitting at the tax office; and he said to him, "Follow me."
		And he left everything,
And he rose and followed him.	And he rose and followed him.	and rose and followed him.
And as he sat at table in the house, behold,	And as he sat at table in his house,	And Levi made him a great feast in his house; and there was a
many tax collectors and sinners	many tax collectors and sinners	large company of tax collectors

Matthew 9:9–10	Mark 2:13–15	Luke 5:27–32
came and sat down with Jesus and his disciples.	were sitting with Jesus and his disciples; for there were many who followed him.	and others sitting at the table with them.

Here again we see exact wording, not just in quotations, but also in narrative descriptions ("sitting at the tax office," "rose and followed him"). When one notices such close wording across Gospels—and there are numerous other examples—the logical explanation is that they have some relationship to one another. It is difficult to believe that three retellings of the encounter, independent of any shared source or relationship, would be so similar and even verbatim at certain points.

The close wording that one finds in the triple tradition is also found in the material shared by Matthew and Luke (but not Mark)—the double tradition.

Table 1.5. Close Wording in the Double Tradition

Matthew 23:37–39	Luke 13:34–35
Jerusalem, Jerusalem, the city that kills the prophets and stones those who are sent to it! How often have I desired to gather your children together as a hen gathers her brood under her wings, and you were not willing! See, your house is left to you, desolate. For I tell you, you will not see me again until	Jerusalem, Jerusalem, the city that kills the prophets and stones those who are sent to it! How often have I desired to gather your children together as a hen gathers her brood under her wings, and you were not willing! See, your house is left to you. And I tell you, you will not see me until the time comes when
you say, "Blessed is the one who comes in the name of the Lord."	you say, "Blessed is the one who comes in the name of the Lord."

Although Matthew and Luke differ at a few places in the pericope in table 1.5 (different Greek terms for "gather together," for example), the bulk of this material is verbatim in each Gospel.

That this shared material is so close in the actual wording has led numerous scholars to suggest that the relationship among the Synoptic Gospels is on some level a literary one. The **literary dependence** among Matthew, Mark, and Luke is a key tenet of multiple theories of how these Gospels are related to one another. Oral traditions about Jesus and his followers may account for some of the shared material, it is reasoned, but can hardly explain the word-for-word overlap evidenced in the three Gospels. In his Gospel, Luke indicates that he used sources in his research (1:1), and these may well have been written sources. Literary dependence among the Synoptics might involve either direct dependence (one Gospel writer using a previous Gospel) or indirect dependence (multiple Gospel writers using the same or similar previous non-Gospel source or sources).

Order of the Pericopae

That the Synoptic Gospels are somehow formally related to one another is seen not just in that they share material but also in that the material they share often appears in identical order. If the arrangement of pericopae were simply a matter of historical material, then one could attribute this to multiple narratives merely being arranged in chronological order—Jesus was born, ministered in Galilee, headed to Jerusalem, was crucified, and so on. However, the Gospel writers often arrange nonnarrative material in identical ways, often including material that may not obviously go together.

In table 1.6, all three Synoptics use the same general order for this shared material. Some pericopae do not appear in one or more Gospels, but even when a pericope is absent from one Gospel (such as "The Coming of Elijah" in Luke), that Gospel picks right back up in step with the other two. This set of examples is, of course, a selective sampling from the Gospels, and they do not always line up so closely in their arrangement. However, generally speaking, the Synoptic Gospels tend to arrange their material in a similar order, which suggests some type of relationship linking them together.

Table 1.6. Order of Pericopae

Pericope	Matthew	Mark	Luke
Peter's Confession	16:13–20	8:27–30	9:18–21
Jesus Foretells His Passion	16:21–23	8:31–33	9:22
"If Any Man Would Come after Me . . ."	16:24–28	8:34–9:1	9:23–27
The Transfiguration	17:1–9	9:2–10	9:28–36
The Coming of Elijah	17:10–13	9:11–13	
Jesus Heals a Boy Possessed by a Spirit	17:14–21	9:14–29	9:27–43a
Jesus Foretells His Passion Again	17:22–23	9:30–32	9:43b–45
Payment of the Temple Tax	17:24–27		
True Greatness	18:1–5	9:33–37	9:46–48
The Strange Exorcist		9:38–41	9:49–50
Warnings concerning Temptations	18:6–9	9:42–50	

Editorial Comments and Decisions

The last piece of evidence that demonstrates a relationship among the Synoptic Gospels consists of what we are describing as "editorial" similarities that are difficult to explain if attributed to chance. An example of this appears in Matthew 24:15 and its parallel in Mark 13:14.[10]

Table 1.7. Editorial Comment 1

Matthew 24:15–16	Mark 13:14
So when you see	But when you see
the desolating sacrilege	the desolating sacrilege
standing in the holy place,	set up where it ought not to be
as was spoken of by the prophet Daniel	
(let the reader understand),	(let the reader understand),
then those in Judea must flee to the	then those in Judea must flee to the
mountains;	mountains;

As with the examples that we have already considered, these two passages share identical wording. However, both passages contain the editorial comment, "Let the reader understand," just prior to the remark about those in Judea fleeing to the mountains. The chances of both Gospel writers independently deciding to insert this comment, using exactly the same wording at approximately the same place in their discourse, are extremely low. It is more likely that Mark and Matthew share some sort of relationship: either one Gospel used the other, or both had access to the same or a similar source.

Another example of shared editorial comments is found in Matthew 26:14// Mark 14:10//Luke 22:3.

Table 1.8. Editorial Comment 2

Matthew 26:14	Mark 14:10	Luke 22:3
Then one of the twelve,	Then Judas Iscariot,	Then Satan entered into
who was called Judas	who was one of the twelve,	Judas Iscariot,
Iscariot,	went to the chief priests	who was one of the twelve;
went to the chief priests.	in order to betray him to them.	

The intriguing part of this parallel is that each of the three Gospel writers found it appropriate to remind his audience that Judas was one of the twelve at this same point in his narrative. Each of the writers had already introduced Judas as a member of the twelve earlier in the narrative (Matt. 10:4; Mark 3:19; Luke 6:15). So the fact that each writer felt the need to remind his audience that Judas was one of the twelve disciples when describing his betrayal of Jesus points to some relationship among the Synoptics.

---

10. Luke's Gospel contains a parallel in 21:20–21, but apart from the line "then those in Judea must flee to the mountains," the parallel is not as close in wording. The point of this example, however, is the line "Let the reader understand," which does not appear in Luke's account.

A Problem?

In light of this evidence, scholars for some time have recognized that the Synoptic Gospels are somehow related to one another. The question involves the type of relationship involved. Was one Gospel written first and used by the other two? Did all three share common sources or traditions? Did the Gospel writers borrow and copy from one another? How do we explain the abundance of shared material and often exact wording found in the Synoptics? The inquiry into the relationship among the Synoptic Gospels, usually on a literary level, has commonly been called the **Synoptic Problem**. Investigations into the Synoptic Problem attempt to explain the similarities (and differences) found in the Synoptic Gospels by articulating a theory of their relationships to one another. The question usually revolves around the topic of which Gospel was written first and how it was used by the other Gospel writers.

Despite the fact that it is well established within New Testament studies, the term "Synoptic Problem" itself is problematic for two reasons. First, the word "problem" implies that there is something potentially wrong with how the Synoptic Gospels relate to one another. Instead of an appreciation for the similarities that one finds between the Synoptics, this term automatically labels their relationship a dilemma and therefore in need of fixing. Second, by labeling it as a problem, one is implying that a solution is possible. As we will see in this volume, the issues are complex, and very good arguments continue to be put forward to support differing theories regarding the relationship of the Synoptics. In short, the term "Synoptic Problem" implies some fault found within the Gospels and suggests that one can offer a solution, much like solving a math equation. If we can use the term "Synoptic Problem" in its best possible manner—to refer to an issue that has garnered much scholarly attention and a variety of opinions—then we welcome its use. The term has become so ingrained in Gospel scholarship that it is difficult to avoid. Therefore we will continue to use it throughout this volume, but we do not wish to imply that the Synoptics are either inherently problematic or that an easy solution is possible.

Theories of the Synoptic Problem

For most of church history it was believed that Matthew's Gospel was the first to be written, as its placement at the beginning of the New Testament suggests.[11] Just about every reference that we have from the earliest interpreters of the Gospels seems to work from the assumption that Matthew's Gospel was the first to be written.[12] In his *Commentary on Matthew*, Origen writes the following:

> I have learned by tradition that the Gospel according to Matthew . . . was written first; and that he composed it in the Hebrew tongue and published it for the converts from Judaism. The second written was that according to Mark, who wrote it according to the instruction of Peter. . . . And third, was that according to Luke, the Gospel commended by Paul, which he composed for the converts from the Gentiles. Last of all, that according to John.[13]

Writing about two hundred years later, Augustine offered the same order in his *Harmony of the Gospels*: "Now, those four evangelists whose names have gained the most remarkable circulation over the whole world, and whose number has been fixed as four . . . are believed to have written in the order which follows: first Matthew, then Mark, thirdly Luke, lastly John" (1.2.4).[14] It must be pointed out that early Gospel interpreters like Origen and Augustine were not interested in the question of the Synoptic Problem as we know it today. They were transmitting the tradition concerning the composition of the Gospels rather than comparing the texts with an eye toward which might have been written first. It is clear, however, that the tradition of the church in the early years of Christianity was that the order of composition for the Gospels was the same as the canonical order we have today: Matthew, Mark, Luke, John.

The Griesbach Hypothesis

The earliest attempt at a solution to the Synoptic Problem is associated with Johann Jakob Griesbach (1745–1812), mentioned above for composing the first synopsis, although earlier scholars had articulated similar theories.[15] The

---

11. For an excellent history of the Synoptic Problem, see David L. Dungan, *A History of the Synoptic Problem: The Canon, the Text, the Composition, and the Interpretation of the Gospels* (New York: Doubleday, 1999).

12. E.g., Eusebius, *Ecclesiastical History* 3.24.

13. Origen, *Commentary on Matthew* 1.1. Translation from John Patrick, *Ante-Nicene Fathers*, vol. 9, ed. Allan Menzies (Buffalo, NY: Christian Literature Publishing, 1896).

14. Translation from S. D. F. Salmond, *Nicene and Post-Nicene Fathers*, vol. 6, ed. Philip Schaff (Buffalo, NY: Christian Literature Publishing, 1888).

15. Most notably, Henry Owen, *Observations on the Four Gospels: Tending Chiefly, to Ascertain the Times of Their Publication; and to Illustrate the Form and Manner of Their*

Griesbach Hypothesis maintains that Matthew was the earliest Gospel, but that it was followed by Luke, and then Mark was the third. This deviates slightly from the early tradition, putting Luke second and Mark as the third Gospel written. Not only does the Griesbach Hypothesis propose an order for the composition of the Gospels, but it also argues that there is a direct literary dependence among the Gospels. So, according to the theory, Luke made use of Matthew's Gospel, and Mark had and used both Matthew's and Luke's Gospels. This theory and ones that posit a similar relationship to Matthew's Gospel are often described as illustrating **Matthean priority**.

Figure 1.1
The Griesbach Hypothesis

The Two Source Hypothesis

In the late nineteenth century, however, scholarly opinion began to sway away from theories of Matthean priority to what has become known as the Two Source Hypothesis. An important turning point in the history of the Synoptic Problem was a seminar dedicated to the topic held by William Sanday at Oxford University beginning in 1894. Meeting several times a year for nine years, Sanday and his graduate students published the massively influential *Studies in the Synoptic Problem* in 1911.[16] By this time the Griesbach Hypothesis had come under harsh criticism, and different areas of the Synoptic Problem were being scrutinized. The **Two Source Hypothesis** (or Two Document Hypothesis, as it was earlier called) argues that Mark was the first Gospel written and was used by both Matthew and Luke.[17] This theory also argues that Matthew and Luke not only used Mark as a source but also shared another source that is lost to us but given the name "Q" in

---

Composition (London: St. Martin's, 1764). On the possible relationship between Owen and Griesbach, see Dungan, *History*, 314–18.

16. William Sanday, ed., *Studies in the Synoptic Problem, by Members of the University of Oxford* (Oxford: Clarendon, 1911).

17. An earlier incarnation of the Two Source Hypothesis was called the Oxford Hypothesis due to its origins with Sanday and his seminar.

scholarly circles. This theory and those like it are said to reflect **Markan priority**.

Figure 1.2
Two Source Hypothesis

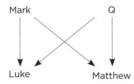

The Two Source Hypothesis also recognizes that Matthew and Luke incorporate unique material found only in their Gospels ("M" and "L"). Thus some scholars refer to the Four Document Hypothesis.

Figure 1.3
Four Document Hypothesis

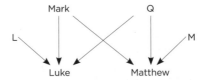

Differentiating between the Two Source/Document and Four Document Hypotheses can lead to confusion, since both really refer to the same basic hypothesis. Furthermore, most proponents of the Two Source Hypothesis would argue that the number of sources involved in the composition of the Gospels is more than two or four. Most adherents to this hypothesis believe that Mark used sources—oral and written—not represented in the diagram above. Some scholars do not limit their understanding of Q to one document but potentially include numerous documents or traditions shared by Matthew and Luke. Thus one should not hold so closely to the number of documents in the titles of these hypotheses. The skeleton of the diagram for the Two Source Hypothesis communicates the basic premise of those who identify as proponents of either the Two Source/Document Hypothesis or the Four Document Hypothesis. Therefore, in an effort to avoid confusion, we will use the title "Two Source Hypothesis" in this volume while acknowledging that some prefer the other title.

There are two major facets of the Two Source Hypothesis, which should be studied independently: Markan priority and the Q document.

Markan Priority

What is known as Markan priority, meaning that Mark's Gospel was the first written, was argued in some form by several scholars but is most closely associated with B. H. Streeter, especially his *The Four Gospels: A Study of Origins*.[18] The arguments in favor of Markan priority will be explored in detail in the chapters that follow as those for and against the hypothesis take up the challenge, but the major arguments are worth summarizing here. According to Streeter, there are four major arguments that Matthew and Luke used Mark's earlier Gospel.[19] First, the fact that so much of Mark's Gospel appears in the other two points to its use and earlier composition. If in fact Mark was written last, Streeter argues, it is difficult to understand why he would have left out so much of Matthew and Luke. Second, the wording of the material shared by all three Gospels (the triple tradition) reveals Matthew and Luke more often being close in verbal agreement to Mark and almost never agreeing against Mark. Third, the arrangement of pericopae demonstrates that Mark's ordering is more original, with the other two following his lead. When Matthew or Luke departs from Mark's order, the other typically maintains the Markan order. This can be seen in table 1.6 above: Luke does not include the "Coming of Elijah" pericope, but Matthew and Mark continue in the same arrangement; later Matthew does not include the "Strange Exorcist" pericope, but Luke and Mark continue in the same order. Streeter's point is that Mark remains what is later called the "middle term," which the other two seem to be following. Fourth, Streeter argues that Mark's language and grammar are often improved upon by Matthew and Luke, which demonstrates the movement by which the Gospels were used.[20]

Streeter's arguments for Markan priority have been picked up and developed by numerous scholars[21] and became widely accepted among New Testament scholars. Markan priority certainly has been the majority opinion regarding

---

18. B. H. Streeter, *The Four Gospels: A Study of Origins, Treating of the Manuscript Tradition, Sources, Authorship, and Dates* (London: Macmillan, 1924), esp. 157–69. Other early proponents of Markan priority include Karl Lachmann, "De ordine narrationum in evangeliis synopticis," *TSK* 8 (1835): 570–90; Heinrich Julius Holtzmann, *Die synoptischen Evangelien: Ihr Ursprung und geschichtlicher Charakter* [The synoptic gospels: Their origin and historical character] (Leipzig: Engelmann, 1863); F. Crawford Burkitt, *The Earliest Sources for the Life of Jesus* (Boston: Houghton, 1910).

19. Streeter, *Four Gospels*, 157–64.

20. Streeter has a fifth argument (that Matthew and Luke used Mark and other sources independently of each other), but it is based upon Markan priority rather than arguing for it (ibid., 164–69).

21. For more arguments in favor of Markan priority, see Metzger, *New Testament*, 81–84. Still one of finest treatments of Markan priority is G. M. Styler, "The Priority of Mark," in C. F. D. Moule, *The Birth of the New Testament*, BNTC (London: A&C Black, 1962), 223–32.

Synoptic origins, but it has not been without its critics.[22] In response to the fact that so much of Mark appears in the other two Gospels, several scholars have argued that this can be explained by understanding Mark as conflating or combining the other two Gospels.[23] Much has been made of the argument regarding the order of pericopae and what this can tell us about the origins of the Gospels. That Matthew and Luke never agree in order against Mark or apart from Mark is commonly presented as a definitive argument for Markan priority. In 1951, however, B. C. Butler criticized this reasoning and showed how several conclusions could be drawn from this evidence.[24] Finally, the argument that Mark's grammar is of a low quality and was improved upon by Matthew and Luke has been disputed, and examples of Mark's superior Greek in instances of shared material have been put forward.

As will be clear in the chapters that follow, Markan priority is an important issue in discussions of the Synoptic Problem. Once heralded as not a mere hypothesis but a fact of Gospel studies, Markan priority has come under fire in recent years, especially from proponents of the Two Gospel Hypothesis (more below). However, for many scholars, Markan priority remains the best answer.

Q

Markan priority is an attempt to account for the triple tradition and to explain the relationship of the three Gospels to one another. Given the premise that Mark's Gospel was written first and used by both Matthew and Luke, one must still account for the double tradition and how these two later Gospels came to share so much material. The Two Source Hypothesis addresses this by arguing that Matthew and Luke shared a common source that is now lost to us. This hypothetical source was given the name Q, short for the German word for "source," *Quelle*. Proponents of Q argue positively that Matthew and Luke appear to share a good deal of material absent in Mark. These same proponents argue negatively that this shared material is not the result of either Matthew or Luke using the other as a source.[25]

---

22. See David L. Dungan, "Mark—The Abridgement of Matthew and Luke," in *Jesus and Man's Hope*, vol. 1, ed. David G. Buttrick (Pittsburgh: Pittsburgh Theological Seminary, 1970), 51–97, esp. 54–74.

23. See David B. Peabody, Lamar Cope, and Allan J. McNicol, eds., *One Gospel from Two: Mark's Use of Matthew and Luke; A Demonstration by the Research Team of the International Institute for Renewal of Gospel Studies* (Harrisburg, PA: Trinity Press International, 2002), 92–96.

24. B. C. Butler, *The Originality of St. Matthew: A Critique of the Two-Document Hypothesis* (Cambridge: Cambridge University Press, 1951), 62–71.

25. For a substantial argument that Luke did not use Matthew as a source, see Joseph A. Fitzmyer, *The Gospel according to Luke I–IX: Introduction, Translation, and Notes*, AB 28 (Garden City, NY: Doubleday, 1981), 73–75.

Since Q is a hypothetical source, there are many more opinions regarding this tenet of the Two Source Hypothesis than the first concerning Markan priority. Some understand Q as a single written document, like Mark's Gospel, that was used by Matthew and Luke. Others use the term "Q" as representative of what were likely numerous sources shared by the two Gospel writers. There is ongoing discussion of whether Q comprises written or oral sources or some combination of both. Attempts have gone into reconstructing Q and understanding its formation.[26] Since the bulk of material shared by Matthew and Luke consists of sayings of Jesus, it is often hypothesized that Q was a "sayings source" that began as oral traditions that were eventually written down.

Proponents of the Two Source Hypothesis demonstrate a range of thinking regarding the contents of Q, but they all appeal to Q as some type of source or sources that explain the shared material found in Matthew and Luke but not in Mark. As noted earlier, the author of Luke's Gospel mentions using numerous sources in his composition. In its simplest form the Q hypothesis argues that the author of Matthew's Gospel also used one or more of those sources.

The Two Gospel Hypothesis

Both tenets of the Two Source Hypothesis—Markan priority and Q—have come under strong attack and help to differentiate the other major proposals for the Synoptic Problem from it and one another. At a time when Markan priority was the clear majority view and sometimes described as an assured result of New Testament criticism, William Farmer published a significant work that challenged the established consensus.[27] Farmer built on the earlier Griesbach Hypothesis by arguing that Matthew was written first, that Luke wrote second and used Matthew's Gospel as a source, and that Mark used both prior Gospels as sources and wrote last. This theory, as articulated by Farmer and his students, has become known as the **Two Gospel Hypothesis** and differentiates itself by the inclusion of oral tradition in its understanding of the Synoptic Problem.

According to the Two Gospel Hypothesis, Matthew used multiple sources when composing his Gospel. Luke used Matthew's Gospel, along with several other sources, which explains the double-tradition material. Mark, writing

26. John S. Kloppenborg, *The Formation of Q: Trajectories in Ancient Wisdom Collections*, SAC (Philadelphia: Fortress, 1987); Christopher M. Tuckett, *Q and the History of Early Christianity: Studies on Q* (Edinburgh: T&T Clark, 1996).

27. William R. Farmer, *The Synoptic Problem: A Critical Analysis* (New York: Macmillan, 1964).

last, used both Matthew and Luke, combining their narratives and offering a shorter account that essentially conflates the earlier Gospels. Proponents of the Two Gospel Hypothesis argue that Mark likely did not use many sources beyond Matthew and Luke's Gospels and employ the term **Markan Overlay** to refer to the material unique to Mark that ties his Gospel together.

Supporters of the Two Gospel Hypothesis have offered numerous criticisms of Markan priority, several of which have been referred to above. A major issue in this discussion is the places where Matthew and Luke agree with each other against Mark's Gospel. These instances, labeled the "**minor agreements**," are thought of as major agreements by proponents of the Two Gospel Hypothesis because they are difficult to explain if Mark wrote first, but they fit well with the premise that Luke directly used Matthew without any connection to Mark. Consider the example in table 1.9.

Table 1.9. Example of Minor Agreement

Matthew 6:21	Mark 8:31	Luke 9:22
From that time on, Jesus began to show his disciples that he must go to Jerusalem and undergo great suffering at the hands of the elders and chief priests and scribes, and be killed, *and on the third day be raised*.	Then he began to teach them that the Son of Man must undergo great suffering, and be rejected by the elders, the chief priests, and the scribes, and be killed, and after three days rise again.	. . . saying, "The Son of Man must undergo great suffering, and be rejected by the elders, chief priests, and scribes, and be killed, *and on the third day be raised*."

The important line of this triple-tradition material is the last one. Just prior to this last phrase, all three Gospels use nearly the exact same wording in Greek as they list the elders, chief priests, and scribes. At the end of their verses both Matthew and Luke use exactly the same wording: "and on the third day be raised." Under the Two Source Hypothesis, one would need to explain how Matthew and Luke, independently of each other, edited Mark's Gospel in the same way, using exactly the same wording.[28] Two Gospel Hypothesis adherents have an easier time explaining this change since, according to their view, Luke would have copied this line from Matthew's text, and Mark decided to deviate from both Matthew and Luke.

---

28. This is easier to explain if one allows that either Luke or Matthew used the other as a source in addition to Mark's Gospel. The Farrer Hypothesis (to be introduced next) can explain such minor agreements by arguing that Luke had access to Matthew's Gospel in addition to Mark's.

The Two Gospel Hypothesis has the longest history of all proposed solutions to the Synoptic Problem, drawing from the earliest interpreters of the Gospels. As was presented above, all the earliest Christian documents that address the issue work from the assumption that Matthew's Gospel was the first to be written. This appears to be the tradition concerning the order of composition of the Gospels that circulated in the early church. While many Synoptic Problem scholars focus on **internal evidence**—that found within the text of the Synoptics—proponents of the Two Gospel Hypothesis have support for their theory from this **external evidence** as well.

The major differentiation of the Two Gospel Hypothesis from the Two Source Hypothesis concerns the order of composition of the Gospels. While those who follow the Two Gospel Hypothesis may challenge the notion of Q in order to expose potential weaknesses in the Two Source Hypothesis, Q is essentially irrelevant to Two Gospel Hypothesis proponents because the double tradition is explained by Luke (writing second) using Matthew's Gospel (written first) as a source. Thus there is no need for a hypothetical source since, according to the Two Gospel Hypothesis, one can point to an actual written source that explains the double tradition.

The Farrer Hypothesis

Much as Farmer's influential work put into question the consensus of Markan priority, an important article by Austin Farrer in 1955 challenged the concept of Q.[29] In this article Farrer argues that Matthew and Luke did not use Mark independently of each other. Rather, he contends that Luke used not only Mark as a source but also Matthew, erasing the need for a hypothetical source (i.e., Q) to explain the double tradition. The **Farrer Hypothesis** agrees with the Two Source Hypothesis that Mark's Gospel was the first written but argues that Luke, written last, also had the Gospel of Matthew as a source (fig. 1.4, p. 22).

Farrer's article initiated a theory of origins of the Synoptic Gospels sometimes referred to as "Markan Priority without Q," but it was Michael Goulder who most fully developed the theory and built upon it.[30] In fact, the hypothesis is sometimes labeled the Farrer-Goulder Hypothesis. In recent years the Farrer Hypothesis has been defended and developed by Mark Goodacre. Francis

29. Austin Farrer, "On Dispensing with Q," in *Studies in the Gospels: Essays in Memory of R. H. Lightfoot*, ed. Dennis E. Nineham (Oxford: Blackwell, 1955), 55–88.
30. Michael Goulder, *Luke: A New Paradigm*, 2 vols., JSNTSup 20 (Sheffield: JSOT Press, 1989).

Figure 1.4
The Farrer Hypothesis

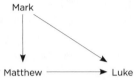

Watson, in his *Gospel Writing*, also presents a version of the Farrer Hypothesis in his reconstruction of the Synoptic tradition.[31]

The arguments for the Farrer Hypothesis center on demonstrating Luke's familiarity with and use of Matthew's Gospel. Much like the arguments for Markan priority, evidence of close wording, similar order of pericopae, and discernible editorial changes are appealed to in order to establish that Luke used Matthew as a source. The minor agreements between Luke and Matthew against Mark are significant for the Farrer Hypothesis because this hypothesis supposedly more easily explains these passages than does the Two Source Hypothesis. For the Farrer Hypothesis, as with the Two Gospel Hypothesis, the minor agreements are the result of Luke's relationship to Matthew's Gospel, in this instance Luke's use of Matthew. In a similar way, the material of the double tradition is supposedly more easily explained in the Farrer Hypothesis if Luke had access to Matthew's Gospel and therefore used it for material of which Mark was not aware.

Oral Tradition

The major explanations of the Synoptic Problem have focused heavily on the literary relationships between the Gospels. The creation of synopses, the close readings of parallel passages, and analysis of exact wordings in the Synoptics all treat the relationships between the Gospels on the literary level. Alongside the advances in the Two Source, Two Gospel, and Farrer Hypotheses have been advances in what we know about **oral tradition** and how it might help explain the Synoptic Problem. Many of these early advances in Synoptic relations occurred within German scholarship and focused on establishing literary relationships. Only later were their theories made to coincide with the rise of **form criticism**, which identified units of texts according to literary patterns and attempted to tie them to oral conventions. In his 1851 introduction to

---

31. Francis Watson, *Gospel Writing: A Canonical Perspective* (Grand Rapids: Eerdmans, 2013), esp. 117–216.

the Gospels, B. F. Westcott, a major English scholar, departed from then-contemporary German criticism by appealing instead to oral tradition to explain the relationships between the Synoptics.[32] Westcott argued that the traditions eventually written down in the Synoptic Gospels originated in the preaching of the apostles. This apostolic tradition safeguarded the faithfulness of the oral transmission. Theories of oral tradition often explain variations in the Gospel accounts by arguing that Jesus delivered similar words on several occasions, often linked to theories of location tradition.[33]

Each hypothesis of the Synoptic Problem presented so far does, to some extent, allow for a level of oral tradition to explain Synoptic relations. Oral tradition may be included in what constitutes Q or M or L—that is, sources that are not canonical Gospels. Most scholars, regardless of which solution to the Synoptic Problem they endorse, agree that oral traditions are behind the Synoptics in some way. That said, the literary relationship is often given greater emphasis as the oral tradition is given peripheral treatment.

Scholars who study the oral tradition behind the Gospels have long worked to give proper emphasis to the role of eyewitness accounts, memory, oral transmission, and traditions about Jesus in early Christianity. Several scholars argue for what is called the **Tradition Hypothesis**, which asserts that the relationship among the Synoptics can be explained purely by oral traditions and sources. However, here again the issue is a matter of emphasis, and most scholars who stress oral traditions combine a theory of oral tradition with literary sources when addressing the Synoptic Problem. For them, any hypothesis of Synoptic relations is necessarily more complex than what is possible to know with certainty. It is likely, they would argue, that the Synoptic writers utilized numerous sources and possibly different variations of oral traditions and eyewitness accounts.

Placing the Four Contributors within the Conversation

This brief overview of the history and major hypotheses and figures of the Synoptic Problem just scratches at the surface of the scholarship and the discussion that have surrounded this important topic. In the essays that follow, leading scholars of the four major views on the Synoptic Problem that we have outlined above present more detailed articulations of these hypotheses

32. Westcott, *Study of the Gospels*, 165–212. On Westcott's proposal, see Stanley E. Porter, "The Legacy of B. F. Westcott and Oral Gospel Tradition," in *Earliest Christianity within the Boundaries of Judaism*, ed. Alan Avery-Peck, Craig A. Evans, and Jacob Neusner (Leiden: Brill, 2016), 326–45.

33. See Bo Reicke, *The Roots of the Synoptic Gospels* (Philadelphia: Fortress, 1986).

and then enter into dialogue with one another. It is an important and potentially productive time in the history of the Synoptic Problem, as all the founders and major early proponents associated with each hypothesis—for example, Holtzmann, Streeter, Griesbach, Farmer, Farrer, Goulder, Westcott, and Reicke—have passed on, and a new generation of scholars has picked up the mantles left behind.

Craig A. Evans, John Bisagno Distinguished Professor of Christian Origins at Houston Baptist University in Houston, Texas, is an accomplished scholar and an expert in Gospel and Jesus studies. In this volume Evans represents what is still probably the majority view among New Testament scholars: the Two Source Hypothesis. He has articulated this stance on numerous occasions, often defending it against other hypotheses of Synoptic relations. His most rigorous defense of the Two Source Hypothesis is found in his Word commentary on the second half of Mark.[34] In an essay titled "Sorting Out the Synoptic Problem: Why an Old Approach Is Still Best," Evans defends the Two Source Hypothesis, especially Markan priority, and points to its ability to explain parallel passages better than any other theory.[35]

Mark Goodacre, Professor of New Testament and Christian Origins in the Department of Religious Studies at Duke University in Durham, North Carolina, is the foremost contemporary scholar articulating and defending the Farrer Hypothesis. In much the same way as Goulder advanced the earlier view of Farrer, Goodacre has advanced the Farrer Hypothesis to such an extent that it is not uncommon to see it referred to as the Farrer-Goulder-Goodacre Hypothesis (or Theory). Goodacre has published numerous works on the topic, including *Goulder and the Gospels* and *The Case against Q*. He has also published the widely used introduction to the Synoptic Problem, *The Synoptic Problem: A Way through the Maze*.[36]

David Barrett Peabody, Professor of Religion at Nebraska Wesleyan University in Lincoln, Nebraska, is a leading scholar in the Synoptic Problem and leading proponent of the Two Gospel Hypothesis. A student of Farmer, Peabody is part of an international team of scholars who have heartily defended the Two Gospel Hypothesis and published two important volumes

34. Craig A. Evans, *Mark 8:27–16:20*, WBC 34B (Nashville: Nelson, 2001), xliii–lviii.

35. Craig A. Evans, "Sorting Out the Synoptic Problem: Why an Old Approach Is Still Best," in *Reading the Gospels Today*, ed. Stanley E. Porter, MNTS (Grand Rapids: Eerdmans, 2004), 1–26.

36. Mark Goodacre, *Goulder and the Gospels: An Examination of a New Paradigm*, JSNT-Sup 133 (Sheffield: Sheffield Academic Press, 1996); Goodacre, *The Case against Q: Studies in Markan Priority and the Synoptic Problem* (Harrisburg, PA: Trinity Press International, 2002); Goodacre, *Synoptic Problem*. See also Mark Goodacre and Nicholas Perrin, eds., *Questioning Q: A Multidimensional Critique* (Downers Grove, IL: InterVarsity, 2004).

on the theory.[37] Peabody has written several key articles supporting different aspects of the Two Gospel Hypothesis, and his published dissertation, *Mark as Composer*, is a landmark in the contemporary expression of the hypothesis.[38]

Rainer Riesner, Professor Emeritus at Dortmund University in Germany, is an expert in theories of oral transmission and has published widely on the role of memory and orality in the composition of the New Testament. In the present volume Riesner argues for an Orality and Memory Hypothesis that takes into consideration oral transmission and practice in order to address the Synoptic Problem. His significant work on the background of Jesus's teaching, *Jesus als Lehrer* (Jesus as teacher), made an important impact on the understanding of how early Jesus traditions were transmitted.[39] In addition to this work, Riesner has published several articles on the topics of Synoptic relations, memory and orality, and early Christian traditions.[40]

Conclusion

The unity and diversity of the Gospels, including similarities and differences in their very wording, have fascinated readers of the New Testament from its earliest interpreters to the present day. The contemporary framework of the Synoptic Problem continues to intrigue scholars, and articulations of fresh theories continue to surface.[41] At the present time, however, four main views

37. Peabody, Cope, and McNicol, *One Gospel from Two*; Allan J. McNicol, David L. Dungan, and David B. Peabody, eds., *Beyond the Q Impasse: Luke's Use of Matthew; A Demonstration by the Research Team of the International Institute for Gospel Studies* (Valley Forge, PA: Trinity Press International, 1996).

38. W. R. Farmer, David L. Dungan, Allan J. McNicol, J. Bernard Orchard, and David B. Peabody, "The Two-Gospel Hypothesis: The Statement of the Hypothesis," in *The Interrelations of the Gospels: A Symposium Led by M.-É. Boismard, W. R. Farmer, F. Neirynck, Jerusalem 1984*, ed. David L. Dungan, BETL 95 (Leuven: Leuven University Press; Peeters, 1990), 125–56; David B. Peabody, "Reading Mark from the Perspectives of Different Synoptic Source Hypotheses: Historical, Redactional and Theological Implications," in Foster et al., *New Studies*, 159–85; Peabody, *Mark as Composer*, NGS 1 (Macon, GA: Mercer University Press; Leuven: Peeters, 1987).

39. Rainer Riesner, *Jesus als Lehrer: Eine Untersuchung zum Ursprung der Evangelien-Überlieferung*, WUNT 2.7 (Tübingen: Mohr Siebeck, 1981).

40. Rainer Riesner, "Jüdische Elementarbildung und Evangelien-Überlieferung," in *Gospel Perspectives*, vol. 1, *Studies of History and Tradition in the Four Gospels*, ed. R. T. France and David Wenham (Sheffield: JSOT Press, 1980), 209–23; Riesner, "From the Messianic Teacher to the Gospels of Jesus Christ," in *Handbook for the Study of the Historical Jesus*, vol. 1, *How to Study the Historical Jesus*, ed. Tom Holmén and Stanley E. Porter (Leiden: Brill, 2011), 405–46.

41. Some recent theories responding to the Synoptic Problem include Delbert Burkett, *Rethinking the Gospel Sources*, vol. 1, *From Proto-Mark to Mark* (London: T&T Clark International, 2004); Burkett, *Rethinking the Gospel Sources*, vol. 2, *The Unity and Plurality of Q*,

on the Synoptic Problem represent the vast majority of scholarship on the subject. We are grateful to have leading scholars representing these views in the present volume.

In what follows, each contributor offers his main essay putting forward his view on the Synoptic Problem. Since the Two Source Hypothesis, and its two tenets—Markan priority and Q—is probably still the majority view among New Testament scholars, Evans's essay is presented first and sets the course for the remaining essays. Goodacre's essay on the Farrer Hypothesis, which shares a major tenet with the Two Source Hypothesis (Markan priority), is placed next. This is followed by Peabody's essay on the Two Gospel Hypothesis, which moves significantly away from Evans's view but shares common features with Goodacre's view, especially in dispensing with Q. The fourth essay is Riesner's articulation of an Orality and Memory Hypothesis, which is both quite distinct in some ways from the other three views and surprisingly similar in others. Instead of immediately following each proposal with responses from the other contributors, as some multiple-views books do, this volume presents all four position essays up front. This allows the reader to be exposed to each view on its own merits without outside voices entering the discussion. Then, after each view's positive proposal has been made, each contributor offers a single essay in response to the other three views. The concluding chapter, written by the editors, summarizes the discussion and presents next steps for future studies on the Synoptic Problem.

SBLECL 1 (Atlanta: Society of Biblical Literature, 2009); James Edwards, *The Hebrew Gospel and the Development of the Synoptic Tradition* (Grand Rapids: Eerdmans, 2009).

2

The Two Source Hypothesis

Craig A. Evans

Introduction

Most New Testament scholars hold to the view that is called either the Two Document Hypothesis or the Two Source Hypothesis. (The latter designation is preferred by many, because not all are convinced that both sources were written documents. I will say more about that later.) This hypothesis holds that the Gospel of Mark was written first and became the principal narrative source of the Gospels of Matthew and Luke. The Two Source Hypothesis also holds that Matthew and Luke made use of a second major non-Markan source, chiefly comprised of the teaching of Jesus. This source is usually called Q (after the German word *Quelle*, "source").[1]

Although some contend that the Two Source Hypothesis carries with it theological or canonical implications, most find in it exegetical and tradition-critical implications, in the sense that the hypothesis aids exegesis and critical inquiry. In my view, this is the most important dimension in the attempt to resolve the question of the relationships of the Synoptic Gospels.

Why is the Two Source Hypothesis the dominant view among New Testament scholars? It is the dominant view because most scholars believe that

1. For a clear and concise description and defense of the Two Source (or Document) Hypothesis, see Robert H. Stein, *Studying the Synoptic Gospels: Origin and Interpretation*, 2nd ed. (Grand Rapids: Baker Academic, 2001), 29–169.

it offers the best explanation of the data. This is not to say that everything is neatly explained; no theory of the relationships of the Synoptic Gospels is free from difficulty. It is only to say that most scholars find that the Two Source Hypothesis encounters the fewest difficulties and, more importantly, offers greater explanatory power.

In what follows I will present arguments in support of (1) the priority of the Gospel of Mark and its use by Matthew and Luke, and (2) the existence of a non-Markan source, usually called Q, that Matthew and Luke drew upon independently of each other. In conjunction with the latter, I will also briefly address the hypothesis that embraces Markan priority but argues against the existence of the non-Markan source known as Q.

Arguments for the Priority of the Gospel of Mark

The major factor in favor of Markan priority lies in its explanatory power: it more easily explains the similarities and differences that we observe when we compare the Synoptic Gospels side by side. Most Gospel scholars believe that the data are better explained as Matthean and Lukan improvements on Mark, rather than the reverse. We see this in hundreds of detailed comparisons, on the one hand, and in the larger theological pictures of Matthean and Lukan theology that emerge. Matthew makes a great deal of sense as a revision and expansion of Mark. So also for Luke.

Scholars who argue that Mark wrote last and made use of Matthew and Luke have not been successful in explaining just what Mark has accomplished. Indeed, in a hefty commentary on Mark, written from the perspective that Matthew was written first, that Luke was written second and used Matthew as a source, and that Mark was written last and used both Matthew and Luke as sources (i.e., the Owen-Griesbach-Farmer Two Gospel Hypothesis), we find some odd conclusions. Although presupposing that Mark was written last and represents a conflation of portions of Matthew and Luke, the commentator frequently finds examples where Mark has preserved the most primitive form of the tradition, which is often said to be independent of Matthew or Luke.[2]

2. C. S. Mann, *Mark*, AB 27 (Garden City, NY: Doubleday, 1986). Here are several examples of what Mann states regarding Markan material: "not derived from Matthew and Luke" (202); "a Petrine reminiscence. . . . The very vivid details . . . all appear to be derived from early tradition" (214); "not derived from Matthew . . . certainly far more vivid in style than Luke's stereotypical account . . . a traditional piece, and the style suggests reminiscence by one of the participants" (217); "Mark's version, with its vivid detail, may owe far more to an original oral reminiscence than to the other evangelists" (218–19); "supplemented by Petrine reminiscences" (222); "some features of the Markan narrative . . . have all the marks of a tradition based on

To the extent that this commentator's analysis of the tradition is on target, his results are more compatible not with Markan posteriority but with Markan priority, in which Mark as the older Gospel is more likely to preserve ancient tradition, and the later Gospels, such as Matthew and Luke, which have edited, revised, and enlarged upon Mark, are more likely to have moved away from the older, more primitive forms of the tradition in their respective efforts to improve upon Mark's language, economy, and clarity. This commentator does not appear to be aware of the extent to which the results of his analysis conflict with the solution to the Synoptic Problem that he has embraced. His exegetical conclusions tend to undermine the very theory upon which he has based his commentary.

In short, the differences we see in Matthew and Luke, when compared with the parallel passages in Mark, are more convincingly explained as stylistic or theological improvements on Mark, whose traditions in places may well be ancient and perhaps even reflective of eyewitness tradition. Let us look at a few examples, keeping in mind the question, "Which solution—Matthean priority or Markan priority—best explains the data?"

Style and Word Choice

I begin with a couple of examples of Mark's writing style and word choice. In his terse account of Jesus's temptation in the wilderness, Mark states, "The Spirit immediately kicked him out into the wilderness" (Mark 1:12). I am not aware of any English translation that renders the verb exactly this way. The RSV reads "drove him out," which sounds a bit more dignified. The verb is *ekballō*, which can be rendered "kick out," "drive out," "throw out," "cast out," and perhaps a few other ways. It occurs sixteen times in the Gospel of Mark (eighteen times, if we include Mark's Long Ending [16:9–20]). The first occurrence is here in 1:12. Most of the occurrences of the verb *ekballō* are in

---

eyewitness reminiscence" (241); "The vividness of the Markan narrative, adding what would appear to be eyewitness detail . . . provides us with an insight into the controversial ministry of Jesus as seen through the eyes of members of his family" (251); "not dependent on Matthew" (261); "vivid details which almost certainly belong to the earliest level of oral tradition and suggest an eyewitness" (274). Many more examples could be cited. For a more recent and better effort to make sense of Mark as a conflation of Matthew and Luke, see David L. Peabody, Lamar Cope, and Allan J. McNicol, eds., *One Gospel from Two: Mark's Use of Matthew and Luke; A Demonstration by the Research Team of the International Institute for Renewal of Gospel Studies* (Harrisburg, PA: Trinity Press International, 2002). A number of reviewers have expressed appreciation for the work of the contributors to this book, but most Gospel scholars remain unconvinced of its thesis—that Mark's Gospel was the last to be written—principally because the differences seen in the triple tradition are easier to explain as Matthean and Lukan improvements on Mark.

reference to casting out demons (ten occurrences in all: 1:34, 39; 3:15, 22, 23; 6:13; 7:26; 9:18, 28, 38). The word is used of Jesus's action in casting out the money changers (11:15) and of the son who is murdered and cast out of the vineyard in the parable of the tenants (12:8). The remaining three occurrences include Jesus driving out the healed leper (1:43), thrusting out of the house those who laugh at him (5:40), and the metaphorical and hyperbolic saying about plucking or casting out an eye that causes one to sin (9:47).

From this survey we see that almost all the occurrences of the verb *ekballō* are in negative contexts. Ten of the sixteen are in reference to casting out evil spirits, and another is in reference to casting out the body of the murdered son of the vineyard. Most of the remaining occurrences are in contexts that are hardly dignified. The verb occurs twenty-eight times in Matthew. Twelve times it refers to casting out demons (Matt. 7:22; 8:16, 31; 9:33, 34; 10:1, 8; 12:24, 26, 27, 28; 17:19). Three times it is used for casting out the wicked into outer darkness (8:12; 22:13; 25:30). Matthew also uses the verb for Jesus's action in driving the money changers out of the temple (21:12) and in reference to the son in the parable who is cast out of the vineyard and then murdered (21:39). Matthew's use of *ekballō* is quite similar to its usage in Mark.

The verb *ekballō* occurs twenty times in Luke, eight times in reference to casting out evil spirits (Luke 9:40, 49; 11:14, 15, 18, 19, 20; 13:32). Jesus is cast out of Nazareth (4:29). He warns his disciples that their names will be "cast out" as evil (6:22). He warns his religious critics that they will find themselves cast out of the kingdom of God (13:28). And like Mark and Matthew, Luke uses *ekballō* to describe Jesus's action against the money changers (19:45) and the parable's murdered son and one of the servants who had been sent to collect what was due (20:12, 15).

I survey the use of *ekballō*, "to cast out," to help us answer the question "Was Mark first or last to write?" If the evangelist Mark was last to write and so made use of both Matthew's and Luke's Gospels, then he was very much aware of how the verb *ekballō* was used. He would have read it forty-eight times in Matthew and Luke, twenty of those times in reference to casting out evil spirits and several times in other very negative contexts. When the evangelist Mark set out to write his version of the gospel, would he have used this verb in reference to Jesus being sent out into the wilderness, to be tested by Satan? Indeed, would he use such a verb in reference to Jesus when in the Gospels before him—Matthew and Luke—far more dignified options were available? According to Matthew, Jesus was "led up by the Spirit into the wilderness" (Matt. 4:1). Matthew's verb is *anagō*. According to Luke, Jesus, "full of the Holy Spirit . . . was led by the Spirit" (Luke 4:1). Luke's verb is *agō*. It is hard to imagine why the evangelist Mark would choose not to use either *anagō* (to lead up) or *agō* (to lead) but rather choose to use *ekballō*, which he would have known is used repeatedly in reference to casting out evil spirits.

It makes far more sense to suppose that the evangelist Mark wrote first and that the evangelists Matthew and Luke made use of Mark. The evangelist Mark made use of *ekballō* in Mark 1:12, his first use of this verb, perhaps not anticipating its later use in reference to casting out evil spirits and other negative contexts. The verb itself is not always negative, and all three Synoptic evangelists use it a few times in more or less neutral settings. But it is understandable that the evangelists Matthew and Luke, having read Mark and having decided to use Mark as their principal narrative source, both chose to use some other verb. Matthew chose "led up," while Luke chose "led." It is much easier to view Matthew and Luke as revisions of Mark than to view Mark as a revision of Matthew and Luke.

We have another example of word choice. All three Synoptic Gospels state that one of Jesus's disciples drew a sword and struck the servant of the high priest. Mark uses the verb *paiō*, "to strike, dash, hit" (Mark 14:47). Matthew and Luke use the verb *patassō*, "to strike" (Matt. 26:51; Luke 22:50). All three evangelists use the word *machaira* for "sword" (or "dagger"). Although Mark's choice of verb is not wrong, it is a bit curious. (It is also used in the parallel at John 18:10.) In the Septuagint (the Greek translation of the Old Testament likely read by the early church), the verb *paiō* is paired with *machaira* once (2 Sam. 20:10). It is never paired with *rhomphaia*, another word for "sword." However, *patassō*, the verb used by Matthew and Luke, is paired with *machaira* nine times in the Septuagint; it is paired with *rhomphaia* sixteen times.

In light of the usage of these verbs, it is not surprising that both Matthew and Luke replace Mark's less suitable *paiō* with the more suitable *patassō*. (Matthew and Luke do use *paiō* elsewhere, in the sense of "beat" with fists or clubs, in Matt. 26:68; Luke 22:64.) If Mark wrote last and had Matthew and Luke before him, it is not easy to explain why he would replace the suitable *patassō*, which would have been in both of his sources, for the somewhat less suitable *paiō*.

Dignity

In favor of Markan priority, one may also invoke the argument from dignity, primarily with respect to Jesus but also in some cases with respect to the disciples. By this I mean places where Mark portrays Jesus in what might seem an undignified light, which is then mitigated to some degree in the parallels in Matthew and Luke. Let us review a few examples.

In the stilling of the storm (Matt. 8:23–27//Mark 4:35–41//Luke 8:22–25), the frightened disciples ask Jesus, according to Mark, "Teacher, is it not a care to you that we perish?" (Mark 4:38). But in Matthew we read, "Save, Lord, we are perishing!" (Matt. 8:25); and in Luke, "Master, Master, we are perishing!" (Luke 8:24). The differences are subtle but important and, on the theory of Markan priority, are not difficult to explain. The potentially disrespectful tone of the disciples' question in Mark ("Is it not a care to you . . . ?") disappears in Matthew and Luke. All three Synoptics preserve the identical form of the verb *apollymetha* (we perish) and have the disciples directly address Jesus. But the minor differences in Matthew and Luke are significant. Whereas Mark has "teacher" (*didaskale*), Matthew has "lord" (*kyrie*) and Luke has "master" (*epistata*). These changes in Matthew and Luke heighten the tone of respect for Jesus.

After Jesus calms the storm, he rebukes his disciples. Mark reads, "Why are you afraid? Have you no faith?" (Mark 4:40). Both Matthew and Luke soften the rebuke. Matthew has, "Why are you afraid, O men of little faith?" (Matt. 8:26). Luke has, "Where is your faith?" (Luke 8:25). Mark's "no faith"—hardly a good thing for the disciples, the future leaders of the Christian movement—is mitigated in Matthew and Luke. According to Matthew, the disciples have "little faith," while in Luke the faith of the disciples seems at the moment of crisis to have been misplaced. At least the disciples have faith; it needs to grow and be at the ready.

I might add that the expression "little faith" is a favorite in Matthew (in addition to Matt. 8:26, see 6:30; 14:31; 16:8; 17:20). Matthew picked it up from his non-Markan source (Q), in the saying about God as clothing even the grass (Matt. 6:30; cf. Luke 12:28). The occurrence in Matthew 6:30, in the context of the Sermon on the Mount, is the first occurrence of "men/man of little faith" in the Gospel of Matthew. The evangelist evidently liked it and so used it four more times. The evangelist Luke, however, apparently was not so fond of the expression and so uses it only in Luke 12:28, in the saying that he found in the non-Markan material and that he and the evangelist Matthew drew upon.

Another instructive passage again involves the disciples in a boat crossing the Sea of Galilee (Matt. 14:24–33//Mark 6:47–52). When the disciples see Jesus walking on the water, they are terrified. Mark explains that "they did not understand about the loaves, but their hearts were hardened" (Mark 6:52). The evangelist's comment has long puzzled interpreters. I suspect that Matthew and Luke were puzzled too. In what way understanding "about the loaves" (whatever that is supposed to mean) would have helped the disciples deal with a frightening and mysterious experience is not clear.

Not surprisingly, Matthew chooses to omit mention of the loaves and the critical comment about the hardened hearts of the disciples. Matthew adds the story about Peter walking on the water and then concludes the episode on a more reassuring note: "And those in the boat worshiped him, saying, 'Truly you are the Son of God'" (Matt. 14:33). Not only has Matthew deleted the negative comment about the disciples, but also he heightens the Christology of the passage. Luke chooses to omit the entire story, though the language of Mark 6:49–50 ("They thought it was a ghost and cried out; for they all saw him and were terrified") may be echoed in the resurrection scene in Luke 24:37 ("They were startled and frightened, and supposed that they saw a spirit").

In another story the boat and bread again come into play (Matt. 16:5–12// Mark 8:14–21). According to Mark, Jesus warns his disciples, "Take heed, beware of the leaven of the Pharisees and the leaven of Herod" (Mark 8:15). The juxtaposition of the Pharisees and Herod (presumably Antipas the tetrarch of Galilee) is curious. It is not surprising that copyists were tempted to "correct" the text, replacing "Herod" with "Herodians." Although this change at least pairs two parties, one still wonders what the Herodians had in common with the religiously conservative Pharisees. Not surprisingly, Matthew replaces Herod with the Sadducees (Matt. 16:6). The Sadducees appear seven times in Matthew but only once in Mark and once in Luke. Six times in Matthew the Sadducees are paired with the Pharisees. Matthew's replacement of Herod with the Sadducees in this passage makes good sense, for he has paired two well-known religious parties, both of which opposed Jesus. Markan priority is again the best explanation of the data. Although it is not hard to explain Matthew replacing Herod with the Sadducees, it would be very difficult to explain Mark replacing the Sadducees with Herod. Although Luke omits the story, he knows of it, which will be shown in a moment.

Other features in the passage also lend support to Markan priority. The Markan Jesus's hard-hitting criticism of the disciples (Mark 8:17–18) is greatly reduced in Matthew (Matt. 16:8b–9a). But more important, the question that is left unanswered in Mark is answered in both Matthew and Luke. Mark's passage ends with Jesus asking his bewildered disciples, "Do you not yet understand?" (Mark 8:21). Much more reassuringly, the evangelist Matthew concludes the story with the words "Then they understood . . ." (Matt. 16:12). Matthew also explains the meaning of the mysterious "leaven of the Pharisees." Whereas Mark never tells his readers what the metaphor means, Matthew explains that it is "the teaching" of the Pharisees (and the Sadducees). And although Luke has omitted the story itself, he has retained the saying, so that in another context Jesus warns his disciples, "Beware of the leaven of the

Pharisees, which is hypocrisy" (Luke 12:1). In their own ways both Matthew and Luke have cleared up perceived problems with Mark's story.

I conclude this section with a couple of observations regarding the interesting story of the Syrophoenician woman who begs help from Jesus on behalf of her daughter (Matt. 15:21–28//Mark 7:24–30). The potential awkwardness of the story is seen in how the woman argues with Jesus and how Jesus underscores Israel's priority over Gentiles. The Markan Jesus says to the woman, "Let the children first be fed, for it is not right to take the children's bread and throw it to the dogs" (Mark 7:27). But the woman will not take no for an answer. She retorts, "Yes, Lord; yet even the dogs under the table eat the children's crumbs" (7:28). Jesus grants the woman her request (7:29).

The evangelist Matthew seems uneasy with aspects of this story. For one thing, it stands in tension with these earlier instructions to the disciples: "Go nowhere among the Gentiles, and enter no town of the Samaritans, but go rather to the lost sheep of the house of Israel" (Matt. 10:5b–6). The evangelist mitigates the tension in a number of ways. First, he identifies the woman as a "Canaanite" (15:22), which links her to the holy land and increases her eligibility for messianic blessing. Second, she addresses Jesus with great respect and with a touch of Christology: "Have mercy on me, O Lord, Son of David" (15:22). The evangelist Matthew has borrowed most of this language from elsewhere in Mark (see Mark 10:47–48). Third, notwithstanding the woman's respectful address, the Matthean Jesus reminds her and his disciples of the priority of his mission: "I was sent only to the lost sheep of the house of Israel" (Matt. 15:24). Fourth, the evangelist Matthew augments the story, recasting Mark's statement that the woman "fell down at his feet" (Mark 7:25) as kneeling before Jesus and again addressing him with respect, "Lord, help me" (Matt. 15:25). After Jesus tells her that the children (of Israel) must first be fed and that their bread should not be thrown to the dogs (15:26) and after her clever reply (15:27), Jesus answers, according to the Matthean evangelist's revision, "O woman, great is your faith! Be it done for you as you desire" (15:28). Jesus will grant the woman her request because of her faith (which is not "little" but "great"). Matthew's alterations and expansions bring the story more fully in step with his theological interests and mitigate the potential awkwardness and lack of dignity that the story in its Markan form may have had.

Interpretation and Unique and Omitted Material

Matthew and Luke make good exegetical sense as interpretations and adaptations of Mark, but Mark makes little sense as an interpretation and conflation of Matthew and Luke. When compared to Mark, Matthew's interest in showing how Jesus fulfills both prophecy and law is plainly evident. When compared to Mark, Luke's interest in showing how Jesus's saving work applies to the marginalized, including Gentiles, is hard to miss. Countless commentaries and scholarly monographs have benefited from the recognition of Markan priority and the respective ways the evangelists Matthew and Luke have made use of the earlier Gospel.

This cannot be said for the hypothesis that views Mark as the last to be written and as drawing on the Gospels of Matthew and Luke. No one has written a detailed commentary that shows how our understanding of Mark is enhanced by seeing how he has blended or omitted Matthean and Lukan materials. Matthean prioritists speak of Peter, the voice behind Mark, as attempting to bring together the divergent Jewish and Hellenistic views of Matthew and Luke, respectively. This is plausible in theory, but there has been no success in showing how exegetically this is actually so. One would think, moreover, that the tradition of authentic Petrine material lying behind Mark fits better with an early Mark, on which later evangelists would rely.

We are told by Matthean prioritists that Mark achieves his unifying goal by blending and editing common material. On this theory we must wonder why Mark omitted so much of Jesus's teaching, which is especially odd given the observation that Mark twelve times refers to Jesus as "teacher" and another nine times mentions his "teaching." Among other things, the evangelist Mark has omitted the Lord's Prayer, the Beatitudes, the Sermon on the Mount/Plain, all of which appear in both Matthew and Luke.

The small amount of material unique to the Gospel of Mark also supports Markan priority. This material consists of Mark 1:1; 2:27; 3:20–21; 4:26–29; 7:2–4, 32–37; 8:22–26; 9:29, 48–49; 13:33–37; 14:51–52. In reviewing this material, one should ask which explanation seems most probable: that Mark added it, or that Matthew and Luke found it in Mark and chose to omit it. The nature of the material supports the latter alternative, for it seems more likely that Matthew and Luke chose to omit the flight of the naked youth (14:51–52), the odd saying about being "salted with fire" (9:48–49), the strange miracle in which Jesus effects healing in two stages (8:22–26), the even stranger miracle where Jesus puts his fingers in a man's ears, spits, and touches his tongue (7:32–37), and the episode where Jesus is regarded as mad and his family attempts to restrain him (3:20–21). If we accept Matthean priority, we would then need to explain why Mark would choose to add these odd, potentially embarrassing materials, only to omit the Lord's Prayer, the Golden Rule, and so forth.

Evidence for the Existence of Q and Its Usage by Matthew and Luke

Thus far adherents of two explanations of the Synoptic Problem will support me in arguing for Markan priority. I of course have in mind adherents of the Two Source Hypothesis, as well as adherents of the Farrer-Goulder-Goodacre Hypothesis, in which it is argued that Mark is the source for Matthew, and Mark and Matthew were the sources utilized by Luke.[3] I must bring this second Markan priority hypothesis into play at this point because its adherents are not persuaded that Q existed. They believe that Matthew's revision and expansion of Mark do not require a non-Markan source, and that Luke's revision and expansion of Mark also entailed drawing upon Matthew. In their view, there is no need to appeal to a non-Markan source of material, which New Testament scholars have traditionally called Q.

Proponents of the Two Source Hypothesis posit a substantial non-Markan source not out of a fascination with lost documents but out of logical necessity: if Mark is prior to Matthew and Luke, and if there is little reason to suppose that Luke used Matthew or vice versa, then one is obliged to account for the material common to Matthew and Luke that they did not get from Mark by appealing to another source (oral or written). This is Q.

I will argue that a source of non-Markan dominical tradition was in circulation no later than the mid-first century (and probably earlier), and that Matthew and Luke drew upon it and upon Mark in the composition of their respective Gospels. I will argue that although Mark Goodacre has greatly improved upon the older arguments of Michael Goulder (who in turn greatly developed the even older suggestion of Austin Farrer), there remain good reasons for hypothesizing the existence of a substantial non-Markan source, on which the evangelists Matthew and Luke drew.

The Probability of the Existence of a Substantial Body of Dominical Tradition

Before turning to the data of the Gospels themselves, I think a solid case can be made for the existence of a body of Jesus's teachings, along with stories

---

3. Austin Farrer, "On Dispensing with Q," in *Studies in the Gospels: Essays in Memory of R. H. Lightfoot*, ed. D. E. Nineham (Oxford: Blackwell, 1955), 55–88; Michael Goulder, *Midrash and Lection in Matthew* (London: SPCK, 1974); Goulder, *Luke: A New Paradigm*, 2 vols., JSNTSup 20 (Sheffield: JSOT Press, 1989); Mark Goodacre, *The Case against Q: Studies in Markan Priority and the Synoptic Problem* (Harrisburg, PA: Trinity Press International, 2002). Other scholars have lent support to this view. Goodacre himself criticizes aspects of Goulder's presentation of the hypothesis. See Mark Goodacre, *Goulder and the Gospels: An Examination of a New Paradigm*, JSNTSup 133 (Sheffield: Sheffield Academic Press, 1996).

about him. Something like Q, portions of which originated during the time of Jesus's public activities and then were gathered and consolidated in the weeks and months after his death and resurrection, is highly probable for a number of reasons. Jesus was a teacher and so presumably gave voice to a body of recognizable and coherent teaching. Given the impression he made on his followers, including and especially his disciples, his teaching would have been treasured. It seems to me that virtually every New Testament scholar would agree with this. Jesus is called "teacher" or "rabbi" throughout the Gospels. Furthermore, his closest followers were his disciples, which means "learners." In short, they learned his teaching. But they did not simply learn it and then keep it to themselves; they learned it and began to teach others.

How this pedagogy took place is now better known thanks to recent studies in Greek education, particularly the *progymnasmata*, in which students are taught how to learn and themselves formulate narratives and speeches. Of special interest is the basic building block in this pedagogy, the *chreia* (i.e., "useful anecdote"), in which the student memorizes small units of a master's teaching and learns how to adapt and apply them in various settings. For the last thirty years or so, scholars have been investigating the presence of the *chreia* form in the Gospels.[4] These studies have helped interpreters better understand how the disciples of Jesus learned and passed on their master's teaching. These studies have also helped us understand better the historiography that lies behind the Gospels.

The relevance of the *chreia* (pl. *chreiai*) at this point lies in the observation that the intention of the *chreia* is to preserve and apply the teaching of a master, *not to invent tradition*.[5] The student (or "tradent," one who preserves or passes on teaching) may expand, contract, and adapt—even paraphrase if necessary—his master's teaching, so long as the teaching is made clear. It is recognized that such editing is necessary if the teaching is to be understood in new settings. This is very much what we see taking place in the Gospels. The evangelists interpret and apply the Jesus tradition. It is edited, rearranged, recontextualized, sometimes paraphrased. Introductory clauses or sentences

---

4. Many studies could be cited, but here I mention only Marion C. Moeser, *The Anecdote in Mark, the Classical World and the Rabbis*, JSNTSup 227 (London: Sheffield Academic Press, 2002); Samuel Byrskog, "The Early Church as a Narrative Fellowship: An Exploratory Study of the Performance of the *Chreia*," *TTKi* 78 (2007): 207–26; Byrskog, "The Transmission of the Jesus Tradition: Old and New Insights," *EChr* 1 (2010): 441–68.

5. The tendency on the part of the tradents not to invent is seen in the fact that the dominical tradition does not address a number of questions and problems faced by the early church, as we see in the Epistles and in the book of Acts. Nowhere does Jesus instruct his disciples regarding the use of spiritual gifts, or provide guidance about Jew-Gentile relations, or qualifications for office, or the role of women, and so on.

are added. Materials are grouped and ordered as needed. Trained by Jesus, or trained by the disciples of Jesus, the tradents and evangelists have learned how to extract from the dominical tradition "what is new and what is old" (Matt. 13:52). All of this is very much in step with Hellenistic pedagogy, which from the time of Alexander had become an important part of Jewish pedagogy.[6]

If there was a dominical tradition (that is, an early tradition about Jesus), which seems highly probable, we should expect it to appear in the early Christian literature, and indeed this we see. Stories and sayings are quoted or alluded to in Paul's Letters and the Letter of James. The Gospel of Mark, in whatever way it may have been linked to Peter, contains a large chunk of dominical tradition, comprising deeds and sayings, including elements of Q. The Gospels of Matthew and Luke contain, in addition to most of Mark, large quantities of non-Markan material. The Synoptic tradition as a whole is coherent and exhibits the verisimilitude we should expect if a body of teaching derived from Jesus of Nazareth had survived and eventually been incorporated into written, published works.

In my judgment, what we have in Mark are Petrine reminiscences and other materials, overlapping with a substantial body of Jesus's (and John's) teaching, which is what scholars call Q. Matthew and Luke made use of Mark and much of Q. Although Matthew and Luke include in their Gospels some Q tradition that overlaps with what is found in Mark,[7] we should assume that Q itself contained a number of overlaps with Mark that Matthew and Luke omitted (though they did not always omit the same things). Matthew and Luke inserted the Q material into the Markan narrative frame as they saw fit. Much of Matthew's Q material has been shaped into his well-known five discourses (three of which are built on Markan material). Luke scatters

6. On this point, see Saul Lieberman, *Hellenism in Jewish Palestine: Studies in the Literary Transmission, Beliefs, and Manners of Palestine in the I Century B.C.E.–IV Century C.E.*, 2nd ed., TSJTSA 18 (New York: Jewish Theological Seminary of America, 1962); Martin S. Jaffee, *Torah in the Mouth: Writing and Oral Tradition in Palestinian Judaism, 200 BCE–400 CE* (New York: Oxford University Press, 2001). One will recall that in the second century BCE a Hellenistic gymnasium was built in Jerusalem itself, which angered religious conservatives (see 2 Macc. 4:12). The religious conservatives may have resisted aspects of Hellenism, but they readily adopted much of its scribal culture and pedagogy. The seven interpretive principles, or middot, attributed to Hillel in fact derive from Hellenistic principles of interpretation.

7. Scholars have identified as many as thirty examples of Mark-Q overlaps. See B. H. Streeter, "Mark's Knowledge and Use of Q," in *Oxford Studies in the Synoptic Problem*, ed. W. Sanday (Oxford: Clarendon, 1911), 165–83; C. M. Tuckett, *Q and the History of Early Christianity: Studies on Q* (Edinburgh: T&T Clark, 1996), 31–34; Stein, *Studying the Synoptic Gospels*, 120–21. Stein remarks, "It would be most unusual if two sources concerning Jesus, such as Mark and Q, did not overlap in some way" (120).

his Q material in much smaller clusters of teaching, often interweaving the teaching with events.

The Non-Markan Material in Matthew and Luke

There are two major arguments for the existence of Q that grow out of the Gospel data themselves. The first relates to the conclusion that Mark's Gospel was first and was used by Matthew. We must ask, then, where did the evangelist Matthew derive the several hundred verses of non-Markan material that we observe in his Gospel? Most scholars find it unlikely that Matthew invented it, either as midrash on Mark or as midrash on Old Testament passages and themes.[8] Matthew is relatively conservative in his treatment of Markan material. Why should we assume that he treats his other material significantly differently? And as has been mentioned above, adaptation not invention was the modus operandi of current pedagogy and its use of the *chreia*. In short, it seems best to explain Matthean content as mostly derived from Mark and a substantial non-Markan source.

The second argument relates to the composition of the Gospel of Luke. Luke too is seen as dependent on Mark. Most scholars think that Luke made use of the non-Markan (though not necessarily identical) source that Matthew utilized. This then explains why Luke follows the narrative thread we find in Mark and why the non-Markan material found in Matthew appears in different locations in the Gospel of Luke. Many scholars also state, sometimes quite emphatically, that Luke must have drawn upon a non-Markan source (i.e., Q) because it is hard to see Luke's non-Markan material as derived from Matthew. Why would Luke have disassembled Matthew's well-structured discourses? And if Luke drew heavily upon Matthew, would we not find many examples of distinctive Matthean redaction and materials in Luke?

Nevertheless, supporters of the Two Source Hypothesis have sometimes too quickly dismissed the possibility that Luke as a revision of Matthew could actually make sense. And this is where Goodacre's recent book has made a useful contribution.[9] He has labored hard to show how Luke may well have done this very thing. Goodacre also identifies and discusses a number of agreements of Matthew and Luke against Mark that cannot be easily dismissed. After all, if Matthew and Luke independently made use of Mark and a non-Markan source, we should expect only minor agreements between Matthew and Luke, where they from time to time make the same change in Mark or the

---

8. Which is the argument in Goulder, *Midrash and Lection*.
9. Goodacre, *Case against Q*.

non-Markan source. Goodacre, however, thinks that some of these "minor agreements" of Matthew and Luke against Mark are not so minor but rather constitute evidence that Luke made use of Matthew. And this seems to be the burden of Goodacre's defense of his case against Q—the argument that Luke made extensive use of Matthew, such that appeals to Q become unnecessary.

Proponents of the Two Gospel Hypothesis and proponents of the Farrer Hypothesis argue against the Two Source Hypothesis on the grounds of the minor agreements between Matthew and Luke against Mark. They reason plausibly that if Matthew and Luke independently made use of Mark, there should be very few agreements, at least very few of significance. (They allow, of course, that in making hundreds of editorial changes to Mark, there would inevitably be many minor agreements, such as adding or subtracting definite articles, changing word order, changing verb tenses, selection of more appropriate vocabulary, and the like.) Supporters of the Two Source Hypothesis agree that this is the most vulnerable point in their hypothesis. (It should also be pointed out that minor agreements are a problem for the Farrer Hypothesis also.)

Proponents of the Two Source Hypothesis usually address the problem of the minor agreements by pointing to evidence of oral tradition, scribal harmonization, and other factors, especially involving the more influential and more widely read Gospels of Matthew and Luke. Some scholars allow for the possibility that, at a late stage in composition, the evangelist Luke may have been influenced by the Gospel of Matthew[10] (though many proponents of the Two Source Hypothesis do not agree with this proposal).

The Use of Q in Matthew and Luke: An Exegetical Test Case

The real test of a hypothesis is its effectiveness, not simply in explaining verbal and statistical data, but especially in making interpretive sense of the text. In my judgment, the hypothesis of Matthew's and Luke's independent uses of the non-Markan material (rather than the hypothesis of Luke's use of Matthew) leads to greater exegetical precision. I will illustrate this by using the story of the healing of the Capernaum official's servant (Matt. 8:5–13//Luke 7:1–10). The appearance of a very similar story in the Gospel of John (John 4:46b–54) encourages us to view the healing story as very early

10. This is argued by Robert H. Gundry, *Matthew: A Commentary on His Literary and Theological Art* (Grand Rapids: Eerdmans, 1982), 4–5; Gundry, "Matthean Foreign Bodies in Agreements of Luke with Matthew against Mark: Evidence That Luke Used Matthew," in *The Four Gospels 1992: Festschrift Frans Neirynck*, ed. F. Van Segbroeck et al., 3 vols., BETL 100 (Leuven: Leuven University Press; Peeters, 1992), 2:1467–95.

and well known. It circulated among first-generation Christians, even if the Q and Johannine versions of the story differed at points. These differences suggest that we have in our possession two distinct streams of tradition, one Synoptic and one Johannine. Here is my literal translation of Matthew's version of the story:

> When he entered Capernaum a centurion came to him, beseeching him, and saying, "Sir, my servant lies at home paralyzed, terribly tormented." And he says to him, "Coming I will heal him." And the centurion, answering, said, "Sir, I am not worthy that you should come under my roof; but only say the word and my servant shall be healed. For I also am a man under authority, having soldiers under me, and I say to this one, 'Come,' and he comes, and to my servant, 'Do this,' and he does it." When Jesus heard this, he marveled and said to his followers, "Truly, I say to you, from no one have I found such faith in Israel. *But I say to you that many will come from east and west, and they shall recline with Abraham and Isaac and Jacob in the kingdom of heaven, but the sons of the kingdom shall be cast into the outer darkness, where there shall be weeping and gnashing of teeth.*" And Jesus said to the centurion, "Go, let it be to you as you have believed." And the servant was healed at that very moment. (Matt. 8:5–13 [emphasis added])

Jesus is quite astonished at the centurion's declaration. He admits, "Truly, I say to you, from no one have I found such faith in Israel" (Matt. 8:10). In Luke's version of the story, Jesus says no more. All that Luke's readers are told is that when those who approached Jesus returned home, they found the servant healed (Luke 7:10; cf. Matt. 8:13). But in Matthew's version Jesus goes on to exclaim, "But I say to you that many will come from east and west, and they shall recline with Abraham and Isaac and Jacob in the kingdom of heaven, but the sons of the kingdom shall be cast into the outer darkness, where there shall be weeping and gnashing of teeth" (Matt. 8:11–12).

Although the saying about many coming from east and west does not appear in Luke's story of the centurion, it does appear in Luke 13:28–30. Most interpreters see this saying as belonging to Q, which Matthew has placed in the context of the exchange with the centurion. The evangelist has added the saying here because it provides the opportunity to elaborate on Jesus's remark that the centurion's faith exceeds the faith found in Israel. Matthew can now hint at the mission to the Gentiles that will later be developed more directly (cf. Matt. 10:16–23; 28:19–20).

Not only will those far away, Gentiles as well as Israelites, enjoy the anticipated banquet of God, but also "the sons of the kingdom shall be cast into the outer darkness" (Matt. 8:12). The "sons of the kingdom" are the Jewish people who live in Israel, to whom, it was supposed, belongs the kingdom of God (see Luke's use of a similar epithet in Luke 13:28). Because they live in the promised land, which was thought in itself to be a blessing, surely they would be the very first to benefit in the restoration of Israel. But no, Jesus says, those far away are more likely to benefit than those right in the land itself.

As already mentioned, Luke's saying about those who will come from east and west appears in a different location. The evangelist has added the saying to the admonition to enter by the narrow door, which in turn is il- lustrated by the parable of the householder who refuses to open the door to those who knock (Luke 13:22–30). The Q saying does not fit especially well with the parable, nor does the parable fit well with the admonition to enter by the narrow door (13:24). The whole passage is likely a Lukan con- struction, with verses 22–23 introducing the teaching, verse 24 providing a warning about entering, verses 25–27 comprising a parable about the danger of the door that will not be opened once shut, verses 28–29 describing the grief of being "thrust out," and verse 30's floating topos ("some are last who will be first," etc.) providing a conclusion to the section. None of this material hangs together well. Its principal purpose is to advance Luke's concern with election.

I find it hard to see why the evangelist Luke, if he had Matthew but not Q before him, chose to remove the saying about being thrust out to make room for the many who come from east and west (Luke 13:28–29) from its fitting context in Matthew 8:5–13. The Matthean form of the story would well suit Luke's theology of election, whereby presumptuous, apparently elect Jews may well be cast out, and less obvious candidates, such as the poor, the sick, and Gentiles, may be included. One immediately thinks of the parable of the great banquet (Luke 14:15–24) and the parable of the rich man and the poor man (16:19–31).

However, if Luke, like Matthew, had a substantial source of non-Markan dominical tradition, in which the story of the Capernaum's official's request and the saying about those coming from east and west were distinct items in different locations, then what we find in Matthew and Luke makes better sense. Matthew, seizing on the implications of the saying about those coming from afar, saw how it could enhance the contrast between the centurion's faith and the lack of faith on the part of many Jews. In that saying Luke saw the idea of being "thrust out" and decided to append the saying to the parable of the closed door and the angry retort, "Depart from me, all you workers of iniquity!" (Luke 13:27).

Other Problems for Non-Q Hypotheses

Other significant problems remain for the Two Gospel and Farrer Hypotheses, in which it is argued that Luke depended directly on Matthew. One is the appearance of archaic tradition in Luke. Such archaisms really cannot be explained as scribal variants; rather, they point to variant forms of tradition. One thinks of Luke's version of the saying "If it is by the finger of God that I cast out demons . . ." (Luke 11:20), compared to Matthew's version, "If it is by the Spirit of God that I cast out demons . . ." (Matt. 12:28). Matthew's "Spirit," in the targumizing style of the time (which often moved away from metaphor and anthropomorphisms), clarifies the meaning of the text. Luke's version is clearly more primitive and probably reflects the very word that Jesus used. Indeed, given Luke's keen interest in the Holy Spirit, one would think that the evangelist would have retained Matthew's form of the saying had he seen it.

A few other examples of archaisms in Luke can be mentioned briefly. Luke's shorter, simpler version of the Lord's Prayer (Luke 11:2b–4; cf. Matt. 6:9–13) is widely regarded as the more primitive form of the tradition. Luke's form of the sending saying, "the Wisdom of God said, 'I will send them prophets and apostles'" (Luke 11:49), is more primitive than Matthew's form, "I send you prophets" (Matt. 23:34), though Matthew updates the tradition as a whole in his own way. Luke has likely preserved the more primitive version, which in Matthew has been edited more creatively. We probably have the same thing where Luke's "the Son of Man will confess" (Luke 12:8), not Matthew's "I will confess" (Matt. 10:32), is original. Likewise, parts of Luke's version of the Last Supper are regarded as more primitive than what we find in Matthew. Scholars have identified a number of other examples where Luke's version of a saying seems to be more primitive than its parallel in Matthew.[11]

In response to these examples, Goodacre speaks of "Luke's knowledge of oral traditions of some of the same material," which makes it "inevitable that, on occasion, Luke will show knowledge of some more primitive traditions."[12] Advocates of the Two Source Hypothesis will readily agree. Luke knew these

---

11. In reviews of Goodacre's *Case against Q*, these examples are discussed by John S. Kloppenborg, "Goulder and the New Paradigm: A Critical Appreciation of Michael Goulder on the Synoptic Problem," in *The Gospels according to Michael Goulder: A North American Response*, ed. Christopher A. Rollston (Harrisburg, PA: Trinity Press International, 2002), 29–59; Kloppenborg, "On Dispensing with Q? Goodacre on the Relation of Luke to Matthew," *NTS* 49 (2003): 210–36; Christopher M. Tuckett, review of *The Case against Q*, by Mark Goodacre, *NovT* 46 (2004): 401–3.

12. Goodacre, *Case against Q*, 64.

primitive extra-Matthean forms of the tradition because he made use of a non-Markan, extra-Matthean tradition that scholars call Q.[13]

Another problem for the Two Gospel and Farrer Hypotheses is having to account for Luke's omission of Matthean material that otherwise accords well with Luke's theology. One wonders why Luke would have omitted the parable of the laborers in the field (Matt. 20:1–16), which among other things is concerned with what is "just" (see vv. 4, 13)? Surely such a parable would have been right at home in Luke's Gospel (e.g., see Luke 23:47, where the centurion declares of Jesus, "Certainly this man was just"). Again, why would Luke have omitted Matthew's parable of the last judgment (Matt. 25:31–46), in view of the evangelist Luke's interest in acts of mercy and generosity (see Luke 10:30–37; 14:12–14; 16:19–31)? Other examples could be cited.[14]

Conclusion

Proposed solutions to the Synoptic Problem will always be to some degree tentative, in no small part because we simply do not possess the original compositions and therefore do not know exactly how the texts of the three Synoptic Gospels read. Besides that problem, we do not know how many "editions" of each Gospel were produced (e.g., which edition of Mark did Matthew use?), the full nature and extent of scribal variants in the copies that were produced in the first century (a period for which we have very little textual evidence), how much harmonization took place, and how much the ongoing oral tradition continued to exert influence on the written Gospels.[15]

Because of factors like these, about which we know almost nothing, we cannot account for every detail. In the words of Joseph Fitzmyer, who has long argued for the Two Source Hypothesis,

13. Commenting on Goodacre's concession regarding primitive tradition in Luke, Tuckett remarks, "If appeal is made too often to parallel traditions (oral or otherwise) available to Luke independently of Matthew, some form of 'Q' starts creeping in by the back door again!" (see Tuckett, review of *The Case against Q*, 403). See also Kloppenborg, "On Dispensing with Q?," 223–25.

14. For further discussion, see Kloppenborg, "On Dispensing with Q?," 222–23; Kloppenborg, review of *The Case against Q*, by Mark Goodacre, *RBL* 5 (2003): 409–15, esp. 412–13.

15. In this connection one should remember Papias's famous comment: "I did not think that what was to be gotten from the books would profit me as much as what came from the living and abiding voice" (in Eusebius, *Church History* 3.39.4 [trans. Arthur Cushman McGiffert, *NPNF*[2] 1:174]). That Papias would speak this way in the early second century, when all four New Testament Gospels were known and in circulation, is quite remarkable. It bears witness to the deep and abiding appreciation that the first two generations of the Christian movement had for dominical tradition in oral form.

Extrinsic, historically trustworthy data about the composition of these Gospels are totally lacking, and the complexity of the traditions embedded in them, the evangelists' editorial redaction of them, and their free composition bedevil all attempts to analyze objectively the intrinsic data with critical literary methods.[16]

Exegetical and theological approaches that are less vulnerable to the interference of scribal variants and harmonizations must be given priority. When these approaches are given priority, the evidence as a whole is better explained by the Two Source Hypothesis than by the other competing hypotheses.[17]

Further Reading

Intermediate

Kloppenborg, John S. *Q, the Earliest Gospel: An Introduction to the Original Stories and Sayings of Jesus*. Louisville: Westminster John Knox, 2008.

McKnight, Scot. *Interpreting the Synoptic Gospels*. Grand Rapids: Baker, 1988.

Stein, Robert H. *Studying the Synoptic Gospels: Origin and Interpretation*. 2nd ed. Grand Rapids: Baker Academic, 2001.

———. "The Synoptic Problem." In *Dictionary of Jesus and the Gospels*, edited by Joel B. Green, Scot McKnight, and I. Howard Marshall, 784–92. Downers Grove, IL: InterVarsity, 1992.

Streeter, B. H. *The Four Gospels: A Study of Origins, Treating of the Manuscript Tradition, Sources, Authorship, and Dates*. London: Macmillan, 1924.

Advanced

Kloppenborg, John S. *Excavating Q: The History and Setting of the Sayings Gospel*. Minneapolis: Fortress, 2000.

———. *The Formation of Q: Trajectories in Ancient Wisdom Collections*. SAC. Philadelphia: Fortress, 1987.

———. *Synoptic Problems: Collected Essays*. WUNT 329. Tübingen: Mohr Siebeck, 2014.

Tuckett, Christopher M. *Q and the History of Early Christianity: Studies on Q*. Edinburgh: T&T Clark, 1996.

———. *The Revival of the Griesbach Hypothesis: An Analysis and Appraisal*. SNTSMS 44. Cambridge: Cambridge University Press, 1983.

16. Joseph A. Fitzmyer, *The Gospel according to Luke I–IX: Introduction, Translation, and Notes*, AB 28 (Garden City, NY: Doubleday, 1981), 63.

17. I thank Greg Monette and John Kloppenborg for reading a draft of this paper and making a number of helpful suggestions.

3

The Farrer Hypothesis

Mark Goodacre

Introduction

The Farrer Hypothesis is in some senses the new kid on the block. The Two Gospel (or Griesbach) Hypothesis and the Two Source (or Two Document) Hypothesis have both been honored by time, while the Farrer Hypothesis (sometimes called "Mark without Q" or "Markan Priority without Q") has only found its feet in recent years. It is named after Austin Farrer (1904–68),[1] whose article "On Dispensing with Q"[2] was a delightful essay that challenged a great orthodoxy in New Testament scholarship, the notion that the Gospels of Matthew and Luke were written independently of each other, which necessitated the postulation of the hypothetical document "Q." Farrer believed that the case for Markan priority was so strong that it did not even require defense. It was one of the established results of New Testament

1. However, the theory actually predates Farrer. See especially E. W. Lummis, *How Luke Was Written* (Cambridge: Cambridge University Press, 1915).

2. Austin Farrer, "On Dispensing with Q," in *Studies in the Gospels: Essays in Memory of R. H. Lightfoot*, ed. D. E. Nineham (Oxford: Blackwell, 1955), 55–88. However, the theory owes most to Michael Goulder. See especially Goulder, *Luke: A New Paradigm*, 2 vols., JSNTSup 20 (Sheffield: JSOT Press, 1989); Goulder, "Is Q a Juggernaut?," *JBL* 115 (1996): 667–81.

scholarship. But Farrer was not convinced that Matthew and Luke accessed Mark independently. He observed that if Luke appeared to be familiar with Matthew's Gospel as well as with Mark, the need for Q disappeared. One could "dispense with Q." His argument sparkled with simplicity, yet it has taken decades for it to be taken seriously in New Testament scholarship. A careful consideration of the evidence, however, shows how strong Farrer's initial impulse was. The evidence for Luke's knowledge of Matthew is strong, and this requires the abandonment of Q.

The Farrer Hypothesis can be represented straightforwardly in a diagram:

Figure 3.1
The Farrer Hypothesis

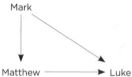

Mark is the first Gospel and is used by both Matthew and Luke. In this key respect the Farrer Hypothesis is similar to the Two Source Hypothesis, which also affirms the priority of Mark. However, the Farrer Hypothesis differs from the Two Source Hypothesis in drawing a direct arrow from Matthew to Luke. This represents Luke's use of Matthew, and it is Luke's knowledge of Matthew that enables one to abandon Q. It should be added, however, that Synoptic diagrams, like the Synoptic theories that they are modeling, are necessarily simpler than the reality that they are attempting to represent. The arrows in the diagram represent the ways in which the Synoptic Gospels are related to one another at the literary level, notwithstanding the complexities that need to be taken into account, such as differing editions of each of the Gospels and the presence of oral traditions that will have supplemented and interacted with the written texts.

This presentation on the Farrer Hypothesis begins by setting in place the cornerstone of Markan priority.[3] It then turns to the evidence for Luke's use of Matthew and concludes by considering some of the standard arguments against the hypothesis.

---

3. There is also a key prior stage, which is to come to terms with the Synoptic Problem itself, to understand the nature of the data. All too often scholars present the Synoptic data in terms of the Two Source Hypothesis, which of course prejudices the conclusions. For an introductory exploration of the Synoptic data, presented without prejudice to any particular solution, see Mark Goodacre, *The Synoptic Problem: A Way through the Maze*, BibSem 80 (London: Sheffield Academic Press, 2001), 33–55.

The Cornerstone: Markan Priority

The notion of a direct literary link between the three Synoptics is demanded by the degree of similarity between them. The triple-tradition material—the passages shared by all three Synoptics—often has the same basic order, and there are striking agreements in wording, as, for example, in the story of the paralytic (Matt. 9:1–8//Mark 2:1–12//Luke 5:17–26), from which this excerpt is taken:

Matthew 9:6	Mark 2:10–11	Luke 5:24
"But in order that you may know that the Son of Man has authority on the earth to forgive sins," then he says to the paralytic, "Arise, take up your bed and go to your house."	"But in order that you may know that the Son of Man has authority on the earth to forgive sins," he says to the paralytic, "I say to you, Arise, take up your pallet and go to your house."	"But in order that you may know that the Son of Man has authority on the earth to forgive sins," he said to the paralytic, "I say to you, Arise and take up your bed and return to your house."

Not only is the wording very close, as is often the case in the Synoptics, but also the three Synoptics agree with one another even in somewhat clumsy Greek syntax with a half-unfinished sentence. This is not independent reporting of the same event; it is direct copying. The key question, however, is whether the extensive agreement between Matthew, Mark, and Luke makes better sense on the theory of Markan priority (Farrer Hypothesis; Two Source Hypothesis), whereby Matthew and Luke copy Mark, or on the theory of Markan Posteriority (Two Gospel Hypothesis), whereby Mark copies Matthew and Luke.

In spite of some strong critiques of some poor arguments in favor of the priority of Mark,[4] this theory remains one of the surest building blocks in New Testament scholarship. There are several good arguments in favor of Matthew's and Luke's dependence on Mark. The strongest are the arguments from omissions and additions and from editorial fatigue. Let us take these in turn.

Omissions and Additions

The two primary alternatives currently on the table are that Mark's Gospel was written first and was used by both Matthew and Luke (Two Source Hypothesis; Farrer Hypothesis), and that Mark's Gospel was written third and was familiar with Matthew and Luke (Two Gospel Hypothesis). Since

---

4. See, e.g., William R. Farmer, "The Current State of the Synoptic Problem," in *Literary Studies in Luke-Acts: Essays in Honor of Joseph B. Tyson*, ed. Richard P. Thompson and Thomas E. Phillips (Macon, GA: Mercer University Press, 1998), 11–36.

a lot of material found in Matthew and Luke is absent from Mark, the student needs to ask whether it is more plausible that this material was added by Matthew and Luke or whether it is more plausible that this material was omitted by Mark.

It is much easier to see the additional material in Matthew and Luke as material that they added to their Markan source. It is harder to imagine this material as Mark's omissions from Matthew and Luke. Matthew and Luke, for example, both feature the Lord's Prayer (Matt. 6:6–13//Luke 11:2–4), but it is absent from Mark. Since its teaching is highly congenial to Mark, and since it has an ideal location into which it could have been inserted (Mark 11:20–25), it is more likely that this is a passage added by Matthew and Luke rather than a passage omitted by Mark from Matthew and Luke. Similarly, other teaching from Matthew's Sermon on the Mount (Matt. 5–7) and Luke's Sermon on the Plain (Luke 6:20–49) might have worked well in Mark's Gospel, and it is not always easy to find explanations for the omissions Mark must have made if his sources were Matthew and Luke.

The issue is focused by the fact that much of the material unique to Mark's Gospel is so strange. Among the passages found only in Mark are the healing of the blind man of Bethsaida (Mark 8:22–26), in which Jesus spits on a man's eyes and heals him in two stages, and the healing of the deaf mute (7:33–36), in which Jesus puts his fingers in a man's ears, and spits and touches his tongue. It is easier to imagine that Matthew and Luke both omitted these passages from Mark, perhaps because of the earthy, physical nature of the healings, than that Mark went out of his way to add these odd passages.

The point relates to the relationship between omissions and additions. If Mark's sources were Matthew and Luke, he has omitted a great deal of congenial material from the combined witnesses of his two sources, while adding material that appears to have a peculiar and primitive-looking profile. The more plausible scenario is that Matthew and Luke were using Mark and that they have omitted this odd, uncongenial material, while adding a great deal of new material of obvious interest and appeal.

Editorial Fatigue

One of the clearest indicators of Markan priority is a phenomenon called "editorial fatigue," whereby an author inadvertently betrays his use of a source by making characteristic changes at the beginning of a passage and then reverting to the source's wording later in the same passage.[5] Thus, in the story of

5. See further Mark Goodacre, "Fatigue in the Synoptics," NTS 44 (1998): 45–58.

John the Baptist's death (Matt. 14:1–12//Mark 6:14–29), Matthew correctly describes Herod as a "tetrarch," in contrast to Mark, who less accurately calls him "king." But then Matthew appears to drift into Mark's wording when, later in the passage, he also calls him "king" (Matt. 14:9). Moreover, Matthew's apparent abbreviation of Mark's story leads to a further peculiarity. In Mark, Herodias wanted to see John killed, but Herod listened to him gladly (Mark 6:19–20); in Matthew, Herod wanted him killed (Matt. 14:5). Matthew's subsequent comment that the king grieved about John's death (Matt. 14:9) therefore makes little narrative sense and appears to be the result of Matthew's editorial fatigue, leading him to drift into the wording of his Markan source (Mark 6:26).

The same phenomenon can be illustrated from Luke's use of Mark. Luke resets the story of the feeding of the five thousand (Mark 6:30–44//Luke 9:10–17) in "a city called Bethsaida," which causes problems when he subsequently appears to drift into the Markan wording: "Send away the crowd, so that they may go into the surrounding villages and countryside to lodge and find provisions because we are here in a desert place" (Luke 9:12; cf. Mark 6:35–36). So now the crowds are no longer in a city but in "a desert place," and the exhortation to send the disciples into the villages and countryside makes little sense. Luke appears to have carried it over from Mark because of editorial fatigue.

Examples like these make good sense on the assumption that Mark's Gospel was used as a source by Matthew and Luke. Observations about editorial fatigue alongside the patterns of omissions and additions make it highly plausible that Mark was the primary literary source for both Matthew and Luke. But Markan priority takes us only part of the way toward a solution of the Synoptic Problem. It effectively explains the many triple-tradition passages, where there are major agreements between all three Synoptics in wording and order, but it does not help with the double-tradition passages, where Matthew and Luke have substantial material that is not present in Mark.

The Origin of the Double Tradition

The double tradition (material shared by Matthew and Luke but not Mark) is the most contentious set of Synoptic data, and explaining the phenomenon is at the heart of the disagreement between Q advocates and Q skeptics. The Two Source Hypothesis postulates that Matthew and Luke used Mark independently of each other. Neither knew the other. And if Matthew and Luke are independent of each other, the double tradition has to have come from a hypothetical source. This source is conveniently labeled "Q," from the German *Quelle*, "source." The Farrer Hypothesis, on the other hand, suggests that they did not write independently of each other. Luke had direct access to Matthew, so Q is unnecessary: Luke copied from Matthew as well as from Mark.

It is worth noting at this point how close the wording in the double tradition can be, not least because those unfamiliar with the data sometimes make vague suggestions about oral-only source material. Sometimes Matthew and Luke have almost 100 percent verbatim agreement in Greek. John the Baptist's preaching provides a good example of the phenomenon:

Matthew 3:7-10	Luke 3:7-9
Offspring of vipers! Who warned you to flee from the coming wrath? Bear fruit therefore worthy of repentance and do not <u>presume</u> to say in yourselves, "We have Abraham as father"; for I say to you that God is able from these stones to raise up children to Abraham. Already the ax is laid at the root of the trees; for every tree not producing good fruit is cut down and cast into the fire.	Offspring of vipers! Who warned you to flee from the coming wrath? Bear fruit therefore worthy of repentance and do not <u>begin</u> to say in yourselves, "We have Abraham as father"; for I say to you that God is able from these stones to raise up children to Abraham. Already the ax is laid at the root of the trees; for every tree not producing good fruit is cut down and cast into the fire.

Here only the words for "presume" and "begin" differ between these two Gospels.[6] This kind of verbatim identity in Greek points to a literary connection of some kind. While it is important to take oral tradition seriously as a factor in the discussion of the Synoptics (see further below), it is essential to grasp that verbatim agreement in Greek of this nature can be explained only by literary dependence.[7] An ill-defined oral source will simply not explain the extensive verbatim agreement satisfactorily. The question, therefore, is whether the literary link is a direct one, from Matthew to Luke (Farrer Hypothesis),[8] or an indirect one (Two Source Hypothesis). Is Luke copying from Matthew, or are both of them copying from Q?

6. Luke uses the plural form *karpous axious* (fruits worthy) and Matthew the singular *karpon axion* (fruit worthy).

7. Note also that terms like "literary dependence" should be used without prejudice to the mode of dependence. It is quite likely, e.g., that Luke dictated his Gospel to a scribe, perhaps in more than one draft. He did not physically copy his source texts as a scribe.

8. The closeness in wording between Matthew and Luke in the double tradition is also congenial to the Two Gospel Hypothesis, which has a direct line between Matthew and Luke. However, the Two Gospel Hypothesis also postulates that Luke was dependent on Matthew in the triple tradition, which generates an anomaly: why is Luke often closer to Matthew when Mark is not present?

The very closeness of the agreement between Matthew and Luke may itself provide a clue about the nature of the relationship. The closer the degree of agreement between two works, the more likely it becomes that the two are directly related. The point can be illustrated by imagining a scenario in which two students hand in essays featuring passages with nearly identical wording. Our first instinct would be to imagine that one had copied from the other, not that both had copied from a hypothetical, unseen third source. Thus, where Matthew and Luke have long strings of sequential agreements in the double tradition, it is natural to suggest that there is a direct link between the two, not that both are dependent on a hypothetical document.

The point is not purely abstract. On the common ground of Markan priority, we have an idea of what Matthew and Luke look like when they are working from a third source. We know what kind of agreement to expect. And in this material, the triple tradition, Matthew and Luke are never as close to each other as they are in the double tradition, and this is true for sayings material as well as narrative. It appears that the double tradition results from Luke having direct access to Matthew, not from mutual knowledge of a lost source. In other words, the agreement between Matthew and Luke is simply too good to be Q.[9]

Luke's Knowledge of Matthew's Structure

The closeness of the wording in much of the double-tradition material suggests a direct link between Matthew and Luke, but this takes us only part of the way. It is important to look at other indications of Luke's knowledge of Matthew. One key issue is that the very shape of Luke's Gospel resembles Matthew's in a way that may be too much to be coincidence. Mark's Gospel begins with John the Baptist's preaching (Mark 1:4–8) and ends, according to most text critics,[10] with the empty tomb (16:1–8). Matthew and Luke, by contrast, both begin their Gospels with birth narratives (Matt. 1–2; Luke 1–2) that set Jesus's miraculous birth in Bethlehem, fulfilling prophecy, with great signs and portents, before fast-forwarding to John's preaching (Matt. 3:1–12; Luke 3:1–20). Similarly, neither Matthew nor Luke stops where Mark stops, instead going on with resurrection appearances and Jesus's commissioning of the disciples (Matt. 28:9–20; Luke 24:9–53). Further, Matthew

9. See further Mark Goodacre, "Too Good to Be Q: High Verbatim Agreement in the Double Tradition," in *Marcan Priority without Q: Explorations in the Farrer Hypothesis*, ed. John C. Poirier and Jeffrey Peterson, LNTS 455 (London: Bloomsbury T&T Clark, 2015), 82–100.

10. For a helpful discussion of the endings of Mark's Gospel, see D. C. Parker, *The Living Text of the Gospels* (Cambridge: Cambridge University Press, 1997), 124–47.

and Luke coincide in filling in what is lacking in Mark's narrative, adding a lot of Jesus's teaching, in parables and discourses, as well as miracle stories and more.

It is quite possible, of course, that Matthew and Luke independently hit on the idea of reworking Mark's Gospel in parallel fashion, structuring their Gospels by adding a prologue dealing with Jesus's birth and an epilogue dealing with his resurrection, and filling in the ministry with lots of extra teaching and other material. These important coincidences, however, should not be lightly brushed aside. It may be that we miss these coincidences because of our familiarity with Matthew's and Luke's Gospels. We assume that it would have been natural or somehow self-evident that a Gospel should begin with stories of Jesus's birth and conclude with stories about resurrection appearances. But John's Gospel does not begin this way; instead of birth narratives, it has a mystical prologue (John 1:1–18) before arriving at John the Baptist's preaching (1:19–28). Nor are there any other extant Gospels that begin in this way. Even Luke himself, in the Acts of the Apostles, appears to think of Jesus's story as beginning not so much with his birth as with the preaching of John the Baptist (Acts 1:21–22; 13:24).

Luke's Agreements with Matthew in Markan Material

The similarities between Matthew's and Luke's Gospels are not enough on their own, of course, to establish a direct link between them. These coincidences suggest a relationship, but they do not establish it. To move the discussion forward, we must take a closer look at the agreements between Matthew and Luke on the passage level. According to the Farrer Hypothesis, Luke knows both Matthew and Mark, so we would be surprised if Luke never showed his knowledge of Matthew in his editing of Mark. And there are many, many examples of Luke apparently showing his knowledge of Matthew in passages that are shared by all three Synoptics.

One of the clearest examples is found in John the Baptist's preaching about the coming Messiah.

Matthew 3:11–12	Mark 1:7–8	Luke 3:15–17
	And he was preaching, and saying,	Now while the people were in a state of expectation and all were wondering in their hearts about John, as to whether he might be the Christ, John answered and said to them all,

Matthew 3:11-12	Mark 1:7-8	Luke 3:15-17
"I, on the one hand, am baptizing you with water for repentance, but he who is coming after me is mightier than I, and I am not fit to remove his sandals;	"After me one is coming who is mightier than I, and I am not fit to stoop down and untie the thong of his sandals. I baptized you with water; but	"I, on the one hand, am baptizing you with water; but one is coming who is mightier than I, and I am not fit to untie the thong of his sandals;
he will baptize you with the Holy Spirit and fire. His winnowing fork is in his hand, and he will clear his threshing floor; and he will gather his wheat into the barn, but he will burn up the chaff with unquenchable fire."	he will baptize you with the Holy Spirit."	he will baptize you with the Holy Spirit and fire. His winnowing fork is in his hand to clear his threshing floor, and to gather the wheat into his barn; but he will burn up the chaff with unquenchable fire."

Here John the Baptist prophesies the coming of Jesus in similar words in all three Synoptics: Jesus is mightier than John, who is not worthy to untie Jesus's sandals, and whereas John baptizes with water, Jesus baptizes with the Holy Spirit. However, Matthew and Luke both add, at exactly the same point, a continuation of John's prophecy that is not found in Mark. This is represented by the underlined words above. They both complete Mark's sentence "He will baptize you with the Holy Spirit" in the same way, by adding "and fire," before adding a whole sentence about judgment, in nearly identical wording. What appears to have happened here is that Matthew has expanded Mark's core narrative and Luke has copied Matthew's expansion, almost word for word.

To explain passages like this, Q theorists suggest that they represent cases where Mark and Q must have "overlapped" in content and wording. Thus Q also had an account of John's prediction about the coming one, expressed in similar wording, and Matthew and Luke independently conflated Mark and Q in exactly the same way. Explanations like this are, of course, possible, but they become increasingly implausible the more often they are invoked to explain the data. The number of passages like this, where Q advocates use the "Mark-Q overlap" explanation, is sizable and includes the baptism (Matt. 3:13–17//Mark 1:9–11//Luke 3:21–22), the temptation (Matt. 4:1–11//Mark 1:12–13//Luke 4:1–13), the Beelzebub controversy (Matt. 12:22–30//Mark 3:20–27//Luke 11:14–23), and the parable of the mustard seed (Matt. 13:31–32//Mark 4:30–32//Luke 13:18–19), among others. Broadly speaking, these are triple-tradition passages in which there are substantive agreements between Matthew and Luke against Mark. They make good sense as passages where Luke shows his knowledge of the way that Matthew reworked passages found in Mark.

It would be a mistake, however, to think that it is only passages like this where Matthew and Luke coincide in their rewording of passages that they derive from Mark. Every single triple-tradition passage features agreements between Matthew and Luke against Mark—agreements in omission, agreements in addition, agreements in order. It is true that where all three Synoptics have the same passage, Mark is usually the "middle term," which means that the majority of agreements are mediated via Mark, but at the same time, there are hundreds of agreements between Matthew and Luke against Mark, and these so-called minor agreements must be taken seriously. Unlike the major agreements that are explained by the theory of "Mark-Q overlap," the minor agreements cannot be explained by appealing to Q.

An example of a minor agreement between Matthew and Luke in the triple tradition is provided by the passage in which Jesus is mocked:

Matthew 26:67–68	Mark 14:65	Luke 22:63–64
Then they spat into his face, and struck him; and some slapped him, saying, "Prophesy to us, you Christ! Who is it that struck you?"	And some began to spit on him, and to cover his face, and to strike him, saying to him, "Prophesy!"	Now the men who were holding Jesus mocked him and beat him; they also blindfolded him and asked him, "Prophesy! Who is it that struck you?"

At the same point in the narrative, Matthew and Luke insert five identical Greek words, here translated by "Who is it that struck you?" Since Q, according to its advocates, did not have a Passion Narrative, this kind of agreement cannot have derived from Q. It is a mystery, therefore, how Matthew and Luke could have independently added this identical sentence to their Markan source. The standard answer given by Q advocates is that there must have been some kind of textual corruption, but since the wording is in every known witness of both Matthew and Luke, this answer is weak.

The presence of a whole range of agreements, from major to minor, between Matthew and Luke against Mark draws attention to the plausibility of the Farrer Hypothesis. If Matthew and Luke were independent of each other, as the Two Source Hypothesis proposes, it is surprising that they coincide in so many ways, and so frequently, in the triple-tradition material.

Returning to Editorial Fatigue

Given the links between Matthew and Luke, it might be asked whether it is indeed more likely that Luke knew Matthew or whether the reverse situation could obtain, that Matthew was familiar with Luke. With respect to Markan priority, one of the elements that proved helpful was the phenomenon of "editorial fatigue" (see above, pp. 50–51). If Luke was familiar with Matthew, are there any signs of Lukan fatigue in his editing of Matthew? Among several cases of editorial fatigue in material shared by Matthew and Luke,[11] the direction of dependence is always from Matthew to Luke.

One of the best examples is Matthew's parable of the talents, paralleled by the parable of the pounds in Luke (Matt. 25:14–30//Luke 19:11–27). Matthew's better-known, more compelling parable has three servants who receive five talents, two talents, and one talent respectively. The one who receives five talents makes five more, the one who receives two makes two more, and the one who receives one hides his in the ground. Those who made more money are warmly commended, and the other is roundly condemned. In Luke's retelling of the parable, there are now ten servants, each of whom is given a pound. This is a characteristic Lukan move; he often has the ratio 10:1 in his Gospel (e.g., Luke 15:8; 17:11–19). But this initial change is not sustained throughout, and Luke's story line soon drifts into Matthew's, and instead of the ten servants, it emerges that there are in fact three, as in Matthew: "the first," "the second," and "the other" (Luke 19:16, 18, 20). Further, in Luke's parable the first two servants receive "cities" as their reward (19:17, 19), the first ten and the second five, whereas in Matthew they are "put in charge of much" (25:21, 23). Moreover, Luke clearly shares Matthew's story line toward the end of the parable:

Matthew 25:28	Luke 19:24
So take the talent from him and give it to him who has the ten talents.	Take the pound from him and give it to him who has the ten pounds.

This line makes perfect sense in Matthew, but it is problematic in Luke. Luke's first servant actually has ten cities now, so a pound extra is nothing, and in any case he has not ten pounds but eleven (Luke 19:16; contrast Matt. 25:20). In cases like this, Luke appears to be secondary to Matthew, which suggests that the arrow should be drawn from Matthew to Luke rather than in the opposite direction.[12]

11. See further Goodacre, "Fatigue," 54–57.

12. Q theorists could of course suggest that here Luke was fatigued with Q rather than Matthew. However, I have not been able to find any examples of editorial fatigue that go

The evidence for Luke's familiarity with Matthew appears strong. The evangelists share the same basic approach to Mark's Gospel, adding a prologue about Jesus's birth, an epilogue about his resurrection, and teaching and narrative in between. They edit Mark in similar ways in individual passages; they often agree together in major ways against Mark, and there is not a passage in the triple tradition that lacks minor agreements between Matthew and Luke against Mark. If the evidence for a direct link between Matthew and Luke appears strong, Luke's editorial fatigue suggests that the direction of dependence is from Matthew to Luke, just as Matthew's and Luke's editorial fatigue has suggested their familiarity with Mark.

Why, Then, Q?

In spite of the evidence for Luke's use of Matthew, the theory of a hypothetical, lost document called Q remains popular. It is worth asking why this is the case. To some extent, its popularity relates to its pedigree. The Q theory has been honored by time, and it has been believed by almost all the great New Testament scholars over the last century and more. It is an attractive hypothesis in that it hopes to shed light on the earliest, most mysterious period of early Christianity and so to provide a promising early source of evidence for the historical Jesus's teaching and ministry. Moreover, the fact that it apparently lacks any passion or resurrection narrative makes it more intriguing in the bid to map early Christian views of Jesus. Could it be that some early Christians valued Jesus's sayings more than his death and resurrection, that the passion-centered Christianity of Paul and others was not mainstream?[13]

The unquestioning use of Q in much exegesis of Matthew and Luke further entrenches belief in Q in the mind-sets of many scholars. Similarly, many students are not even introduced to alternatives to Q in their introductory New Testament courses. The textbooks are often ignorant about the Farrer Hypothesis and dismissive of alternatives to the Two Source Hypothesis. Moreover, Q has become ever more "tangible" in recent years, now with its

---

in the opposite direction, and in this context my point is to note that Luke is secondary to Matthew, given the occasional suggestion that Matthew might have been familiar with Luke.

13. Q is often aligned with an early and independent *Gospel of Thomas* in a bid to anchor this model of Christian origins in the first century. I have argued that there are problems with this approach: first, because of major generic differences between Q and the *Gospel of Thomas* (see my *The Case against Q: Studies in Markan Priority and the Synoptic Problem* [Harrisburg, PA: Trinity Press International, 2002], 170–85); and second, because *Thomas* was familiar with the Synoptic Gospels (see my *Thomas and the Gospels: The Case for Thomas's Familiarity with the Synoptics* [Grand Rapids: Eerdmans, 2012]).

own verse-numbering system, its own critical edition, its own editorial history, and its own community.[14] In the face of this kind of confidence, it is always useful to remind ourselves that there is no ancient, external evidence of any kind for Q's existence. There are no textual witnesses, no fragments, no patristic citations—nothing. It is purely a scholarly construct, a hypothetical text.

This is not to say that Q is problematic purely because it is hypothetical. If a hypothetical text were to provide the best way of making sense of the internal data in the Synoptic Gospels, it would clearly be worth taking seriously. What Q's hypothetical status should encourage us to do is to take a careful look at the internal data of the Synoptic Gospels themselves. The Q hypothesis is based on the proposition that Matthew and Luke edited Mark independently of each other, a proposition that requires a hypothetical text to explain Matthew's and Luke's substantive agreements with each other. The arguments against Luke's use of Matthew, and so in favor of the existence of Q, cluster around four major claims: (1) Luke shows no knowledge of Matthew's special material; (2) Luke shows no knowledge of Matthew's editorial reworking of Mark; (3) Luke's order is unintelligible if he used Matthew; and (4) sometimes Matthew, sometimes Luke, has the more original form of a double-tradition saying.[15] All these claims are problematic, and I will address each one in turn.

Is Luke Ignorant of Matthew's Special Material?

A lot of material is unique to Matthew, appearing in his Gospel alone. This is generally labeled as Matthew's special material, or "M" for short. Q theorists argue that if Luke used Matthew, it is strange that he shows no knowledge of this material, and especially the details of Matthew's birth narrative (Matt. 1–2) and resurrection narrative (Matt. 28:1–20). A prime example is provided by Matthew's story of the magi visiting Jesus at his birth (Matt. 2:1–12). These magi are clearly non-Jewish, and, given Luke's Gentile-friendly agenda, it is thought odd that Luke, had he known Matthew, would have omitted so congenial a tale.[16]

14. See especially James M. Robinson, Paul Hoffmann, and John S. Kloppenborg, *The Critical Edition of Q: Synopsis including the Gospels of Matthew and Luke, Mark and Thomas with English, German, and French Translations of Q and Thomas* (Minneapolis: Fortress, 2000); John S. Kloppenborg, *Excavating Q: The History and Setting of the Sayings Gospel* (Minneapolis: Fortress, 2000).

15. For statements of the case for the existence of Q, see especially Christopher M. Tuckett, *Q and the History of Early Christianity: Studies on Q* (Edinburgh: T&T Clark, 1997), 1–39; Kloppenborg, *Excavating Q*, 11–54.

16. See, e.g., Robert H. Stein, *Studying the Synoptic Gospels: Origin and Interpretation*, 2nd ed. (Grand Rapids: Baker Academic, 2001), 111.

The argument is circular and problematic. On the Farrer Hypothesis, Luke takes over a great deal of material from Matthew. The material that he takes over is the double-tradition material, the passages that Two Source theorists attribute to Q. By definition, Luke does not have any of Matthew's unique material. The key question, therefore, is whether the double tradition looks like the kind of material we would expect Luke to take over from Matthew, and whether Matthew's special material looks like passages that Luke might leave behind. This is exactly what we find. Matthew's special material often has a non-Lukan profile, and it is easy to see why Luke would have chosen not to include it in his Gospel. In the aforementioned case of the visitation by the magi (Matt. 2:1–12), for example, it is true that Luke likes stories about Gentiles approaching Jesus, as his version of the centurion's boy, from Matthew, illustrates (Matt. 8:5–13//Luke 7:1–10), but it is not true that we would expect Luke to feature magi as heroes in his Gospel. His attitude toward magi (astrologers, magicians, sorcerers) is negative. One of the villains in Acts of the Apostles is Simon Magus (Acts 8:9–24). Luke gives magi and sorcerers bad press (see Acts 13:6, 8; 19:19).

Further, while it is true that Luke's birth narrative takes a different course from Matthew's, difference does not equate with ignorance. The points of contact between the two should be taken seriously (Mary and Joseph, Bethlehem, the virginal conception, and so on), as should the verbal correspondences like this:

Matthew 1:21	Luke 1:31
She will give birth to a son, and you [sg.] shall call him Jesus.	You will give birth to a son, and you [sg.] shall call him Jesus.

This is the kind of agreement that cannot be attributed to Q, since its advocates argue that it did not have a birth narrative. It appears, then, that Luke has carried this over from Matthew, and there is a subtle indication of this in the form of the address. In Matthew, this prophecy is made to Joseph and refers to Mary's birth and Joseph's naming of the child. Since it was the men who named their sons (cf. Luke 1:62–63), the singular address to Mary, in Luke, is less appropriate.

The detail, however, runs the risk of distracting attention from the general issue, which is that Luke's differences from Matthew do not require Luke's independence from Matthew. If Luke's birth narratives were not so well loved in the history of Christianity, it would be easier to understand the argument that he should have used more of Matthew's birth narrative. The same point is true of the resurrection stories. Although there are points of contact with his predecessors' accounts, Luke's points of divergence from Mark and Matthew result in some of the most memorable narratives of Jesus's resurrection, especially the story of the disciples on the road to Emmaus, which is unsurpassed as a literary masterpiece and in which the travelers come to recognize their walking companion as the resurrected Jesus, now made present in the breaking of bread (Luke 24:13–34).

Is Luke Ignorant of Matthew's Modifications of Mark?

It is often said that Luke cannot have known Matthew because he appears to be ignorant of the way in which Matthew modifies his Markan source. In other words, the triple-tradition material points to Luke's use of Mark, while the double tradition points to Luke's use of Q. There are several examples of Matthew's editing of Mark that one might have expected Luke to parallel, such as Peter's walking on the water (Matt. 14:28–31), Jesus's commendation of Peter (Matt. 16:16–19), and Pilate's wife's dream (Matt. 27:19).[17]

There are two major difficulties with this argument, one relating to the general point and one relating to the examples cited. The general point is that Luke does feature many of Matthew's modifications of Markan material, as we saw above (pp. 54–55) in cases such as John's prediction of a coming one (Matt. 3:11–12//Mark 1:7–8//Luke 3:15–17), where Matthew and Luke insert almost exactly the same wording at exactly the same point. Cases like this are excluded from consideration by Q advocates, however, because they are placed in a separate category of their own, "Mark-Q overlap." Examples of "Mark-Q overlap" are actually examples of triple-tradition passages where Matthew and Luke agree with each other in major, substantive ways, and there are several such passages, the temptation story and the Beelzebub controversy being among the better known. It appears that Luke generally prefers the Markan version of passages that he shares with Matthew, but there are occasions where he prefers the Matthean version. It is therefore false to talk about Luke's ignorance of Matthew's versions of Markan material.

There are also difficulties with the examples that Q advocates provide to make this argument. It is true, for example, that Luke has no parallel to Peter's walking on the water (Matt. 14:28–31), but he also has no parallel to the entire passage in which Jesus walks on the water (Matt. 14:22–32//Mark 6:45–52), so it is hardly surprising that he does not feature Matthew's episode with Peter. Similarly, it is true that Luke lacks Jesus's glowing commendation of Peter

---

17. A typical and influential formulation of this argument is found in Joseph A. Fitzmyer, *The Gospel according to Luke I–IX: Introduction, Translation and Notes*, AB 28 (Garden City, NY: Doubleday, 1981), 73–74. For other versions and discussion, see my *Case against Q*, 49–54.

(Matt. 16:16–19), but he also lacks the famous rebuke of Peter that follows on from it and that features in both Matthew and Mark (Matt. 16:22–23// Mark 8:32–33). In other words, Luke treads his own path in the passage, and he has his own story about Peter to tell later on, in both the Gospel (Luke 22:31–32) and Acts. The absence of a given Matthean passage in Luke is no more telling than the absence of a given Markan passage in the same context. Thus we should conclude not that Luke is ignorant of Matthew's additions to Mark, but rather that he includes some passages (the so-called Mark-Q overlap passages) and excludes others, just as he does with Mark's Gospel itself.[18]

Is Luke's Reordering of Matthew Unintelligible?

Q advocates argue that Luke's ordering of the double-tradition material is incomprehensible if he has taken it over from Matthew. Although we do not know what order the material had in the hypothetical Q, the presumption is that Luke's order broadly resembles Q's order, while Matthew reworked Q extensively. The argument focuses especially on Matthew's Sermon on the Mount (Matt. 5–7). It is argued that Luke surely would not have destroyed this Matthean masterpiece, keeping only some of it in his Sermon on the Plain (Luke 6:20–49), omitting some of it, and scattering the remainder to different contexts later in his Gospel. For an evangelist to have behaved in this way is unthinkable.[19]

There are several difficulties with the argument. It is based on a value judgment, a kind of contemporary aesthetic preference for Matthew's Sermon on the Mount that is unlikely to have been shared by Luke. The Sermon on the Mount is the longest uninterrupted monologue anywhere in the Synoptic Gospels, and however greatly we may admire it, it is unreasonable to expect Luke to have wished to reproduce it wholesale. He structures his Gospel differently and has far more narrative drive and dramatic variety than Matthew. Luke's discourses are regularly broken up with related parables and narratives. Thus one passage from the Sermon on the Mount, on the topic of care and anxieties (Matt. 6:25–34), is relocated in Luke 12:22–31, where it appears after the special Lukan parable of the rich fool (12:13–21), which deals with the same theme of riches, possessions, and God's provision in the context of a larger discussion about discipleship and heaven (12:32–34). It would be difficult to imagine a more appropriate location for this passage from the Sermon on the

18. Indeed, the theory of Markan priority has long had to deal with the fact that Luke has made one massive omission from Mark covering Mark 6:45–8:26. Since Q is unseen, no "omissions" can be observed, which naturally lends the theory a certain unfair advantage.

19. See, e.g., Christopher M. Tuckett, "Synoptic Problem," ABD 6:263–70, esp. 268.

Mount. Similarly, Luke relocates the teaching about prayer from the Sermon on the Mount (Matt. 6:9–13//Luke 11:1–4; Matt. 7:7–11//Luke 11:9–13) into its own special section on the theme of prayer (Luke 11:1–13), adding the unique Lukan parable about the friend at midnight (Luke 11:5–8), which is also about prayer. Once again, it is a perfect relocation of material from the Sermon on the Mount that is not at all unintelligible.

The difficulty in part with the argument about Luke's order is that it arises from unrealistic expectations about how Luke would have proceeded. If indeed Mark was the first Gospel, it may be that Luke had known it for longer than he had known Matthew, or that he admired its narrative structure over Matthew's. When faced with a book like Matthew's, which takes a unique course in reworking Mark's narrative, it is easy to imagine Luke following Matthew's basic idea and broad plan—adding birth narratives and resurrection stories and filling in the intervening narrative—while mining Matthew's non-Markan material for use in new, narratively compelling contexts.

Moreover, a careful look at Luke's attitude toward Mark's order is telling. Although Luke broadly retains the order of Mark's narrative passages, he behaves a little differently with Mark's sayings material. So when reworking Mark's parable chapter (Mark 4:1–34), Luke retains some of Mark's material (Mark 4:1–25//Luke 8:4–18: sower, mysteries, lamp), omits some (Mark 4:26–29: seed growing secretly; 4:33–34: speaking in parables), and relocates the remainder (Mark 4:30–32//Luke 13:18–19; cf. Matt. 13:31–32). The overall effect is that Luke's version of Mark's parable chapter is drastically shorter than Mark's. We observe the same kind of behavior in Luke's treatment of Matthew's sayings material. It is just that it is on a much larger scale, given the massive scope of the Matthean discourses like the Sermon on the Mount. Although Luke produces his own version of Matthew's sermon as the Sermon on the Plain (Luke 6:20–49), he omits some (like Matt. 5:33–37, on oaths; Matt. 6:16–18, on fasting) and redistributes the rest (like the material on prayer and possessions [see above]). Overall, Luke's reordering of Matthew makes perfect sense once one uses some imagination and pays attention to Luke's editorial practices elsewhere. Far from being a reason to invoke a hypothetical document, it is key to understanding how Luke's Gospel is constructed.

Does Luke's Double Tradition Sometimes Appear More Primitive?

One final argument against Luke's use of Matthew is dubbed "alternating primitivity." This is the argument that sometimes Matthew and sometimes Luke has the more original form of double-tradition sayings. This makes sense only on the Q hypothesis, it is alleged, because it illustrates the way in which the evangelists vary in their faithfulness to their source Q. Sometimes Matthew is closer to Q, and sometimes Luke is closer to Q. There is no difficulty for the Farrer Hypothesis in cases where Matthew appears to be more primitive than Luke, but there would appear to be a problem in cases where Luke looks more primitive. A textbook example of alleged greater Lukan primitivity is provided by the first beatitude:

Matthew 5:3	Luke 6:20
Blessed are the poor in spirit because theirs is the kingdom of the heavens.	Blessed are the poor because yours is the kingdom of God.

Here it is suggested that Luke reflects the Q wording, "Blessed are the poor," while Matthew "spiritualizes" the beatitude, changing "the poor" to "the poor in spirit." The argument, however, is without merit. It is characteristic of Luke to feature Jesus commending "the poor." Luke's Jesus begins his first major sermon in this way, with Jesus anointed to proclaim good news to "the poor" (Luke 4:18), and the fates of the poor and the rich are regularly reversed, just as they are here with Luke's addition of a woe to the rich (6:24), in passages like the Magnificat (1:52–53: "the rich are sent away empty") and the parable of the rich man and Lazarus (16:19–31). It is not at all surprising that Luke would redact Matthew in this way.[20]

However, the difficulties with the argument from alternating primitivity are not purely related to "poor" examples. There is a more fundamental flaw with the way that the argument conceptualizes the Synoptic Problem. While it is important to understand that the Synoptics are related to one another at a literary level, and to see what kind of literary relationship is involved, it is nevertheless a mistake to ignore oral traditions as a factor in the development of the Synoptics. The argument from alternating primitivity works with a narrowly literary understanding of the way that the evangelists worked, so that every variation between them is refracted through a literary prism.

There is a basic confusion between literary priority and the age of traditions in much Synoptic scholarship. It is a confusion that can be illustrated with the example of the Lord's Prayer (see the table on p. 65).

Here advocates of the Q hypothesis point to the variations between Matthew's and Luke's versions of the prayer by suggesting that each copied the prayer from Q, and that Luke's version is generally closer to the original Q

20. In some versions of the argument, scholars also appeal to *Gospel of Thomas* 54, which also has "Blessed are the poor"; however, *Thomas* probably is relying on Luke. See my *Thomas and the Gospels*, 50–52. On the beatitude as a whole, see further my *Case against Q*, 133–51.

Matthew 6:9–13	Luke 11:2–4
Our Father in heaven,	Father,
hallowed be your name.	hallowed be your name.
Your kingdom come.	Your kingdom come.
Your will be done,	
on earth as it is in heaven.	
Give us this day our daily bread.	Give us each day our daily bread.
And forgive us our debts,	And forgive us our sins,
as we also have forgiven our debtors.	for we ourselves forgive everyone indebted to us.
And do not bring us to the time of trial,	And do not bring us to the time of trial.
but rescue us from the evil one.	

wording, to which Matthew added embellishments. So Luke follows Q's simple address, "Father," and Matthew embellishes this by writing "Our Father in heaven," and so on.

The difficulty with this kind of approach is that it acts as if the only way that Matthew or Luke could have gained access to the prayer is via the literary text that they were copying. In cases like this, however, it is straightforward to imagine that Luke might have been influenced not solely by his Matthean source material but also by the way that the prayer was prayed in his church. A similar phenomenon can be observed in Luke's version of the eucharistic discourse, where Luke departs from Mark in ways that may suggest familiarity with parallel oral traditions (Matt. 26:26–29//Mark 14:22–25//Luke 22:14–20). In other words, while it is always important to take the Synoptic Problem seriously as a literary problem, it is also important to remember that there is a key difference between literary priority and tradition history, a difference that arguments about "alternating primitivity" can all too easily forget.

Conclusion

The Farrer Hypothesis has significant advantages over the competing theories. Unlike the Two Gospel Hypothesis, it recognizes the powerful arguments for the priority of Mark's Gospel. It builds on some of the best scholarship of the last century or more, with Matthew and Luke understood as creatively and critically expanding and reworking the Gospel of Mark. Unlike the Two Source Hypothesis, it is able to explain the data plausibly without appealing to a hypothetical, unattested document, Q. And it has the potential to make the best sense of the interaction between literacy and orality that characterizes early Christianity, recognizing that extensive agreements in wording and order among literary works can reasonably be explained only in terms of direct contact between texts, while understanding the key role played by oral tradition in the formation of the Gospel tradition.

The only disadvantage of the Farrer Hypothesis is that, with a pedigree of less than a century, the theory is still young, and the wheels of scholarship turn slowly. But theories come and go, and the advantage of recognizing both the priority of Mark and Luke's use of Matthew is that it acknowledges that its competitors—the Two Gospel and the Two Source Hypotheses—each got something right. The evidence for the priority of Mark remains overwhelming. The evidence for Luke's use of Matthew is so strong that it can no longer be brushed aside or explained away. The time has come to build on the cornerstone of Markan priority and to dispense with Q.

Further Reading

Intermediate

Farrer, Austin. "On Dispensing with Q." In *Studies in the Gospels: Essays in Memory of R. H. Lightfoot*, edited by D. E. Nineham, 55–88. Oxford: Blackwell, 1955.

Goodacre, Mark. *The Case against Q: Studies in Markan Priority and the Synoptic Problem*. Harrisburg, PA: Trinity Press International, 2002.

———. *The Synoptic Problem: A Way through the Maze*. BibSem 80. London: Sheffield Academic Press, 2001.

Goulder, Michael. "Is Q a Juggernaut?" *JBL* 115 (1996): 667–81.

Sanders, E. P., and Margaret Davies. *Studying the Synoptic Gospels*. London: SCM; Philadelphia: Trinity Press International, 1989.

Advanced

Foster, Paul, et al., eds. *New Studies in the Synoptic Problem: Oxford Conference, April 2008; Essays in Honour of Christopher M. Tuckett*. BETL 239. Leuven: Peeters, 2011.

Goodacre, Mark. "Fatigue in the Synoptics." *NTS* 44 (1998): 45–58.

Goulder, Michael. *Luke: A New Paradigm*. 2 vols. JSNTSup 20. Sheffield: JSOT Press, 1989.

Poirier, John C., and Jeffrey Peterson, eds. *Marcan Priority without Q: Explorations in the Farrer Hypothesis*. LNTS 455. London: Bloomsbury T&T Clark, 2015.

Watson, Francis. *Gospel Writing: A Canonical Perspective*. Grand Rapids: Eerdmans, 2013.

4

The Two Gospel Hypothesis

David Barrett Peabody

Introduction: Basic Features of the Two Gospel Hypothesis

Advocates of the Two Gospel Hypothesis conclude that the first of the canonical Gospels to be written was that attributed to Matthew; the second, that attributed to Luke; and the third, that attributed to Mark.

Advocates of the Two Gospel Hypothesis affirm that Matthew,[1] although written first, utilized a variety of source materials, but deny that any of Matthew's sources were any of the other, now-canonical Gospels. After Matthew's Gospel was written, both Luke and Mark utilized the work of predecessors in composing their own later Gospels. As the second of the canonical Gospels to be written, Luke utilized Matthew's Gospel and a considerable amount of non-Matthean source material, while Mark, writing third, utilized both Matthew's and Luke's Gospels as primary sources and blended or (to use an applicable literary term) "conflated" them, with the addition of very little other source material. Nevertheless, Mark did contribute a significant and distinctively Markan layer of literarily unifying material to his Gospel, as an

---

1. The full names "Matthew," "Luke," and "Mark" are used here to indicate the author of the Gospels that now carry their names, even though these Gospels remain, strictly speaking, anonymous compositions.

important and perhaps concluding step in its composition. Advocates of the Two Gospel Hypothesis have come to call this layer of Mark's text the "Markan Overlay"; it contains many significant and relatively easily identifiable, frequently repeated, Markan linguistic characteristics, some of which are quite sophisticated literary devices.

One of the latter literary devices is Mark's use of the Greek word for "again," *palin*, in a retrospective manner to unite two or more literary contexts in his Gospel.[2] What is remarkable about this literary characteristic of Mark's Gospel is that not one of the fifteen occurrences of this particular usage of the retrospective "again" appears in the parallel text of either Matthew's or Luke's Gospels, even though parallel contexts are frequent. On the Two Source Hypothesis, what is the likelihood that two authors, writing independently of each other (*ex hypothesi*, Matthew and Luke) while utilizing a common source (Mark's Gospel), would have managed to omit every one of these fifteen occurrences of this very important compositional, literary characteristic? One might imagine that Matthew and Luke have omitted some of the examples of this most significant Markan literary characteristic, but their common omission of every appearance of it seems highly unlikely, given the presuppositions of those who hold to the Two Source Hypothesis.

Internal Literary Evidence Favoring the Two Gospel Hypothesis

Direct Literary Dependence between and among the Synoptic Gospels

The most impressive sample of direct literary dependence between any two Synoptic Gospels is perhaps the preaching of John the Baptist (Matt. 3:7b–10//Luke 3:7b–9; Mark's Gospel has no parallel text here).

In this literary context there is verbatim agreement between Matthew's and Luke's Gospels for a total of sixty-two words in Greek, in the same word order and in the same Greek grammatical forms. Within this literary unit is only one lexical disagreement between the two Gospels, that of a single vocabulary item. In English this one lexical disagreement is on a word often

---

2. See (1) Mark 2:1 (cf. 1:21); (2) Mark 2:13–14 (cf. 1:16); (3) Mark 3:1 (cf. 2:1; 1:21); (4–6) Mark 3:20 (cf. 3:7–10; 2:13; 2:1–2; 1:45); (7) Mark 4:1–2 (cf. 2:13; 1:16); (8a) Mark 5:21 (cf. 5:1; 4:35–36); (8b) Mark 5:21 (cf. 4:1–2; 3:20; 3:7–10; 2:13; 2:1–2; 1:45); (9) Mark 7:14 (cf. 3:20); (10) Mark 7:31 (cf. 7:24); (11) Mark 8:1 (cf. 6:34); (12a) Mark 8:13 (cf. 8:10); (12b) Mark 8:13 (cf. 6:45); (13) Mark 10:1 (cf. 4:1–2; 2:13); (14) Mark 10:1 (cf. 3:7–8); (15) Mark 10:10 (cf. 9:28; 7:17; 4:10); (16) Mark 10:32 (cf. 9:35; 6:7; 3:13–15); (17) Mark 11:27 (cf. 11:15; 11:11a; 11:1a; 10:33a; 10:32a).

Matthew 3:7b–10	Luke 3:7b–9
You brood of vipers! Who warned you to flee from the wrath to come? Bear *fruit worthy* of repentance. Do not *presume* to say to yourselves, "We have Abraham as our ancestor"; for I tell you, God is able from these stones to raise up children to Abraham. Even now the ax is lying at the root of the trees; every tree therefore that does not bear good fruit is cut down and thrown into the fire.	You brood of vipers! Who warned you to flee from the wrath to come? Bear *fruits worthy* of repentance. Do not *begin* to say to yourselves, "We have Abraham as our ancestor"; for I tell you, God is able from these stones to raise up children to Abraham. *And* even now the ax is lying at the root of the trees; every tree therefore that does not bear good fruit is cut down and thrown into the fire.

translated "presume" in Matthew 3:9, which is contrasted with a word often translated "begin" in the parallel context in Luke 3:8.[3]

On the Oral Tradition Hypothesis, the same and similar contents in the Gospels of Matthew, Luke, and Mark are hypothesized to be the result of each Synoptic evangelist's independent usage of common oral traditions, rather than what appears to advocates of the Two Source, Two Gospel, and Farrer Hypotheses to be the results of direct or indirect literary dependence between and among these three Gospels. Furthermore, in the case of the Two Source Hypothesis, Matthew and Luke were also literarily dependent upon a nonextant literary source commonly referred to as "Q," a shorthand label for the German word *Quelle*, which simply means "source." John Kloppenborg, an advocate of the Two Source Hypothesis, for various reasons and following a significant amount of research into this nonextant document, including its layering into several developing versions over time, has suggested calling this "The Sayings Gospel, Q," rather than continuing to label it simply a "source" for Matthew and Luke.[4]

Most advocates of the hypotheses considered in this volume do allow for the influence of oral tradition during the development of the Synoptic Gospels. In the example just mentioned (Matt. 3:7b–10//Luke 3:7b–9), dependence on oral tradition alone may be possible, but it seems unlikely, even if one acknowledges, as advocates of the Two Gospel Hypothesis do, that the memories of peoples who depend upon oral tradition have been demonstrated to be significantly better than those dependent upon written

3. In addition, Matt. 3:8 has "fruit worthy," the noun and its modifying adjective both being singular in Greek, while Luke 3:8 has "fruits worthy," the noun and its modifying adjective both being plural in Greek, but even here the vocabulary items are identical. Otherwise, Luke also supplies a supplementary Greek *kai* (translated "and," "even," or "also" in Luke 3:9) before "ax"; cf. Matt. 3:10, where no *kai* appears at this location.

4. See John S. Kloppenborg, *Excavating Q: The History and Setting of the Sayings Gospel* (Minneapolis: Fortress, 2000), esp. 11–38.

literature—at least among the members of the very few living nonwriting cultures in the world today. In any case, although some today may be accustomed to making a clear distinction between oral and written culture, there is good evidence, in ancient written sources, that this was not a clear distinction in the ancient world.

In antiquity written literature typically seems to have been read aloud, even in private. This is reflected, for instance, in the story of Philip and the Ethiopian eunuch, as recorded in Acts 8:27b–35, which relates that Philip "heard him reading the prophet Isaiah" (v. 30). It is, therefore, no miracle that Philip knew what this eunuch was reading if Philip heard him reading aloud. A supporting example of such reading aloud even when in private, from as late as the end of the fourth into the early fifth century CE, is found in Augustine's *Confessions* 6.3.3. During one particular visit to his teacher, Ambrose, at his home in Milan, Augustine reported that he observed Ambrose reading, and, although "his eyes glanced over the pages, and his heart searched out the sense, his voice and tongue were silent." If this were not something odd in Augustine's previous experiences of readers and reading in his own time, he probably would not have thought it worth taking note of.

Isolating Linguistic Characteristics to Establish a Literary Style

Every author has a group of distinctive and, occasionally, even some unique linguistic characteristics—such as vocabulary items, grammatical constructions, turns of phrase, and so forth—that, when collected and studied carefully, can reveal a considerable amount about the literary style of that author. The sum of the many literary characteristics of an author may be said to be that author's literary style, and, like the personality of any author, some elements of their literary style might be shared with other authors, even without consulting another's work. However, the entire sum of an author's literary characteristics—her or his literary style—can rarely, if ever, be completely duplicated. Nevertheless, the literary style of an author, which can be revealed either in oral communication or in written documents if the content containing it is sufficiently extensive, has been so successfully isolated by some students of language that even the identity of the author of otherwise anonymous letters pertinent in cases of criminal activity has been successfully established. Less dramatically, many college professors can somewhat easily spot a term paper that has been plagiarized and subsequently can track down the original source for that plagiarized term paper either in some other student's previously submitted work, or in a published work, or in some online electronic text.

Isolating linguistic characteristics of a Gospel writer can help to establish that author's literary style and can assist in separating the author's hand from that of his or her sources. Unfortunately—apart from Eduard Zeller (1814–1908), who came to advocate the Two Gospel Hypothesis partly on the basis of his linguistic research—most of the other source critics of the Gospels in nineteenth-century Germany (who came to advocate the Two Source Hypothesis) did not, at the outset of their investigations, avoid presupposing a solution to the Synoptic Problem as part of their methodology for isolating the linguistic characteristics of each Synoptic evangelist. Therefore, when these same source critics later utilized the linguistic characteristics of the several Synoptic evangelists, which were determined by presuming a particular solution to the Synoptic Problem at the outset—typically the Two Source Hypothesis—these arguments for solving the Synoptic Problem were clearly circular, and the results of such efforts were predetermined from the outset.

Zeller himself published several lists of what he believed were the linguistic characteristics of each of the three Synoptic evangelists. These characteristics were isolated primarily on the basis of the frequency of their occurrence within each Gospel. Following Zeller's assembly of these lists, he then looked for whether one evangelist's linguistic characteristics appeared in the text of another evangelist only where there was verbatim agreement—that is, evidence of literary dependence between these two texts. Then he researched the text of the second evangelist to discover whether this other evangelist might have utilized the same literary characteristic(s), not only in contexts where there was evidence of copying, but also in other contexts where there was no parallel in the other Gospel.

Zeller then argued that the first evangelist who utilized a particular literary characteristic only in a passage or passages where a second evangelist also utilized it in parallel passages was most likely the copyist, while a second evangelist who utilized this same literary characteristic not only in passages where the other also had it in parallel but also in literary contexts independent of the other was, most likely, the source of the usage in the previously examined Gospel. Although Zeller does not spell out why he came to these conclusions, one may surmise that his thinking followed a logical line of reasoning. Every occurrence of a literary characteristic that appears only in passages where the other evangelist also utilizes it in parallel can be explained by copying. On the other hand, occurrences of a literary characteristic that appear not only in parallel but also in contexts independent of the other evangelist are more likely explained as original to that composition.

Unfortunately, but perhaps inevitably in the realm of literary criticism, the results of Zeller's tests with the individual literary characteristics of each pair of evangelists did not always indicate the same direction of literary dependence between them. Therefore Zeller ultimately chose to weigh the evidence in order to draw his conclusions. That is, whichever evangelist had the least amount of literary evidence that potentially indicated copying was, most likely, the source for one or two of the other Synoptic evangelists. The Gospel with the greater amount of literary evidence indicating copying most likely used the other Gospel(s) as source material.

The specific results of Zeller's experiments with the texts of the Synoptic Gospels were that it was much more likely that Mark was dependent upon Matthew's Gospel rather than the reverse; and much more likely that Mark was also dependent upon Luke's Gospel rather than the reverse. Zeller also argued, on the basis of his evidence, that Luke was more likely dependent upon Matthew's Gospel rather than the reverse, although the weight of this evidence was not as strong as that which favored Mark's dependence upon the other two Gospels.[5]

Evidence of Conflation in Mark's Gospel

On the Two Gospel Hypothesis, the author of the third Gospel to be written, Mark, reveals not only his literary dependence upon both the Gospels of Matthew and Luke by his inadvertent borrowing of many linguistic characteristics from each of his predecessors' literary styles, but also that he clearly blended or conflated the two Gospels together for the great bulk of his content. Mark did this in two major ways. First, Mark chose to make alternating agreements with the Gospels of Matthew and Luke in terms of the order of the pericopae[6] that Mark chose to include within his Gospel. Below is a chart of the evidence of Mark's alternating agreement between his two Gospel sources throughout the Markan Gospel in terms of the order of pericopae. Although J. J. Griesbach made a partial chart of such evidence, he did not provide the more comprehensive evidence provided here (see table, pp. 73–76).

In a second and complementary way, while conflating the Gospels of Matthew with Luke, Mark also frequently made alternating use of the actual

5. Eduard Zeller, "Studien zur neutestamentlichen Theologie 4: Vergleichende Übersicht über den Wörtervorrath der neutestamentlichen Schriftsteller," *Theologische Jahrbücher* 2 (1843): 443–543.

6. The word "pericope" comes from two Greek words meaning "to cut around." Thus a pericope is a literary unit that has integrity even when it is cut out of the running text of a Gospel (either literally or figuratively) and can stand alone and have meaning as an isolated literary unit.

Mark's Pericope Order Maintains Alternating Agreements
with the Gospels of Matthew and Luke

Matthew	Mark	Luke
Matt. 1:1–2:23 • Section begins with a genealogy and birth and infancy narratives	Mark 1:1 • Noting these contradictory orders, genealogies, and birth and infancy narratives, Mark omits both	Luke 1:1–3:38 • Parallel birth and infancy narratives of both John the Baptist and Jesus • Section ends with a genealogy
Prophecies about John • Matt. 11:10; cf. Mal. 3:1 • Matt. 3:3; cf. Isa. 40:3	Conflated Prophecies about John and "The Way" • Mark 1:2–3	Prophecies about John • Luke 7:27; cf. Mal. 3:1 • Luke 3:4–5; cf. Isa. 40:3–5
John the Baptist • Matt. 3:1–17	"Beginning with the Baptism of John" • Mark 1:4–11	John the Baptist • cf. Luke 3:1–22
Three-Stage Temptation • Matt. 4:1–11	Abbreviated Temptation • Mark 1:12–13 (Duality "in[to] the desert")	Three-Stage Temptation • Luke 4:1–13
Jesus's Ministry Begins, Calls First Disciples • Matt. 4:12–22	John Arrested/ Jesus's Ministry Begins, Calls First Disciples • Mark 1:14–20	Jesus's Ministry Begins • Luke 4:14–16a
Sermon on Mount • Matt. 4:23–7:29	Contradictory Inaugural Sermons, So Mark Omits Both	Sermon in Nazareth • Luke 4:16b–30
	Healings and Teachings • Mark 1:21–3:5	Healings and Teachings • Luke 4:14–6:11
Plot to Kill Jesus • Matt. 12:14–16	First Step in Plot to Kill Jesus • Mark 3:6–12	
Proof from Prophecy • Matt. 12:17–21		
	Call of the Twelve • Mark 3:13–19	Call of the Twelve • Luke 6:12–19
	• Absence from Mark of Sermon on the Plain, which complements previous absence of Sermon on the Mount from Matthew's Gospel	Sermon on the Plain • Luke 6:20–7:1
Jesus's Wisdom • Matt. 12:22–13:23	Jesus's Wisdom • Mark 3:20–4:20	

GRAY BOXES = Mark's shifting parallels, now with Matthew, now with Luke

Matthew	Mark	Luke
• cf. Matt. 5:14–16; 6:22–23; 7:1–2; 10:26–27; 13:12	Wisdom Sayings • Mark 4:21–25	Wisdom Sayings • Luke 8:16–18
Parable of Wheat and Tares • Matt. 13:24–30	Parable of Seed Growing Secretly • Mark 4:26–29	
Parable of Mustard Seed Transitional Statement • Matt. 13:31–35	Parable of Mustard Seed Conclusion of Jesus's Wisdom • Mark 4:30–34	
[Jesus's True Relatives, Matt. 12:46–50 above]	[Jesus's True Relatives, Mark 3:31–35 above] • Mark agrees with Matthew's version of this story in terms of order; therefore, Mark omits the same story here in Luke 8:19–21	Jesus's True Relatives • Luke 8:19–21
	Jesus's Acts of Power • Mark 4:35–5:43	Jesus's Acts of Power • Luke 8:22–56
Transition with Retrospective on Jesus's Wisdom and Power • Matt. 13:54–58	Transition with Retrospective on Jesus's Wisdom and Power • Mark 6:1–6a	
(cf. Matt. 9:35–10:16)	Commissioning of Twelve Apostles • Mark 6:6b–13	Commissioning of Twelve Apostles • Luke 9:1–6 (cf. 10:1–16)
	Retrospective on John the Baptist • Mark 6:14–16	Retrospective on John the Baptist • Luke 9:7–9
Death of John the Baptist • Matt. 14:3–12	Death of John the Baptist • Mark 6:17–29	(cf. Luke 3:18–20)
	Apostles' Return • Mark 6:30–31 See Bethsaida below at Mark 6:45 and 8:22	Apostles Return • Luke 9:10 Withdrawal to Bethsaida
Feeding of the Five Thousand • Matt. 14:13–21	Feeding of the Five Thousand • Mark 6:32–44	Feeding of the Five Thousand • Luke 9:11–17
Feeding and Healing • Matt. 14:22–16:12; cf. 18:3	Departure to Bethsaida • Mark 6:45 Feeding and Healing • Mark 6:45–8:21	Luke 9:18–50

Matthew	Mark	Luke
	Arrival in Bethsaida • Mark 8:22 Blind Man Healed • Mark 8:22–26	
Matt. 18:6–19:15 Note that this section begins with Matt. 18:1–2, 4–5. Mark places missing verse (Matt. 18:3) at Mark 10:15	"On the way," Jesus reveals his identity • Mark 8:27–10:16 Parallel w/ Matt. 18:1–2, 4–5 in Mark 9:33–37	cf. Lukan Travel Narrative • Luke 9:51–18:14
From Decalogue to Shema • Matt. 19:16–22:40	From Decalogue to Shema • Mark 10:17–12:34	
Sadducees Mock Jesus's Teaching on Resurrection • Matt. 22:23–33	Sadducees Mock Jesus's Teaching on Resurrection • Mark 12:18–27	Sadducees Mock Jesus's Teaching on Resurrection • Luke 20:27–40 End of Pericope (Luke 20:40): **"No One Dared Any Longer to Question Him."**
A Lawyer Asks Jesus about the Greatest Commandment • Matt. 22:23–40	A Scribe Asks Jesus about the Greatest Commandment • Mark 12:28–34 End of Middle Pericope (Mark 12:34): **"No One Dared Any Longer to Question Him."** (Mark = Middle Term)	A Lawyer Asks Jesus What He Must Do to Inherit Eternal Life [Luke 10:25–28]
Jesus Questions the Scribes' Claim That the Messiah is the Son of David • Matt. 22:41–46 End of Pericope (Matt. 22:46): "Nor Did Anyone **Dare Any Longer to Question Him** from That Day."	Jesus Questions the Scribes' Claim That the Messiah is the Son of David • Mark 12:35–37	Jesus Questions the Scribes' Claim That the Messiah is the Son of David • Luke 20:41–44
Woes to Pharisees • Matt. 23:1–36		

Matthew	Mark	Luke
	Widow's Mite Opening of Inclusio with Female Examples • Mark 12:37b–44	Widow's Mite • Luke 21:1–4
Eschatological Discourse • Matt. 24:1–25:30	Eschatological Discourse • Mark 13:1–37 *Note that Mark creates an inclusio of female examples around this section by pulling from both sources' orders (Luke 21:1–4//Mark 12:37b–44; Matt. 26:1–12// Mark 14:1–9).	Eschatological Discourse • Luke 21:5–36
Woman Anoints Jesus • Matt. 26:1–12	Woman Anoints Jesus • Mark 14:1–9	Woman Washes Jesus's Feet [cf. Luke 7:36–50]
Judas Plots Betrayal of Jesus • Matt. 26:14–16	Judas Plots Betrayal of Jesus • Mark 14:10–11	Judas Plots Betrayal of Jesus • Luke 22:1–6
Preparation for Passover • Matt. 26:17–19	Preparation for Passover • Mark 14:12–16	Preparation for Passover • Luke 22:7–13
Passion Narrative • Matt. 26:20–28:8	Passion Narrative • Mark 14:17–16:8	Passion Narrative • Luke 22:14–24:8
Post Resurrection Appearances • Matt. 28:9–20	"Until He Was Taken Up from Us" • Mark 16:9–20 (Mark's text follows Luke's Gospel with details drawn from Matt. 28)	Post Resurrection Appearances • Luke 24:9–53

wording of both sources within individual pericopae. One famous example of this is available here in English translation (see the table on pp. 77–78).

A careful review of these two elements of Mark's method of conflation—(1) alternating agreements with the Gospels of Matthew and Luke in terms of the order of pericopae, and (2) alternating agreements in terms of the very wording within individual pericopae—reveals that typically (3) the Gospel whose pericope order Mark was primarily following at any given time also typically shows Mark's greater dependence upon the actual wording of that same Gospel. This conforms exactly to what one would expect to take place, assuming the validity of the Two Gospel Hypothesis.

Advocates of the Two Source Hypothesis, however, have yet to provide a satisfactory explanation for these complementary alternating agreements

Jesus Heals Many Sick

KEY TO CODING: solid underlining = verbatim agreement
dotted/dashed underlining = same lexeme but different grammatical form

	Matthew 8:16–17		Mark 1:32–34		Luke 4:40–41
1a	And when evening had come	1a	And when evening had come		
		1b	when the sun had set	1b	And as the sun was setting
2a	they brought to him	2a	they brought to him		
		2b	all those having illnesses	2b	all those who had persons with infirmities
2c	many demon possessed	2c	and the demon possessed.		
				4c	with various diseases
				2a	were leading them to him.
		3	And the whole city was gathered at the door.		
	and		And		And on each one of them, after he had laid on his hands,
		4a	he healed many	4a	he was healing them.
		4b	who had illnesses		
		4c	with various diseases		
		4d	and many demons	4d	And even demons
4e	he cast out the spirits	4e	he cast out		were coming out from many
	by a word.				crying out and saying, "You are the Son of God."
		5	and he did not allow the demons to speak because they knew him.	5	And he commanded not to permit them to speak because they knew him to be the Christ.
2b	And all those				
4b	who had illnesses				
4a	he healed;				

Matthew 8:16-17	Mark 1:32-34	Luke 4:40-41
2b thus was fulfilled the word 4c through Isaiah the prophet, "He bore our infirmities and carried our diseases."		

of Mark with Matthew's and Luke's Gospels, both in terms of alternating agreements in pericope order and in the order of wording within pericopae. Specifically, how would it have been possible for two authors—Matthew and Luke, working independently of each other, according to the Two Source Hypothesis—to divide the text of their common source, Mark's Gospel, so neatly between them? This accidental explanation of such literary evidence seems incredible when one considers the kind of evidence displayed in the two charts above. The alternating agreements of Mark with the two other Gospels is clearly more easily explained on the basis that Mark, being in control of his two sources by writing third, has neatly blended or conflated the texts of these two earlier Gospels together in composing his Gospel (Two Gospel Hypothesis), than it is on the Two Source Hypothesis, which alleges that Mark's two kinds of alternating agreements between the Gospels of Matthew and Luke are the accidental results of Matthew and Luke independently utilizing Mark's Gospel.

Major advocates and defenders of the Two Source Hypothesis are well aware that if Matthew and Luke were, in fact, literarily dependent upon each other, there would be no need either to posit the hypothetical "Sayings Gospel, Q" to explain the close literary relationships in the many contexts shared by the Gospels of Matthew and Luke that are not paralleled in Mark's Gospel, or even to explain those literary contexts that are paralleled in Mark's Gospel. In short, the Two Source Hypothesis would no longer need to be posited at all. The Farrer Hypothesis fares better than the Two Source Hypothesis on this point because it argues that although Mark wrote the first Gospel, Matthew directly utilized Mark's Gospel, and Luke directly utilized both. In short, the Farrer Hypothesis also has no need for Q and thus "dispensed" with it in the classic 1955 essay by Austin Farrer that described this part of his source hypothesis for the Synoptic Gospels.[7]

---

7. Austin Farrer, "On Dispensing with Q," in *Studies in the Gospels: Essays in Memory of R. H. Lightfoot*, ed. D. E. Nineham (Oxford: Blackwell, 1955), 55–88.

A Limited Number of Literary Units That Are Unique to Mark

On the Two Gospel Hypothesis, Mark chose to include only a very few whole pericopae within his Gospel that were not drawn from Matthew's Gospel or Luke's Gospel or both. In short, only a limited number of whole pericopae in Mark's Gospel cannot be traced back to either Matthew's or Luke's Gospel or, quite frequently, to both. In the eighteenth century Johann Jakob Griesbach accepted only twenty-four verses in five literary contexts (three stories and two parables) in Mark's Gospel as not coming from the other two Gospels. These contexts were Mark 3:7–12; 4:26–29; 7:32–37; 8:22–26; 13:33–36 (see the illustrative chart above). However, Griesbach came to his conclusion without considering the many examples of special Markan periphrasis (longer phrasing in place of a possible shorter expression) within many other pericopae with no parallel in Matthew's Gospel or Luke's Gospel. This material has since become part of what eventually came to be called the "minor agreements" of Matthew's and Luke's Gospels against the Gospel of Mark.

On the Two Gospel Hypothesis—because Luke had already utilized Matthew's Gospel, prior to Mark's use of both Matthew's and Luke's Gospels—the Gospels of Matthew and Luke already shared quite a number of the same stories about Jesus's birth, life, ministry, death, and resurrection. As a result, many of these shared pericopae also appear in a common pericope order. Luke's prior use of Matthew's Gospel would naturally also have made Mark's conflation of the Gospels of Matthew and Luke much easier than it might have been, had the shared content and sequence of pericopae in the Gospels of Matthew and Luke been more different than they are.

Markan Overlay and Mark's Appearance of Literary Unity

As perhaps the penultimate or even the final step in his compositional procedure, Mark, on the Two Gospel Hypothesis, either intentionally or unintentionally seems to have glossed his conflated text of Matthew's and Luke's Gospels with his own distinctive linguistic characteristics. Such linguistic features found within Mark's Gospel—repeated words, grammatical constructions, theological motifs, and so on—have been termed the "Markan Overlay" to highlight their distinctive presence. This often serves to give Mark's Gospel not only its distinctive literary "flavor" or "color," as scholars in the nineteenth century sometimes referred to these features of the Markan text, but also the appearance of a literary unity. This sets Mark's Gospel apart from the other two Synoptics, each of which more readily reveals the fact that these Gospels were composed from more than one source, and, perhaps, whose authors may even have utilized some somewhat contradictory source materials. This seems to be especially the case when considering the sources that Matthew may have utilized in an apparent attempt to promote unity within a sometimes-quarreling early Christian community. One example of such quarrels, according to the New Testament, was that between the followers of Paul in conflict with the followers of James, "the brother of the Lord" (see Gal. 1:19; cf. Matt. 13:55–56//Mark 6:3).

The So-Called Minor Agreements of the Gospels of Matthew and Luke against Mark's Gospel

As suggested above, a major objection to the Two Source Hypothesis over at least the last century and a half has been the so-called minor agreements of the Gospels of Matthew and Luke against Mark's Gospel in those passages in which all three of these evangelists are telling the same story with many of the same or similar words. The kinds of minor agreements that often are found within these passages may now be divided into two basic and substantially filled categories: (1) the so-called positive minor agreements (common Matthean and Lukan changes or additions to Mark's Gospel) and (2) the so-called negative minor agreements (common Matthean and Lukan omissions from Mark's Gospel). These are anomalous if one claims, as advocates of the Two Source Hypothesis do, that Matthew and Luke made independent use of their two main and commonly utilized sources, Mark's Gospel and Q.

Beginning in 1925 with the work of B. H. Streeter, who carefully divided the positive minor agreements known to him at the time into several categories in order to "divide and conquer,"[8] advocates of the Two Source Hypothesis have tended to suggest that these positive minor agreements are simply the result of independent and therefore accidental agreements between Matthew and Luke in either changing or supplementing Mark's Gospel with exactly the same or similar words in their literary contexts parallel to Mark's Gospel. However, in more recent discussions of the Synoptic Problem, advocates of the Two Source Hypothesis have had to turn to explaining not only the positive agreements but also the negative agreements, which may be identified as those contexts in Mark's Gospel where Matthew and Luke have also accidentally,

---

8. B. H. Streeter, *The Four Gospels: A Study of Origins, Treating of the Manuscript Tradition, Sources, Authorship, and Dates* (London: Macmillan, 1924), esp. Streeter's style of "divide and conquer" by his categorization and atomization of the evidence, 293–331. For a significant critique and history of the Two Source Hypothesis and numerous arguments against Streeter's style of argumentation, see William R. Farmer, *The Synoptic Problem: A Critical Analysis* (New York: Macmillan, 1964), esp. in chap. 4, "An Analysis of Streeter's Contribution to the Two-Document Hypothesis," 118–77.

yet independently, agreed in omitting the same word or words and sometimes entire sentences or paragraphs.

A classic example of a significant positive minor agreement is the fact that both Matthew and Luke have added the question "Who is it that struck you?" in the context of Jesus's precrucifixion mistreatment and mocking by Roman soldiers (see Matt. 26:68//Luke 22:64; cf. Mark 14:53–65, where Mark has no parallel to this sentence either here or anywhere else in his Gospel).

Matthew 26:67-68	Mark 14:65	Luke 22:63-64
Then they spat into his face, and struck him; and some slapped him, saying, "Prophesy to us, you Christ! Who is it that struck you?"	And some began to spit on him, and to cover his face, and to strike him, saying to him, "Prophesy!"	Now the men who were holding Jesus mocked him and beat him; they also blindfolded him and asked him, "Prophesy! Who is it that struck you?"

Advocates of the Two Gospel Hypothesis would argue that, in this literary context, Luke inferred from Matthew's Gospel that Jesus was blindfolded at the time of this mockery and added this detail to his text. Thus, perhaps, Luke made the context of this taunting question more understandable in his Gospel. Mark, however, accepted the detail of the blindfold from Luke 22:64 (cf. Mark 14:65) but omitted the question (Matt. 26:68//Luke 22:64), which may have motivated Luke to add the detail of the blindfold in the first place. Mark may have then made the significant omission of this question from the Gospels of Matthew and Luke because of the somewhat contrasting contexts within their parallel pericopae, in which Jesus is blindfolded in one and not the other.

The German New Testament scholar Andreas Ennulat has calculated that there are now more than a thousand documented literary contexts in the Synoptic Gospels where such "minor agreements," both positive and negative, appear in parallel contexts in the Gospels of Matthew and Luke against their alleged source, Mark's Gospel.[9] This is clearly far too many to be explained by Matthew's and Luke's independent and accidental agreement to change Mark's Gospel in either exactly the same way or, sometimes, in similar ways. According to the Two Gospel Hypothesis, however, these minor agreements are to be explained by Luke's direct use of Matthew's Gospel and Mark's subsequent utilization of both Matthew's and Luke's Gospels. In such cases, by copying from both sources, Mark sometimes changed the common text of

9. Andreas Ennulat, *Die "Minor Agreements": Untersuchungen zu einer offenen Frage des synoptischen Problems*, WUNT 2.62 (Tübingen: Mohr-Siebeck, 1994).

the Gospels of Matthew and Luke, omitted some common material from them, and, at the same time, was free to supplement the texts of his two sources. In fact, such changes and supplements are repeated throughout Mark's Gospel and often reflect the distinctive literary style of its author.

External Evidence in Support of the Two Gospel Hypothesis

Prior to the closing decades of the eighteenth century, no scholar of either church or academy ever suggested that Mark's Gospel was the earliest of the canonical Gospels to be composed. Rather, the uniform tradition was that the Gospel attributed to the apostle named "Matthew" was the first of the four written Gospels that later were canonized, and the apostle named "John" wrote the last Gospel of these four. There was no debate about the sequence of composition of the Gospels of Matthew and Mark prior to the final decades of the eighteenth century, when G. C. Storr at the University of Tübingen first began to advocate the priority of Mark's Gospel in the sequence of the composition of the canonized Gospels.[10] Before Storr's challenge, the only debate about the sequence of the composition of the four canonized Gospels was about who wrote second and who wrote third. Specifically, was it Mark or Luke who wrote second, and the other third?

Some of the early church's beliefs about the order of composition of the four eventually canonized Gospels are reflected in some early orders in which they were subsequently placed in the canon. For instance, some early Latin canons of the four Gospels, made prior to the publication of Jerome's official Latin translation for the Western church, the Vulgate, adopted the canonical order of the Gospels attributed to Matthew, John, Luke, and Mark. This order may reflect two aspects of respect for the authors of these four Gospels. The first can be called an "order of dignity." This signifies that those Gospels presumed to be written by two of the twelve apostles of Jesus—Matthew and John—were placed in the canon prior to the Gospels believed to be by authors who were only presumed to be "apostolic men" (disciples of apostles rather than apostles themselves). Luke was one of these two such apostolic men because he was believed to be the follower of Paul (see Col. 4:14; 2 Tim. 4:11). The other of these two was Mark, who was believed to be the follower of Peter (see 1 Pet. 5:13).

This first order of dignity, which sought to place apostles (Matthew and John) prior to the apostolic men (Luke and Mark), may have then been

---

10. Gottlob C. Storr, *Über den Zweck der evangelischen Geschichte und der Briefe Johannis* (Tübingen: J. F. Herrbrandt, 1786).

combined with a second "order of composition": Matthew's Gospel before John's, and Luke's Gospel before Mark's. The order we find in Origen and later church fathers may, by way of contrast, reflect an evangelistic order: Mark's Gospel (related to Peter's witness) was subsequently placed second, and Luke's Gospel (related to Paul's witness) was placed third. That is, the plan to go "first to the Jews [the Gospel of Mark], and then to the Gentiles [Luke-Acts]" may have been reflected in the then generally accepted canonical sequence: the Gospels of Matthew, Mark, Luke, John.

The earliest external witness to the relative importance of the Gospels of Matthew and Mark to each other is that of Papias of Hierapolis (60–130 CE), who, according to his testimony as it is preserved in the *Church History* of Eusebius of Caesarea (ca. 260–340 CE), said this about each of these Gospels:

> For Matthew composed the Logia [sayings] in a Hebraic style; but each recorded them as he was in a position to do. (Eusebius, *Church History* 3.39.16)

> Mark, being the recorder of Peter, wrote accurately, but not in order, whatever he [Peter] remembered of the things either said or done by the Lord. For he [Mark] had neither heard the Lord nor followed him, but later [followed] Peter, as I said; who used to make his discourses according to the *chreias*,[11] but not making, as it were, a literary composition of the Lord's sayings; so that Mark did not err at all when he wrote certain things just as he (Peter) recalled them. For he had but one intention, not to leave out anything he had heard nor to falsify anything in them. (Eusebius, *Church History* 3.39.15)

Eusebius did not record anything comparable in his *Church History* from Papias about the Gospels of Luke and John, so one can make a comparison only between these two comments from Papias about the Gospels attributed to Matthew and Mark, as Eusebius has preserved them. Here Papias defends the Gospel of Mark against some who have criticized it. Specifically, there appears to be evidence here that some early Christians had criticized Mark's Gospel for (1) having omitted some material from his Gospel, and/or (2) having falsified some matters, and perhaps even (3) having erred about some matters, or (4) not having given an accurate account of the order of events in Jesus's life. Papias, however, claims that Mark intended to write not a literary composition but, more simply, only a record of whatever Peter

---

11. A *chreia* is an ancient literary form that consists of a short historical context, followed by a pithy saying, attributed to a known historical figure. In some contexts, however, it can simply be translated in the plural as "needs."

had recalled and proclaimed about Jesus and passed on to Mark in an order of recollection by Peter.

However, to determine an omission, error, or inaccuracy of the order of events in Mark's Gospel, one would need a norm for establishing what should have been said by Mark. From Eusebius's account of Papias's testimony, the Gospel of Matthew could certainly have been that norm from which these critiques of Mark's Gospel might have been derived or at least supported.

The earliest testimony from the early church fathers that explicitly discusses the sequence in which the Gospels were composed is that of "the primitive elders" passed on by Clement of Alexandria (ca. 150–215 CE), as preserved in Eusebius's *Church History* 6.14.5–7. Clement's testimony from "the primitive elders" affirms that those Gospels with genealogies (such as the Gospels of Matthew and Luke and, perhaps, others with genealogies, either noncanonical or now lost) were written prior to others.[12] Therefore one might conclude that, among the eventually canonized Gospels, Mark's Gospel, John's Gospel, and perhaps any and all other Gospels that do not contain genealogies were composed after those, like the Gospels of Matthew and Luke, that did. This understanding of Clement's testimony was explicitly remembered and preserved in the church's memory and passed on both in some of the works of the ninth-century Irish monk Sedulius Scottus (fl. 840–60 CE)[13] and in the work of Isidore of Seville (ca. 560–636 CE).[14]

At the turn of the fifth century, in book 4 of his famous *Harmony of the Gospels*, Augustine of Hippo concluded, on the basis of his own independent, careful, and detailed verse-by-verse comparative analysis of the texts of all four canonical Gospels, that it was more probable to view the Gospel of Mark as a Gospel that combined elements of Matthew's and Luke's Gospels than it was to view Mark's Gospel simply as an abbreviation of Matthew's that had no relationship to the Gospel of Luke at all—as Augustine had affirmed earlier in book 1 of this same work, perhaps under the influence of some of his predecessors' claims about this matter, such as Origen or Irenaeus of Lyons.

Specifically, in book 1 of his *Harmony of the Gospels*, Augustine passed on a tradition of the church that Matthew wrote the first Gospel; that Mark

12. For a well-researched, different, and challenging interpretation of this testimony from Clement, preserved in Eusebius, consult Stephen C. Carlson, "Clement of Alexandria on the 'Order' of the Gospels," *NTS* 47 (2001): 118–25.

13. See PL 103, cols. 279–860, esp. 283–84.

14. PL 83, col. 175. For comments on Sedulius Scottus and his views of Synoptic relationships, see Giuseppe Giovanni Gamba, "A Further Reexamination of Evidence from the Early Tradition," in *New Synoptic Studies: The Cambridge Gospel Conference and Beyond*, ed. William R. Farmer (Macon, GA: Mercer University Press, 1983), 17–35, esp. 23–25.

wrote second and abbreviated Matthew's Gospel; that Luke—without a companion, such as Matthew had with Mark—wrote third; and that John wrote last, with each successive evangelist making use of the work of his predecessors. In this same early context in book 1 of his *Harmony of the Gospels*, Augustine also assigned the four beasts of Ezekiel 1:4–11 and Revelation 4:6–7 (lion, ox, man, eagle) to each of the four evangelists and their Gospels, as follows. First, since Augustine viewed Matthew as depicting Jesus's regal human nature, Augustine appropriately assigned the lion, the king of beasts, to the Gospel of Matthew. Second, since Augustine viewed Luke as depicting Jesus's priestly human nature, his Gospel should appropriately be assigned the ox, a symbol of priestly sacrifice. Third, since Mark, like Matthew and Luke, had also depicted Christ's human nature, but without specifically focusing on either the regal or the priestly humanity of Jesus, Mark's Gospel should most appropriately be assigned the neutral human figure. And John's Gospel, which Augustine read as depicting the divine nature of Christ rather than the human nature on which the other three canonical Gospels focused, should appropriately be assigned the eagle, the creature of the heavens.

But Augustine's first impressions, prior to working carefully through the whole of each of the four canonical Gospels himself, were based on his initial use of Eusebius's canons in order to find his way from a context in one Gospel to a parallel context in one, two, or three of the others. After Augustine had systematically worked through all four of these Gospels himself, he did not change his assignments of these creatures to each of the four Gospels, but he did change his mind about why these assignments were even more appropriate than he had first thought. Specifically, Augustine changed his mind about how Mark was related to Matthew and to Luke. In book 1, Augustine had assigned the lion, the king of beasts, to Matthew because, in Augustine's view at that time, Matthew's Gospel had particularly depicted Christ's regal human nature. Then Augustine assigned the man to Mark because the kingly, human Jesus depicted in Matthew's Gospel required a courtier, the man. Luke, in turn, received the ox as his symbol because Luke's Gospel was about Christ's priestly human nature, Augustine reasoned in book 1, and because the Jewish high priest always entered the holy of holies in the Jerusalem temple alone—that is, without anyone to accompany him, as Matthew had Mark.

Although Mark was also described in book 1 of Augustine's *Harmony of the Gospels* as the "abbreviator" of Matthew, by the time he reached book 4.10.11, Augustine's rationale for his assignments of these four living creatures of Ezekiel and Revelation to the four canonical Gospels had changed, presumably on the basis of his subsequent, very careful comparative analyses of the four canonical Gospels in their various interrelationships. Specifically, throughout the *Harmony of the Gospels*, Augustine had first worked through all the material to which all four of the canonized Gospels bore concurrent testimony; next, where any three had the same or similar literary units; then, where any two were in agreement; and finally, where any one of the four canonical Gospels had something not found in the other three.

Whereas in book 1 Augustine noted that Luke needed no courtier, foot follower, or abbreviator, as Matthew had Mark, in book 4, after all that comparative work, Augustine concluded that the assignment of the man to Mark was even more appropriate because Mark's Gospel was related both to Matthew's kingly portrayal of the human Christ and to Luke's sacerdotal portrayal of the human Christ. And in book 4, Augustine used the metaphor of Mark "walking with both" Matthew and Luke, even as Augustine had described Mark as Matthew's "foot follower" in book 1, but left Luke, symbolically speaking, standing alone—without a companion, count, footman, or (in literary terms) abbreviator, as Augustine early in his work variously described Mark in his relationship to Matthew.

Therefore toward the end of his *Harmony of the Gospels*, in the context of book 4.10.11, Augustine concluded that Mark's Gospel was actually related to both Matthew and Luke because, although Mark shared many similar texts with Matthew, as pointed out in Eusebius's canons, he also shared much similar material with Luke. Just before Augustine took up his last type of material to be considered—those passages that only John had recorded among the four canonical evangelists—we have what can appropriately be described as an early, but clear, Augustinian observation of something that Henry Owen, Johann Jakob Griesbach, and Friedrich Andreas Stroth, along with a number of later advocates of the Two Gospel Hypothesis, also observed: Mark shared texts not only with Matthew but also with Luke. Augustine's later and, as Augustine himself described it, "more probable" view of the interrelationships among the Gospels of Matthew, Mark, and Luke is, in fact, not the hypothesis traditionally attributed to him in virtually all handbooks on the Gospels: that Matthew wrote first; Mark wrote second, abbreviating Matthew; Luke wrote third, making use of both Matthew and Mark; and John wrote last, being aware of all three of his predecessors. That view is now sometimes called the "traditional Augustinian hypothesis," but that is not what Augustine himself claimed as his own, more probable, view of the interrelations of the Gospels. That hypothesis does not, in fact, reflect what was Augustine's best and most thoroughly supported view of the interrelations among the canonical Gospels, as Augustine himself expresses it (see *Harmony of the Gospels* 4.10.11, and in specific contrast with Augustine's earlier but eventually self-doubted views that appear in *Harmony of the Gospels* 1.2.3–6; 1.3.6; 1.6.9). Instead, Augustine reasoned that Mark made use of both the Gospels of Matthew and Luke, sharing material from both.

Conclusion

Advocates of the Two Gospel Hypothesis support their position on the Synoptic Problem by appealing not only to the internal evidence contained in the texts of the Synoptic Gospels, as advocates of all positions on the Synoptic Problem must do, but also to much of what is often called external evidence—that is, comments recorded by a significant number of important scholars of the church for about the first 1,750 years of the church's history. Significant internal evidence points in the direction of the Gospel of Matthew being the first composed, followed by Luke's Gospel and then Mark's. This includes numerous linguistic characteristics of the Gospel of Mark, such as use of *palin* (again) in parallel passages where it is not found in the other two Gospels. There is further evidence that Mark conflated the Gospels of Matthew and Luke as sources for his composition. Finally, one may point to the so-called minor agreements, both positive and negative, where Matthew's and Luke's Gospels agree against Mark's Gospel, which are not explained in any satisfactory way by advocates of Markan priority.

The Two Gospel Hypothesis alone finds support among the early church fathers and church tradition leading up to the eighteenth century. Such external evidence includes testimonies from members of some of the earliest Christian communities, including such lights as Papias of Hierapolis in Asia Minor, Clement of Alexandria in Egypt, and Augustine of Hippo in North Africa and Rome, along with further testimonies that continue in both church and academy for the better part of seventeen hundred years. However, most advocates of most other solutions to the Synoptic Problem choose not to discuss this kind of evidence, presumably because advocates of no other source theory of the Gospels can find much, if any, support for their views from it.[15]

15. Other illustrative and more detailed work dealing with the external evidence includes David B. Peabody, "Augustine and the Augustinian Hypothesis: A Reexamination of Augustine's Thought in *De consensu evangelistarum*," in Farmer, *New Synoptic Studies*, 37–64; Gamba, "Further Reexamination," 17–35; Bernard Orchard and Harold Riley, *The Order of the Synoptics: Why Three Synoptic Gospels?* (Macon, GA: Mercer University Press, 1987), esp. Orchard's part 2, "The Historical Tradition," 111–226. There are also sections on this in the volumes that came out of the Jerusalem Conference on the Interrelations of the Gospels in 1984 and the Oxford Conference on the Synoptic Problem in 2007. See David L. Dungan, ed., *The Interrelations of the Gospels: A Symposium Led by M.-É. Boismard, W. R. Farmer, F. Neirynck, Jerusalem 1984*, BETL 95 (Leuven: Leuven University Press; Peeters, 1990), esp. William R. Farmer, "The

Further Reading

Intermediate

Bellinzoni, Arthur J., Jr., ed., with the assistance of Joseph B. Tyson and William O. Walker, Jr. *The Two-Source Hypothesis: A Critical Appraisal*. Macon, GA: Mercer University Press, 1985.

Dungan, David L. *A History of the Synoptic Problem: The Canon, the Text, the Composition, and the Interpretation of the Gospels*. New York: Doubleday, 1999.

Farmer, William R. *The Gospel of Jesus: The Pastoral Relevance of the Synoptic Problem*. Louisville: Westminster John Knox, 1994.

McNicol, Allan J., David L. Dungan, and David B. Peabody, eds. *Beyond the Q Impasse: Luke's Use of Matthew; A Demonstration by the Research Team of the International Institute for Gospel Studies*. Valley Forge, PA: Trinity Press International, 1996.

Peabody, David B., Lamar Cope, and Allan J. McNicol, eds. *One Gospel from Two: Mark's Use of Matthew and Luke; A Demonstration by the Research Team of the International Institute for Renewal of Gospel Studies*. Harrisburg, PA: Trinity Press International, 2002.

Advanced

Farmer, William R. *The Synoptic Problem: A Critical Analysis*. New York: Macmillan, 1964.

Longstaff, Thomas R. W., and Page A. Thomas, eds. *The Synoptic Problem: A Bibliography, 1716–1988*. NGS 4. Macon, GA: Mercer University Press, 1993.

Meijboom, Hajo Uden. *A History and Critique of the Origin of the Marcan Hypothesis, 1835–1866: A Contemporary Report Rediscovered*. Translated and edited by John J. Kiwiet. NGS 8. Macon, GA: Mercer University Press; Leuven: Peeters, 1993.

Sanders, E. P., ed. *Jesus, the Gospels, and the Church: Essays in Honor of William R. Farmer*. Macon, GA: Mercer University Press, 1987.

Stoldt, Hans-Herbert. *History and Criticism of the Marcan Hypothesis*. Translated and edited by Donald L. Niewyk. SNTW. Macon, GA: Mercer University Press, 1980.

Two-Gospel Hypothesis: The Statement of the Hypothesis; [Section] 1. The Tradition of the Church," 125–56, and B. Orchard, "Response to H. Merkel," 591–604; Paul Foster et al., eds., *New Studies in the Synoptic Problem: Oxford Conference, April 2008; Essays in Honour of Christopher M. Tuckett*, BETL 239 (Leuven: Peeters, 2011), esp. D. B. Peabody, "Reading Mark from the Perspective of Different Synoptic Source Hypotheses: Historical, Redactional and Theological Implications," 159–85.

5

The Orality
and Memory Hypothesis

Rainer Riesner

Introduction

The role of orality and memory is sometimes underdeveloped or ignored in discussions on the formation of the Synoptic Gospels.[1] The emphasis on the literary relationship (or dependence) between Matthew, Mark, and Luke to explain their origins often downplays the oral tradition of Jesus's sayings and deeds that certainly existed in the earliest Christian communities. The use of memory to accurately pass down a teacher's message or historical event was a feature of both Greco-Roman and Jewish culture. It was common for teachers or philosophers, like Jesus, to use various rhetorical and mnemonic devices while speaking to help make their content memorable. Note taking was another early practice intended to assist in memorization and ensure accuracy in the retelling of events. A tradition of Jesus's sayings and narratives of his life (especially of his passion) was characterized by a flexible stability and can be seen not only in the Gospels but also in the writings of Paul, the Epistle of James, the First Epistle of Peter, and other early Christian writings.

1. But see Werner H. Kelber and Samuel Byrskog, eds., *Jesus in Memory: Tradition in Oral and Scribal Perspectives* (Waco: Baylor University Press, 2009).

Various theories attempting to respond to the Synoptic Problem are often problematic as they seek to identify the literary dependence among the Gospels. The Tradition Hypothesis, which argues that each Gospel writer relied exclusively on oral tradition and eyewitness memory, also fails to articulate a fully nuanced description of the relationship between the Synoptics. The solution, I propose, lies somewhere between the Tradition Hypothesis and a Multisource Hypothesis, but with a strong emphasis on the oral tradition of Jesus that, while sometimes put in writing rather early, was passed down through the early Christian communities. The Synoptic Gospels are not mutually dependent, and their similarities can be explained outside of direct literary dependence. When one understands the role of oral tradition and eyewitness memory in the first century, along with the clear indications of a Jesus tradition in early Christian writings, a different picture emerges. Rather than being dependent upon one another, the three Synoptic Gospel writers each partially used the same intermediary sources, both oral and written.

Oral Gospel Tradition: A Short History of Research

The scholarly interest in oral tradition as a source of the Synoptic Gospels started in the eighteenth century. Up to that point, the classical Augustinian hypothesis was universally accepted: Matthew wrote first, Mark was an abridgement of this Gospel, and Luke knew both of his predecessors (Augustine, *Harmony of the Gospels* 1.2.3–4). In the time of the Enlightenment this solution was being challenged, as were other traditional historical assumptions. Johann Gottfried Herder (1744–1803), having inspired the intellectual movement of Romanticism, investigated folkloristic oral traditions of different nations. For Herder, the main source of the Synoptic Gospels was a body of oral tradition. Herder's hypothesis was further argued in much greater detail by Johann Karl Ludwig Gieseler (1792–1854), who pointed to the analogy of the oral traditions of the Jewish rabbis.[2] But later on, David Friedrich Strauss affirmed that it is not possible to differentiate between oral tradition, legend, and myth. As a reaction to this, liberal scholars investigating the so-called historical Jesus tried to reconstruct the earliest written sources. The result was the Two Document Hypothesis, with Mark and a hypothetical sayings source (Q) as sources for Matthew and Luke. Conservative scholars mainly held fast to the Augustinian hypothesis. However, some of them, like Brooke Foss Westcott, considered an oral tradition as providing the major explanation

---

2. Johann Carl Ludwig Gieseler, *Historisch-kritischer Versuch über die Entstehung und die frühesten Schicksale der Evangelien* (Leipzig: Engelmann, 1818).

for the Synoptic Problem.[3] The so-called Tradition Hypothesis was popular in some Catholic circles as well.

At the end of the nineteenth and the beginning of the twentieth century, German scholarship dominated New Testament studies. The Two Source Hypothesis was therefore accepted in England and France, even by some liberal Catholics. Nevertheless, around the time of the First World War some felt that the meticulous reconstruction of written sources had reached a dead end. Under the heading *Formgeschichte* (form history), the question of oral tradition reentered mainline New Testament studies. According to Rudolf Bultmann (1884–1976), the Synoptic tradition was an anonymous tradition that originated in the early Christian communities and was shaped by their needs.[4] In consequence of his view, influenced by the collectivism of the day, one could know very little about Jesus. Martin Dibelius (1883–1947) believed that eyewitnesses had some influence on the tradition, so he thought more positively of its historical reliability.[5] Someone who felt even more positive about it was the third form-critical pioneer, Martin Albertz (1883–1956).[6] To him it seemed to reflect an attempt at conservation of the material that the Synoptic tradition was handed down in short, isolated, and fixed units. Each of these three scholars combined form criticism with some variant of the Two Source Hypothesis.

Generally, English-speaking scholars were more conservative than Germans. Vincent Taylor (1887–1968) combined form criticism with a strong insistence on the role of eyewitnesses.[7] Especially influential was Burnett Hillman Streeter (1874–1937). He expanded the Two Document Hypothesis into a Four Document Hypothesis, assigning the special material of Luke and Matthew to two written sources, L and M. Streeter could also write, "In Jerusalem it is on the whole likely that the sayings [of Jesus] would for some considerable time be handed down in oral tradition after the manner of the sayings of the Rabbis."[8] This aspect was stressed by the Scandinavian scholar Harald Riesenfeld (1913–2008) in an influential paper, "The Gospel

---

3. Brooke Foss Westcott, *An Introduction to the Study of the Gospels* (London: Murray, 1851).

4. Rudolf Bultmann, *Die Geschichte der synoptischen Tradition*, 2nd rev. ed. (1921; Göttingen: Vandenhoeck & Ruprecht, 1931); ET, *The History of the Synoptic Tradition*, trans. John Marsh (Oxford: Blackwell, 1963).

5. Martin Dibelius, *Die Formgeschichte des Evangeliums*, 2nd rev. ed. (1919; Tübingen: J. C. B. Mohr, 1933); ET, *From Tradition to Gospel*, trans. Bertram Lee Woolf (London: Ivor Nicholson & Watson, 1934).

6. Martin Albertz, *Die Botschaft des Neuen Testaments I/1: Die Entstehung des Evangeliums* (Zollikon-Zürich: Evangelischer Verlag, 1947).

7. Vincent Taylor, *The Formation of the Gospel Tradition*, 2nd ed. (London: Macmillan, 1935).

8. B. H. Streeter, *The Four Gospels: A Study of Origins, Treating of the Manuscript Tradition, Sources, Authorship, and Dates* (London: Macmillan, 1924), 230.

Tradition and Its Beginnings," at an Oxford congress[9] and amply argued by his pupil Birger Gerhardsson (1926–2013).[10] The Catholic exegete Heinz Schürmann (1922–2010)[11] showed that the pre-Easter circle of Jesus's disciples was already a sociological entity, in form-critical terminology a *Sitz im Leben* (life setting), for handing down the sayings of their Master. In response to the criticism that the later rabbinic practice was an anachronistic analogy, I pointed to the traditional methods in popular Jewish education connected with the family and the synagogue.[12] Samuel Byrskog, a pupil of Gerhardsson, made the insights of modern oral-history research fruitful for Gospel studies.[13]

In the 1970s a new interest in the Synoptic Problem became apparent, as testified to by a number of international congresses. William Farmer and his followers championed a revised form of the Griesbach Hypothesis.[14] The Two Gospel Hypothesis argues that Matthew came first and was used by Luke, and that, as the last Synoptist, Mark used both of the other two. Also, the hypothesis of Austin Farrer[15] experienced a revival, especially through the work of Mark Goodacre.[16] In dispensing with the hypothetical sayings source Q, it is argued that Mark was used by Matthew and both of those Gospels by Luke. French-speaking scholars Marie-Émile Boismard[17] and Philippe Rolland,[18] and

9. Harald Riesenfeld, "The Gospel Tradition and Its Beginnings" (1957), reprinted in *The Gospel Tradition: Essays*, trans. E. Margaret Rowley and Robert A. Kraft (Oxford: Blackwell, 1970), 1–30.

10. Birger Gerhardsson, *Memory and Manuscript: Oral Tradition and Written Transmission in Rabbinic Judaism and Early Christianity* [1961]; *with, Tradition and Transmission in Early Christianity* [1964], trans. Eric J. Sharp, BRS (Grand Rapids: Eerdmans, 1998); Gerhardsson, *The Reliability of the Gospel Tradition* (Peabody, MA: Hendrickson, 2001).

11. Heinz Schürmann, "Die vorösterlichen Anfänge der Logientradition: Versuch eines form-geschichtlichen Zugangs zum Leben Jesu," in *Der historische Jesus und der kerygmatische Christus: Beiträge zum Christusverständnis in Forschung und Verkündigung*, ed. Helmut Ristow and Klaus Matthiae (Berlin: Evangelische Verlagsanstalt, 1960), 342–70.

12. Rainer Riesner, *Jesus als Lehrer: Eine Untersuchung zum Ursprung der Evangelien-Überlieferung*, WUNT 2.7, 3rd rev. ed. (1981; Tübingen: Mohr Siebeck, 1988); Riesner, "From the Messianic Teacher to the Gospels of Jesus Christ," in *Handbook for the Study of the Historical Jesus*, vol. 1, *How to Study the Historical Jesus*, ed. Tom Holmén and Stanley E. Porter (Leiden: Brill, 2011), 405–46.

13. Samuel Byrskog, *Story as History—History as Story: The Gospel Tradition in the Context of Ancient Oral History*, WUNT 123 (Tübingen: Mohr Siebeck, 2000).

14. William R. Farmer, *The Synoptic Problem: A Critical Analysis* (New York: Macmillan, 1964).

15. Austin Farrer, "On Dispensing with Q," in *Studies in the Gospels: Essays in Memory of R. H. Lightfoot*, ed. D. E. Nineham (Oxford: Blackwell, 1955), 55–88.

16. Mark Goodacre, *The Synoptic Problem: A Way through the Maze*, BibSem 80 (London: Sheffield Academic Press, 2001).

17. M.-É. Boismard, A. Lamouille, and P. Sandevoir, *Synopse des quatre Évangiles en français: Avec parallèles des Apocryphes et des Pères*, vol. 2, *Commentaire*, 2nd ed. (Paris: Cerf, 1980); Marie-Émile Boismard, *L'Évangile de Marc: Sa préhistoire*, ÉB 26 (Paris: Lecoffre, 1994).

18. Philippe Rolland, *Les premiers évangiles: Un nouveau regard sur le problème synoptique*, LD 116 (Paris: Cerf, 1984).

also English-speaking exegete Delbert Burkett,[19] defend variants of a Multiple Source Hypothesis. Most scholars connected with the so-called Third Quest for the historical Jesus, like Gerd Theissen and John P. Meier, remain adherents of the Two Document Hypothesis. But some, like James D. G. Dunn[20] and his pupil Terence C. Mournet,[21] allow for a strong influence of the oral tradition even in the editing of the Synoptic Gospels. Evangelical scholars such as Darrell L. Bock[22] and Craig A. Evans[23] combine the Two Source Hypothesis with eyewitness testimony and a rather fixed pre-Synoptic oral tradition.

Even the Tradition Hypothesis in its purest form is defended today. Eta Linnemann[24] and F. David Farnell[25] explain the Synoptic evidence only by the different memories of eyewitnesses. To a certain degree their views are influenced by dogmatic assumptions on the inerrancy of the Scriptures. Other scholars argue on purely scientific grounds for the Tradition Hypothesis. Bo Reicke (1914–87)[26] produced literary-critical arguments, whereas Karl Jaroš and Ulrich Victor[27] attempt to show that a direct interdependence of the Synoptics is ruled out statistically. On the grounds of wide comparisons with oral tradition and insights of memory psychology, Armin Baum argues for an oral tradition as the main solution of the Synoptic Problem.[28] Studies of memory have multiplied in psychology and other social sciences and have now been introduced to Gospel studies.[29] Unfortunately, there seems to be no

19. Delbert Burkett, *Rethinking the Gospel Sources*, vol. 1, *From Proto-Mark to Mark* (London: T&T Clark International, 2004); Burkett, *Rethinking the Gospel Sources*, vol. 2, *The Unity and Plurality of Q*, SBLECL 1 (Atlanta: Society of Biblical Literature, 2009).

20. James D. G. Dunn, *The Oral Gospel Tradition* (Grand Rapids: Eerdmans, 2013).

21. Terence C. Mournet, *Oral Tradition and Literary Dependency: Variability and Stability in the Synoptic Tradition and Q*, WUNT 2.195 (Tübingen: Mohr Siebeck, 2005).

22. Darrell L. Bock, "The Words of Jesus in the Gospels: Live, Jive, or Memorex?," in *Jesus under Fire: Modern Scholarship Reinvents the Historical Jesus*, ed. Michael J. Wilkins and J. P. Moreland (Grand Rapids: Zondervan, 1995), 73–100.

23. Craig A. Evans, *Mark 8:27–16:20*, WBC 34B (Nashville: Nelson, 2001).

24. Eta Linnemann, *Is There a Synoptic Problem? Rethinking the Literary Dependence of the First Three Gospels*, trans. Robert W. Yarbrough (Grand Rapids: Baker, 1992).

25. F. David Farnell, "The Case for the Independence View of Gospel Origins," in *Three Views on the Origins of the Synoptic Gospels*, ed. Robert L. Thomas (Grand Rapids: Kregel, 2002), 226–309.

26. Bo Reicke, *The Roots of the Synoptic Gospels* (Philadelphia: Fortress, 1986).

27. Karl Jaroš and Ulrich Victor, *Die synoptische Tradition: Die literarischen Beziehungen der drei ersten Evangelien und ihre Quellen* (Cologne: Böhlau, 2010).

28. Armin D. Baum, *Der mündliche Faktor und seine Bedeutung für die synoptische Frage: Analogien aus der antiken Literatur, der Experimentalpsychologie, der Oral Poetry-Forschung und dem rabbinischen Traditionswesen*, TANZ 49 (Tübingen: Francke, 2008).

29. Alan Kirk and Tom Thatcher, eds., *Memory, Tradition, and Text: Uses of the Past in Early Christianity*, SemeiaSt (Atlanta: Society of Biblical Literature, 2005); Dale C. Allison, *Constructing Jesus: Memory, Imagination, and History* (Grand Rapids: Baker Academic, 2010); Chris Keith, *Jesus' Literacy: Scribal Culture and the Teacher from Galilee*, LNTS 413 (London: T&T Clark, 2011).

consensus about the reliability of human memories.[30] There exists a strong trend, influenced by the philosophy of postmodernism, to consider memory only as a wholly subjective construction. However, this view can be challenged, as especially the case of early Christianity illustrates.[31]

Memory in Hellenistic-Roman Pedagogy

The training of the memory was an important subject on all three levels of Hellenistic-Roman education.[32] Quintilian, the famous Roman pedagogue in the first century CE, had the highest level of education in mind, that of philosophy and rhetoric, when he wrote about a pupil in an elementary grade:

> He will remember such aphorisms even when he is an old man, and the impression made upon his unformed mind will contribute to the formation of his character. He may also be entertained by learning the sayings of famous men and above all selections from the poets, poetry being more attractive to children. For memory is most necessary to an orator, as I shall point out in its proper place, and there is nothing like practice for strengthening and developing it. (*Institutes of Oratory* 1.1.35–36)[33]

Rote learning was seen not as a merely mechanical exercise but rather as part of the formation of human character. It was especially important to know "the sayings [*dicta*] of famous men." Quintilian also stressed that it is easier to memorize short texts (aphorisms) and, above all, poetry, and that a continual training of the memory is necessary. In order to be a persuasive rhetor in antiquity, it was important to be not only original but also well versed in the accepted traditions of society. Quintilian commented on lawyers with good rhetorical training pleading in a trial: "They will be in the agreeable position of being able to quote the happy sayings of the various authors, a power which they will find most useful in the courts" (*Institutes of Oratory* 2.7.4). If a certain hearer knew authoritative texts by heart, it was possible for a speaker not only to cite

30. Alexander J. M. Wedderburn, *Jesus and the Historians*, WUNT 269 (Tübingen: Mohr Siebeck, 2010), 189–224.

31. Barry Schwartz, "Christian Origins: Historical Truth and Social Memory," in Kirk and Thatcher, *Memory, Tradition, and Text*, 43–56; Robert K. McIver, *Memory, Jesus, and the Synoptic Gospels*, RBS 59 (Atlanta: Society of Biblical Literature, 2011).

32. Teresa Morgan, *Literate Education in the Hellenistic and Roman Worlds*, CamCS (Cambridge: Cambridge University Press, 1998), 245; William A. Johnson, *Readers and Reading Culture in the High Roman Empire: A Study of Elite Communities*, CCS (Oxford: Oxford University Press, 2010), 118–20, 200–202.

33. Translations taken from *The "Institutio oratoria" of Quintilian*, vol. 1, trans. H. E. Butler, LCL 124 (London: Heinemann; Cambridge, MA: Harvard University Press, 1920).

these texts but also to allude to them. The Roman poet Ovid claimed that he imitated the earlier Virgil, intending that his borrowing would be recognized by his readers or listeners (Seneca the Elder, *Suasoriae* 3.7). The training of the memory was also emphasized in Greek education (Plato, *Euthydemus* 276D), as it was also in Hellenistic Judaism (Philo, *Dreams* 1.205). From a viewpoint based on modern experience, it is not easy to believe the amount of oral material that educated people in antiquity were able to master.

Oral Instruction and Tradition in Pious Second Temple Judaism

The Maccabean crisis was a watershed moment in the history of Palestinian Judaism, as the Syrian ruler Antiochus IV, with the help of the Jerusalem upper class, tried to force Hellenism on the Jews (167–164 BCE). Even before the crisis, the urban population was attracted to Hellenistic culture, including Greek education and religious syncretism (1 Macc. 1:11–15; 2 Macc. 4:7–17). Pious Jews, the *hasidim*, faced the challenge and projected a program of popular Torah education (11QPs^a 18.1–8 [Ps. 154:3–19]). The book of Deuteronomy had already outlined such a program.[34] Deuteronomy stressed the duty of fathers to teach their sons the precepts by heart: "You shall put these words of mine in your heart and soul. . . . Teach them to your children, talking about them when you are at home and when you are away, when you lie down and when you rise" (Deut. 11:18–19). David M. Carr comments on this command:

> The process envisioned here is one of self- and child-education through constant vocal repetition. Since children in the ancient world typically were included in their parents' daily activities, parents constantly reciting a text would put that text not only on their own hearts but on their children's hearts as well.[35]

Rote learning in Old Testament language was called "writing on the tablets of the heart" (Prov. 3:1–3; 7:3), and from there stems the English idiom "learning by heart."[36]

From the *hasidim* split came the Essenes and the Pharisees, but all three movements understood a program for Torah education in different ways. As a consequence, religious learning in pious Judaism was a question of belonging

34. Karin Finsterbusch, *Weisung für Israel: Studien zum religiösen Lehren und Lernen im Deuteronomium und seinem Umfeld*, FAT 44 (Tübingen: Mohr Siebeck, 2005).

35. David M. Carr, *Writing on the Tablet of the Heart: Origins of Scripture and Literature* (Oxford: Oxford University Press, 2005), 136.

36. Jocelyn Penny Small, *Wax Tablets of the Mind: Cognitive Studies of Memory and Literacy in Classical Antiquity* (London: Routledge, 1997), 131–36.

not to the upper class but to a religious party.[37] The pre-70 CE synagogue in Palestine was not just a communal house of assembly, as some scholars assume, but rather a place of worship and study.[38] The Pharisees founded their own synagogues to propagate their understanding of the Torah. Since in the Shabbat service Jewish men were allowed to read and to preach from the Holy Scriptures, the synagogue was combined with an elementary school (*b. Hag.* 15a–b). The synagogue servant often worked as an elementary teacher, training boys to read and write (*m. Shab.* 1:3–4). Antiquity provides no evidence that the training in reading did not comprise some writing at the same time. Reading Old Testament texts without vocalization was not easy. The texts had to be learned by heart so that they could be read fluently and without mistakes. Some scrolls were available in every synagogue, not just for the service but also for the preparation of the readings and learned discussions (Acts 17:10–11). As a result of continuous Scripture readings, a pious Jewish man would learn long passages of Scripture by heart (Josephus, *Ag. Ap.* 2.175; *Ant.* 4.210–11). Of course, the memorization of Old Testament texts and the sayings of teachers was even more challenging in the circles of the scribes (Hebrew *soferim*, Greek *grammateis*). The pre-Maccabean priest Jesus Ben Sira made it the duty of a scribe "to preserve the speech of notable men" (Sir. 39:2). A good example of the capacity of memory is Paul, the former student of Rabbi Gamaliel the Elder (Acts 22:3), who apparently was able to cite long passages of Scripture from memory.

The Qumran texts open a window into early Jewish education and text production. The Essenes emphasized Torah education within their movement:

> And in the place in which the Ten assemble there should not be missing a man to interpret the law day and night, always, one relieving another. And the Many shall be on watch together for a third of each night of the year in order to read the book, explain the regulation, and bless together. (1QS 6.6–8)[39]

Among the Essene groups, not just the sons but also the women and the children had to learn from the readings of the Holy Scriptures and the sectarian literature (1QSa 1.4–8). In addition to biblical texts, wisdom sayings

---

37. Albert I. Baumgarten, *The Flourishing of Jewish Sects in the Maccabean Era: An Interpretation*, SJSJ 55 (Leiden: Brill, 1997), 114–36.

38. Lee I. Levine, *The Ancient Synagogue: The First Thousand Years* (New Haven: Yale University Press, 2000), 124–59; Anders Runesson, "Synagogue," in *Dictionary of Jesus and the Gospels*, ed. Joel B. Green, Jeannine K. Brown, and Nicholas Perrin, 2nd ed. (Downers Grove, IL: IVP Academic, 2013), 903–11.

39. Translation taken from Florentino García Martínez and Eibert J. C. Tigchelaar, eds., *The Dead Sea Scrolls Study Edition*, vol. 1, *1Q1–4Q273* (Leiden: Brill, 1997), 83.

and hymns were memorized.[40] Most likely the extended family of Jesus cultivated the piety of the older *hasidim*, who had some things in common with the Essenes but were not identical with them.[41] The Enochic literature and the *Testaments of the Twelve Patriarchs* were cherished in these circles (see Jude 14). Both the books of *Enoch* (e.g., *1 En.* 76:14; 82:2) and the *Testaments of the Twelve Patriarchs* (e.g., *T. Levi* 4:5; *T. Dan* 6:9) strongly stress the duty of the fathers to teach their sons. The Jewish historian Flavius Josephus, as a younger contemporary of the apostles, could boast:

> Should anyone of our nation be questioned about the laws, he would repeat them all more readily than his own name. The result, then, of our learning by heart [*ekmanthanontes*] of the laws from the first dawn of intelligence is that we have them, as it were, engraved in our souls. (*Ag. Ap.* 2.178 [AT])

This statement certainly contains some exaggeration, but the truth expressed by Josephus is confirmed by the Jewish philosopher Philo (*Embassy* 210) and also by anti-Jewish pagan writers like Seneca (*On Superstition* [Augustine, *City of God* 6.10]) and Juvenal (*Satires* 14.101–2).

Indications of Oral Gospel Tradition in the New Testament

To the troubled church of Corinth, Paul, around 54 CE, wrote:

> I would remind you, brothers [including sisters], of the gospel [*euangelion*] that I proclaimed to you, which you received [*parelabete*], in which you also stand, through which also you are being saved, if you hold to the wording [*tini logō*] in which I proclaimed it to you. . . . For I handed down [*paredōka*] to you under the first things what also I have received [*parelabon*]. (1 Cor. 15:1–3)

Then the apostle cites a series of statements, a technique he knew from his rabbinical training, indicating certain traditions about Jesus's death, burial, and resurrection appearances (1 Cor. 15:3–7). There are some important things to be noted. Paul could call a summary of the last part of Jesus's life *euangelion*. The apostle reminds the Corinthians that at the foundation of the community (around 50 CE), he taught them some Jesus traditions as part of "the first things." This is confirmed by 1 Corinthians 11:23–24: "I received [*parelabon*] from the Lord what I also handed down [*paredōka*] to you"; then Paul cites

---

40. Carr, *Writing on the Tablet of the Heart*, 228–37.
41. Gabriele Boccaccini, *Beyond the Essene Hypothesis: The Parting of the Ways between Qumran and Enochic Judaism* (Grand Rapids: Eerdmans, 1998), 16.

the eucharistic words of Jesus in a form independent from, but very near to, the Lukan version (Luke 22:19–20). The formulation "from the Lord" (*apo tou kyriou*) points back to Jesus as the originator of the tradition (1 Cor. 11:23). Paul is silent concerning those functioning as intermediaries from whom he received the eucharistic words; but 1 Corinthians 15:5–7 shows that the Jesus tradition was connected with known persons such as Peter, James, and the Twelve. Obviously it was not an anonymous tradition. The nearest philological parallel to the Greek words *paralambanō* (to receive) and *paradidōmi* (to hand down) are the Hebrew technical terms *qibbel* and *masar*, denoting a cultivated oral tradition (*m. Abot* 1:1). This is in agreement with Paul's insistence on the "wording" (1 Cor. 15:2) of the catechetical formula in 1 Corinthians 15:3–5. In addition, the strong verbal agreements between the Pauline and the Lukan forms of the eucharistic words point to a cultivated tradition.

In 50 CE Paul wrote to the Christian community in the Macedonian metropolis of Thessalonica: "Now concerning the times and the seasons, brothers and sisters, you do not need to have anything written to you. For you yourselves know very well that the day of the Lord will come like a thief in the night" (1 Thess. 5:1–2 NRSV). The eschatological instruction of the community comprised words of Jesus as Paul had explicitly said before (1 Thess. 4:15; cf. Matt. 24:30–31). In 1 Thessalonians 5:2 the apostle could merely allude to the parable of "the thief in the night" (Matt. 24:43//Luke 12:39); due to their previous learning (see 1 Thess. 4:1–2), the Thessalonians were able to identify this allusion. According to the "criterion of embarrassment," this parable must be genuine.[42] If one pays attention to such allusions, it becomes obvious that the apostle Paul knew more Jesus traditions than a few explicit citations.[43] The same allusiveness characterizes other New Testament writings, such as the Letter of James (James 5:12; cf. Matt. 5:34–35, 37) or the First Epistle of Peter (1 Pet. 4:14; cf. Matt. 5:11–12//Luke 6:22–23). Chances are high that they originate from those two eyewitnesses of the life of Jesus. Paul was converted in about 31/32 CE and received his first instruction in the conservative Jewish Christian community of Damascus (cf. Acts

---

42. The "criterion of embarrassment" is a scholarly method for discerning which sayings and actions of Jesus in the Gospels are historically accurate. This criterion "focuses on the actions or sayings of Jesus that would have embarrassed or created difficulty for the early Church. The point of the criterion is that the early Church would hardly have gone out of its way to create material that only embarrassed its creator or weakened its position in arguments with opponents" (John P. Meier, *A Marginal Jew: Rethinking the Historical Jesus*, vol. 1, *The Roots of the Problem and the Person* [New York: Doubleday, 1991], 168).

43. David Wenham, *Paul: Disciple of Jesus or Founder of Christianity?* (Grand Rapids: Eerdmans, 1995); Rainer Riesner, "Back to the Historical Jesus through Paul and His School (The Ransom Logion—Mark 10.45, Matthew 20.28)," *JSHJ* 2 (2003): 171–99.

22:12–16).[44] A cultivated Jesus tradition was apparently handed down from very early on, but for the dates of its beginnings, one must look back into pre-Easter times.[45]

Jesus as Teacher and His Memorable Sayings

In the Gospel tradition it is remembered that Jesus was addressed with the Hebrew/Aramaic designation *rabbi* (e.g., Matt. 26:25, 49; Mark 9:5; John 1:49). The Gospels truthfully reflect the situation in first-century Palestine, where *rabbi* was not yet a fixed title, bound to academic studies and ordination, but rather an actual address for a revered teacher, translated into Greek with the vocative *didaskale* (John 1:38). Jesus preached in the synagogues, entered into discussions with the scribes, and assembled a circle of disciples like other contemporaneous Jewish teachers. According to classical scholar George Kennedy,

> Most speakers who present a cause to different audiences at different places, as Jesus did preaching in Palestine, develop a basic speech which encapsulates their main views in a way that proves effective. . . . Jesus was engaged in oral teaching, and he frequently repeated himself.[46]

This reconstruction is confirmed by Philo's description of a teacher in an Essene-like community of the Egyptian Therapeutes: "His instruction proceeds in leisurely manner; he lingers over it and spins it out with repetition, thus permanently imprinting the thoughts in the souls of the hearers" (*Cont. Life* 76).[47] Jesus followed the method of the Old Testament prophets but also the method of later Jewish wisdom teachers like Ben Sira who encapsulated their message in short, poetically structured sentences, called *meshalim* in Hebrew. Jesus would start a longer speech with such a summary and then, in the process of elaboration, repeat it several times. Such a summary could also serve as the conclusion of a speech or a discussion (cf. Mark 7:1–15). Jesus might have drawn attention to these summaries in different ways: by raising his voice (Luke 8:8; John 7:37), by the request to listen (e.g., Mark 4:3; 7:14),

---

44. Rainer Riesner, *Paul's Early Period: Chronology, Mission Strategy, Theology* (Grand Rapids: Eerdmans, 1998), 59–74.

45. Riesner, "From the Messianic Teacher," 405–46.

46. George A. Kennedy, *New Testament Interpretation through Rhetorical Criticism* (Chapel Hill: University of North Carolina Press, 1984), 68.

47. Translation from *Philo*, vol. 9, trans. F. H. Colson, LCL 363 (London: Heinemann; Cambridge, MA: Harvard University Press, 1941).

or with the introductory formula "Truly [*amen*], I say to you . . . ," which was typical for him. Most of the time the evangelists preserved the Semitic expression *amen* (meaning "something is certain"), standing not at the end but at the beginning of a statement (the so-called nonresponsorial *amen*), as an original speech form of Jesus.

To make his teaching summaries memorable, Jesus used poetical and mnemonic devices.[48] About 80 percent of the independent word units in the Synoptic tradition are rather short and arranged in different forms of *parallelismus membrorum* (poetic parallelism), the foremost model of Old Testament and Jewish poetry. Jesus used all kinds of parallelism—synonymous, antithetical, synthetic, and climactic—but most characteristic for him was antithetical parallelism. A number of parallelisms could be combined into stanzas to create a kind of teaching poem (e.g., Matt. 6:25–34; 7:7–11). Often parallelism was complemented by a chiastic structure, which was one of the most common memory aids not only in Old Testament times but also throughout antiquity.[49] Here is one example that could easily be memorized even if Jesus uttered it only once:

> If anyone will *follow me*
> he must deny himself
> and take up his cross
> and *follow me*! (Matt. 16:24)[50]

Even in the Greek form of the sayings of Jesus, one may detect a certain rhythm. A retroversion into Aramaic or Hebrew makes clear, indeed, that he used different forms of rhythm for different kinds of teaching.[51] Two stresses made sayings very urgent; three stresses are characteristic for wisdom sayings; and four stresses were employed in the instructions of the disciples. Strong emotions in laments, warnings, and exhortations, but also the emotions in beatitudes and hymnody, were put into the *qinah*-metrum (three plus two stresses), which was used in the Old Testament lament for death. Sometimes there are also hints of end rhymes, alliterations, assonances, and paronomasia.

To impress his sayings on the mind and the memory of his hearers, Jesus used rhetorical features such as overstatement, hyperbolic speech, puns, similes,

---

48. Riesner, *Jesus als Lehrer*, 392–403; Robert H. Stein, *The Method and Message of Jesus' Teachings*, 2nd ed. (Louisville: Westminster John Knox, 1994), 26–32.

49. Carr, *Writing on the Tablet of the Heart*, 152.

50. The two verbs "follow" translate two different but synonymous Greek expressions going back to the same Semitic expression: *opisō elthein* (16:24a) renders verbally the Hebrew *halakh acharei* (cf. CD 4.19), whereas *akolouthein* (16:24d) is more elegant Greek.

51. Joachim Jeremias, *New Testament Theology*, trans. John Bowden (New York: Scribner, 1971).

proverbs, riddles, paradoxes, irony, questions, and a fortiori conclusions.[52] Some of the short parabolic sayings served as teaching summaries, but most of the parables were premeditated oral texts for reflection (cf. Matt. 13:24, 31, 33). Generally the parables are longer than the teaching summaries. While not entirely lacking poetic features, the parables are memorable mainly through their vivid narrative and impressive images.[53] A typical narratological feature was the confrontation between two different types of persons, such as the Pharisee and the tax collector (Luke 18:10–14) or a younger and an older son (Luke 15:11–32). In ancient rhetoric, certain symbolic numbers served as mnemonic devices.[54] Jesus told the story about ten bridesmaids (Matt. 25:1–12), four kinds of soils (Mark 4:3–8), and three sendings of slaves (Mark 12:2–5). Apparently it was characteristic for Jesus to make use of double parables, sometimes describing two different situations, one typical for men and the other for women (Matt. 13:31–33; Luke 15:3–10). Many of the specific traits of the parables fit into the social and religious situation of first-century Palestine.[55] The longer the parables are, the greater the variations between the different Synoptic versions (e.g., Matt. 21:33–44//Mark 12:1–11//Luke 20:11–18). This evidence cannot be explained sufficiently by the redaction of the evangelists but rather points back to the previous stage of oral tradition.

In their form and content, the Synoptic sayings and parables of Jesus show many peculiarities that clearly distinguish them from other early Christian literature. One may even speak of "Jesus' idiolect."[56] These characteristics point back to only one originator of this tradition. This tradition apparently was handed down as an isolated, cultivated, and even "holy" one, which preserved these characteristics.[57] Although today one needs to stress that Jesus did teach in both the Hebrew and the Aramaic languages and sometimes even in Greek, Matthew Black's statement remains true:

> Jesus did not commit anything to writing, but by His use of poetic form and language He ensured that His sayings would not be forgotten. The impression they make in Aramaic is of carefully premeditated and studied deliverances; we have to do with prophetic utterance of the style and grandeur of Isaiah,

52. Stein, *Method and Message*, 7–26.

53. Baum, *Der mündliche Faktor*, 232–43.

54. Carr, *Writing on the Tablet of the Heart*, 73.

55. Brad H. Young, *Jesus and His Jewish Parables: Rediscovering the Roots of Jesus' Teaching*, TI (New York: Paulist Press, 1989); Klyne R. Snodgrass, *Stories with Intent: A Comprehensive Guide to the Parables of Jesus* (Grand Rapids: Eerdmans, 2008).

56. Gerald Mussies, "Jesus' Idiolect: A Survey," *TD* 26 (1978): 254–58.

57. J. Arthur Baird, *Holy Word: The Paradigm of New Testament Formation*, ed. Craig A. Evans and Stanley E. Porter, JSNTSup 224 (London: Sheffield Academic Press, 2002).

cast in a medium which can express in appropriate and modulated sound the underlying beauty of the sentiment or the passion of which the thought arose.[58]

Disciples and Teachers as Tradition Bearers

Some scholars believe that the rural communities of Galilee stood behind the traditions in the Gospel of Mark and were the first bearers of the Jesus tradition.[59] Of course, sayings of Jesus and stories about him were circulating among those communities, but that was not the main stream of the tradition that was incorporated into the Synoptic Gospels. The criticism of the collectivism of classical form criticism holds true in this case:

> The idea of the folk community taken up by form criticism was not . . . an analytical concept based on empirical ethnographic studies, but a constructive concept rooted in a romantic notion of history and culture, a view characterized by a nostalgic concept of primitive societies uncorrupted by civilization.[60]

Some scholars emphasize anew the role of eyewitnesses and earwitnesses as being the tradition bearers and informants of the Gospel writers.[61] Indeed, in the manner of a historian of antiquity (cf. Josephus, *J.W.* 1.1–3; *Ant.* 1.1–4), Luke in the preface to his Gospel claims that he received the tradition of such primary witnesses (Luke 1:1–4). And in Romans 10:14–17 Paul gives an outline of a chain of tradition reaching from "the word of Christ" through the apostles to their hearers. The shorter or longer poetically structured sayings of the Old Testament prophets were already memorized and then later collected and written down in the circle of their disciples.[62] The fact that this analogy to Jesus's circle of disciples holds true may become evident by sev-

58. Matthew Black, *An Aramaic Approach to the Gospels and Acts*, 3rd ed. (Oxford: Clarendon, 1967), 185.
59. N. T. Wright, *Jesus and the Victory of God*, COQG 2 (Minneapolis: Fortress, 1996), 133–37; James D. G. Dunn, *Christianity in the Making*, vol. 1, *Jesus Remembered* (Grand Rapids: Eerdmans, 2003), 139–75.
60. Harry Y. Gamble, *Books and Readers in the Early Church: A History of Early Christian Texts* (New Haven: Yale University Press, 1997), 15–16.
61. Richard Bauckham, *Jesus and the Eyewitnesses: The Gospels as Eyewitness Testimony* (Grand Rapids: Eerdmans, 2006); Martin Hengel, "The Lukan Prologue and Its Eyewitnesses: The Apostles, Peter, and the Women," in *Earliest Christian History: History, Literature, and Theology*, ed. Michael F. Bird and Jason Maston, WUNT 2.320 (Tübingen: Mohr Siebeck, 2012), 533–88.
62. Samuel Byrskog, *Jesus the Only Teacher: Didactic Authority and Transmission in Ancient Israel, Ancient Judaism and the Matthean Community*, ConBNT 24 (Stockholm: Almquist & Wiksell, 1994), 39–45, 55–63.

eral observations. The prophets claimed divine authority for their words by using the introductory formula "Thus says the LORD. . . ." Like the prophets, Jesus taught without relying on other human authorities, but with the even greater authority given by God (see Mark 1:22, 27). This is clearly expressed in a hymnic speech in two stanzas, characterized by chiastic parallelism (Luke 10:21–22 [cf. Matt. 11:25–27]):

> I thank you, Father, Lord of heaven and earth,
> > because you have hidden these things from the wise and intelligent
> > and have revealed them to infants;
> yes, Father, for such was your gracious will.

> All things have been handed down [*paredothē*] to me by my Father;
> > and no one knows who the Son is except the Father,
> > or who the Father is except the Son
> > and anyone to whom the Son chooses to reveal him.

To his sympathizers who believed in Jesus's prophetic or even messianic authority, his sayings were of the utmost importance. Jesus himself stressed the divine wisdom (Matt. 12:42//Luke 11:31; Matt. 11:16–19//Luke 7:31–35) and the eschatological quality (Mark 8:38//Luke 9:26; Matt. 7:24–27//Luke 6:47–49) of his words on several occasions. So even during the temporary pre-Easter situation, there existed a strong authoritative motive to preserve the sayings of Jesus.

Jesus assembled a group of men to follow him as "the only teacher" (Matt. 23:8–10) at all times (Mark 3:14). He called these men "disciples"—in Greek, *mathētai*, from the Hebrew *talmidim* or Aramaic *talmidajja*, that is, "learners" (e.g., Matt. 10:24–25//Luke 6:40; Luke 14:26–27)—because they should learn from his words and from his example (see Matt. 11:28–30). On different occasions the disciples would hear the teaching summaries that Jesus repeated and could memorize them easily. When Jesus sent them out to the villages to act as his "sent ones" (Greek *apostoloi*, Hebrew *shelikhim*), they themselves became tradents, teachers of the words of their master. On this occasion Jesus formulated a certain chain of tradition reaching over from God through Jesus and the disciples to their hearers. Apparently this stern saying was cast in the memorable form of a two-stress rhythm or the *qinah*-metrum (Luke 10:16 NRSV):

> Whoever listens to you
> listens to me,
> and whoever rejects you

> rejects me,
> and whoever rejects me
> rejects the one who sent me.

After the so-called Galilean crisis, Jesus, like the prophet Isaiah before him (Isa. 8:16), withdrew into the inner circle of disciples consisting of twelve men (Mark 8:37–38; John 6:60–66). He gave them an esoteric instruction about his messianic identity and the meaning of his future passion and death.

After Easter in 30 CE, the remaining eleven disciples around Peter formed the leadership of the seminal messianic community in Jerusalem (Acts 1:13). They built a bridge of living tradition between the time before and after Easter. Surely what Luke called "the teaching of the apostles" (*didachē tōn apostolōn*) in Acts 2:42 comprised Jesus traditions. Besides the teaching summaries and parables of Jesus, they spoke to their fellow Jews about the controversies and the mighty deeds of their master. Partly intentionally and partly due to their constant use, these stories developed into more fixed forms. In this regard, a remark of Papias of Hierapolis is very interesting, reporting that Peter taught the Jesus traditions in the form of *chreiai* (Eusebius, *Church History* 3.39.15). According to the definition of ancient rhetoric, these are memorable units concentrated on the most important point (Theon of Alexandria, *Progymnasmata* 5; Quintilian, *Institutes of Oratory* 1.9.3–5). For the recitation in communal gatherings (see 1 Cor. 11:25), a kernel of a Passion Narrative was already shaped in Jerusalem, as can be deduced from Paul (see above, "Indications of Oral Gospel Tradition in the New Testament"). There were two other groups in the primitive community of Jerusalem that cultivated their special memories: members of the extended family of Jesus and some female followers from Galilee (Acts 1:14). Of course, the Galilean sympathizers of Jesus also shared the same memories. Most of the newly founded messianic communities in the Judean coastal plain, in Samaria and beyond, had no eyewitnesses and earwitnesses in their midst. They were in need of trustworthy oral traditions. Converted scribes (cf. Matt. 13:52) and others, especially trained or gifted teachers (1 Cor. 12:28), may have played a special role in passing on Jesus traditions.

The Use of Informal Written Notes

Some scholars maintain that a wide gap between the oral and the written existed in antiquity, but that assertion seems, at least partially, to be anachronistic:

"Oral performance of story and narrative, supposedly a feature of 'oral culture,' was often aided and abetted by a written text. 'Orality' may at times have had a text under its cloak."[63] In the schools of philosophers it was very common for disciples to take notes on the teachings of their masters (Epictetus, *Discourses* 1.1–2; Porphyry, *Life of Plotinus* 4.12). The same procedure is known from early rabbinic circles.[64] Such notes were called *hypomnēmata* in Greek and *commentarii* in Latin. Books and notes served as aids to memorize sayings and stories in Hellenistic-Roman culture, and the same is true for Judaism (2 Macc. 2:25; Josephus, *Ant.* 4.209–11; 20.118). Estimations of literacy in Roman Jewish Palestine oscillate between minimalist[65] and maximalist views.[66] Since at least some of the pre-Easter sedentary sympathizers of Jesus were literate, it is not unlikely that some of them took notes of Jesus's teachings already at this early date.[67] In the opinion of a classicist:

> It would have been a much less demanding task for regular hearers of Jesus or of the Apostles to hold in memory a significant part of the teaching they had repeatedly heard and to recite it or write it down at any time there was reason to do so, such as when a congregation was deprived of apostolic teaching.[68]

Indeed, with the rapid expansion of the messianic movement from Palestine to Syria, to Phoenicia and to Cyprus (Acts 9:1–2; 11:19), and probably even to Rome (see Acts 2:10) in the first decade, written notes as memory aids became a necessity. The codex form of the Gospels, very unusual for books with religious content, may go back to such notebooks (see 2 Tim. 4:13).[69] Because of the widespread use of note taking in antiquity, it does not seem possible to solve the Synoptic Problem by a pure Tradition Hypothesis. Additionally, there are many strong agreements in Greek wording and syntax that speak for some kind of literary relationship between the Synoptic Gospels.

63. H. Gregory Snyder, *Teachers and Texts in the Ancient World: Philosophers, Jews and Christians* (London: Routledge, 2000), 177.

64. Gerhardsson, *Memory and Manuscript*, 157–63; Martin S. Jaffee, *Torah in the Mouth: Writing and Oral Tradition in Palestinian Judaism, 200 BCE—400 CE* (Oxford: Oxford University Press, 2001), 100–125.

65. Catherine Hezser, *Jewish Literacy in Roman Jewish Palestine*, TSAJ 81 (Tübingen: Mohr Siebeck, 2001).

66. Alan Millard, *Reading and Writing in the Time of Jesus*, BibSem 69 (Sheffield: Sheffield Academic Press, 2000).

67. Ibid., 185–229.

68. George A. Kennedy, "Classical and Christian Source Criticism," in *The Relationships among the Gospels: An Interdisciplinary Dialogue*, ed. William O. Walker (San Antonio: Trinity University Press, 1978), 142.

69. Gamble, *Books and Readers*, 49–66.

Intermediate Synoptic Sources

The following sketch of the way that the Jesus tradition developed from the eyewitnesses to the three Synoptic Gospels is surely a simplification of a much more complex history.[70] Peter, as the leader of the primitive Jerusalem community, played a crucial role in the formation of a shorter or even longer Passion Narrative.[71] Several remarkable agreements exist in the use of Isaiah 53 in the probably genuine First Epistle of Peter and the pre-Synoptic Passion Narrative. Over time the Passion Narrative was expanded into a story of Jesus following a geographical scheme: first Galilee and then Jerusalem (see Acts 10:36–43). Already in Jerusalem, the bilingual Greco-Palestinian John Mark was in close contact with Peter (Acts 12:12) and later served as an editor of the memories of the mentioned pillar apostle (Papias, in Eusebius, *Church History* 3.39.15). During the first missionary journey of Barnabas and Paul, John Mark accompanied them as a *hypēretēs* (Acts 13:5)—that is, a bearer of Jesus traditions.[72] At an early date John Mark would have been able to compose a kind of Proto-Mark in Greek. In Galilee and southern Syria, this Proto-Mark was supplemented with other locally remembered Jesus traditions (especially Mark 6:45–8:26, absent from Luke). In the great community of Antioch, mixed with Jewish and Gentile Christians (Acts 11:20–26), Proto-Mark was combined with a Greek tradition of the words of Jesus. Matthew, the former tax collector (Matt. 9:9), might have played some role in writing down a collection of sayings and stories (Papias, in Eusebius, *Church History* 3.39.16). The extended family of Jesus (see Acts 1:14) developed its own strongly Hebraizing Jesus tradition (see Luke 2:19, 51; 24:18 [cf. Hegesippus, in Eusebius, *Church History* 3.11]).

Luke, the physician and part-time coworker of Paul, was in contact with John Mark (see Philem. 24; Col. 4:10, 14; 2 Tim. 4:11) and so could have obtained a somewhat reworked copy of Proto-Mark. Luke combined it with the source he knew from Antioch (Proto-Mark and sayings tradition) and the source stemming from the Jerusalem/Judean-based extended family of Jesus (see Acts 21:18). With his double work, the Gospel and Acts, Luke served Pauline communities around the Aegean Sea (see *Anti-Marcionite Prologues*). In Syria (see Matt. 4:24) the Gospel of Matthew was edited as a compilation of the Syro-Galilean version of Proto-Mark, the Antiochean source, and another special tradition. After the death of Peter as a martyr, John Mark

---

70. Riesner, "From the Messianic Teacher," 434–43.

71. Martin Hengel, *The Four Gospels and the One Gospel of Jesus Christ: An Investigation of the Collection and the Origin of the Canonical Gospels* (London: SCM, 2000), 153–57.

72. Riesner, *Jesus als Lehrer*, 63.

edited his Gospel for the Roman churches (Irenaeus, *Against Heresies* 3.1.1).
In combining a shorter edition of Proto-Mark, which was used by Luke, with
the longer Syro-Galilean version, Mark created a kind of Gospel harmony.
All three Synoptic Gospels could have been edited before the destruction of
Jerusalem in 70 CE,[73] and they were written for far-removed communities in
the Roman Empire. Given the quite close temporal proximity of editing and
the great geographical distance of origin, one may be able to explain why the
Synoptic Gospels are not mutually dependent.

Figure 5.1

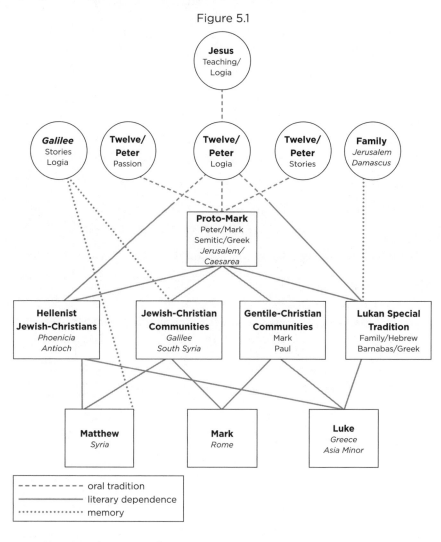

73. Evans, *Mark 8:27–16:20*, lxiii.

One may ask why none of the pre-Synoptic sources conjectured by adherents of the Multiple Source Hypothesis have survived. Of course, this is not a very strong argument if it is proposed by advocates of the Q hypothesis. Wayne Meeks gives an apt answer to this problem:

> Many of the intermediate forms that have been suggested by various critics over the past few decades . . . could more readily be understood as private or limited-circulation *aides-mémoire* than as "published" compositions. . . . The *hypomnēma* stands on the fluid border between tradition and "literature."[74]

The informal intermediate sources mainly served the Christian teachers (see Matt. 13:52) and private persons as memory aids. In the middle of the second century CE, Justin Martyr twice called the Gospels *apomnēmoneumata* (*First Apology* 66.13; 67.8); these are published works based on notes. The canonical Gospels were copied and widely circulated among the Christian communities. This made these first-century works different from the works of the second century and the later apocryphal gospels that were known mainly in the more limited circles of the initiates. Even the much-disputed *Gospel of Thomas* is dependent on the canonical Gospels,[75] but while it seldom relies on extracanonical oral traditions, even these are strongly contaminated by gnostic teachings.

The Mutual Independence of the Synoptics

After a possible historical scenario for an independent composition of the three Synoptic Gospels has been established, their mutual independence must be argued for on literary-critical grounds. Of the two pillars of the Two Source Hypothesis, Markan priority is the stronger one. But this may not be unshakable, and it also affects the Farrer Hypothesis.

Matthew 16:25	Mark 8:35	Luke 9:24
Who wants to save his life will lose it, but who loses his life for my sake	Who wants to save his life will lose it, but who loses his life for my sake *and for the gospel*	Who wants to save his life will lose it, but who loses his life for my sake
will find it.	will save it.	will save it.

74. Wayne Meeks, "*Hypomnēmata* from an Untamed Skeptic: A Response to George Kennedy," in Walker, *Relationships among the Gospels*, 159–60.

75. Simon J. Gathercole, *The Composition of the Gospel of Thomas: Original Language and Influences*, SNTSMS 151 (Cambridge: Cambridge University Press, 2012).

The Markan surplus "and for the gospel" is clearly a redactional feature. The Greek *euangelion* (gospel) is a preferential word in Mark. He uses it seven times (Mark 1:1, 14, 15; 8:35; 10:29; 13:10; 14:9), with only two parallels in Matthew. Both Matthew 24:14 and Mark 13:10 probably go back to a written source of apocalyptic sayings. In Matthew 26:13 and Mark 14:9 *euangelion* renders a Semitic term (*besorah*), probably used by Jesus himself. Luke makes use of the verb *euangelizō* (to proclaim good news), but he never uses the substantive *euangelion* in his Gospel. Mark, having published his Gospel during the Neronian persecution, stresses the subject of persecution and perseverance in the Gospel by his redactions (cf. also Mark 10:29–30; cf. Matt. 19:29//Luke 18:29–30). Many other Markan redactional features are absent from Matthew and Luke.[76] To give another example: Mark likes the connecting word "again," *palin* in Greek, referring back to previous events. While there are fifteen examples of this special usage in Mark, Matthew and Luke have none in their parallels. Presupposing Markan priority, one has to assume that Matthew and Luke, like modern literary critics, independently recognized the Markan redaction every time and deleted it. This is an improbable explanation. The canonical Mark apparently was not the source for either Matthew or Luke. A Greek Proto-Mark can sufficiently explain the triple tradition behind the Synoptics.

In other cases, Matthean redaction is absent from both Mark and Luke.[77] Matthew has a clear preference for the verb *proserchomai* (to approach). By using this word, he especially stresses the reverence for Jesus as a teacher. Matthew uses *proserchomai* no less than fifty-two times, with only five parallels in Luke and three in Mark. Another example is the use of the common word *ekeithen* (from where). Matthew has it twelve times, with only two Markan parallels and one parallel in Luke. This is all the more astonishing because both evangelists do not shy away from using the term elsewhere. Matthew uses it three times and Luke two times apart from the parallels to Mark. Matthean priority as the foundation of the Augustinian hypothesis and the Two Gospel Hypothesis does not seem tenable, and neither is the supposition of the Farrer Hypothesis, which holds that Luke used Matthew. For both the Two Source and the Farrer Hypotheses, it is also difficult to explain why Luke left out the story of the Syrophoenician/Canaanite woman (Mark 7:24–30// Matt. 15:21–28), which would be so apt for his theological aims (praise of women, inclusion of the Gentiles).

76. Burkett, *From Proto-Mark to Mark*, 7–42.
77. Ibid., 43–59.

The existence of the sayings source Q has been strongly challenged in recent times.[78] If one wishes to retain something like a written source for the material common to Matthew and Luke, one should integrate some important observations. If the double tradition starts with the historical introduction of the baptism and the temptation of Jesus (Matt. 3:13–4:11//Luke 3:21–22; 4:1–13) and comprises other narrative elements besides, this fact might argue against a mere sayings source.[79] The many minor agreements point in the same direction of a source comprising the story of Jesus, even including his passion. These minor agreements are agreements between Matthew and Luke against Mark in the material common to all three. There were apparently broad overlaps between the triple and the double tradition. At many places in the double tradition we find strong differences in wording between Matthew and Luke. A possible explanation is that "Q" material frequently overlaps not only with Markan material but also with Matthew's and Luke's special sources.[80]

Conclusion

From Jesus, the messianic teacher, to the Synoptic Gospels and beyond, there existed an oral tradition characterized by a flexible stability. The tradition of the sayings of Jesus was rather fixed, whereas narratives were handed down with greater flexibility. From an early date there was an interplay between the oral and the written. Informal notes served as memory aids. One should not forget that "it is rather in literate societies that verbatim memory flourishes."[81] The evangelists knew their materials from both oral traditions and written sources. Even the textual tradition of the Synoptics is sometimes influenced by the ongoing oral tradition. The copyists assimilated texts to the version they knew from memory, or sometimes they introduced bits of oral traditions (e.g., Luke 6:4 Codex D; 9:55–56 Codex K). The Synoptic Gospels are not mutually dependent but partially used the same intermediary sources. According to the foreword to his Gospel, Luke relied on the traditions of the eyewitnesses and many written accounts (Luke 1:1–4). This also indicates that the Synoptic phenomenon is best explained by a combination of the Tradition Hypothesis and the Multiple Source Hypothesis.

78. Mark Goodacre and Nicholas Perrin, eds., *Questioning Q: A Multidimensional Critique* (Downers Grove, IL: InterVarsity, 2004).

79. Stephen Hultgren, *Narrative Elements in the Double Tradition: A Study of Their Place within the Framework of the Gospel Narrative*, BZNW 113 (Berlin: de Gruyter, 2002).

80. Burkett, *Unity and Plurality of Q*, 113–206.

81. Jack Goody, *The Interface between the Written and the Oral*, SLFCS (Cambridge: Cambridge University Press, 1987), 189.

Further Reading

Intermediate

Bauckham, Richard. *Jesus and the Eyewitnesses: The Gospels as Eyewitness Testimony*. Grand Rapids: Eerdmans, 2006.

Dunn, James D. G. *The Oral Gospel Tradition*. Grand Rapids: Eerdmans, 2013.

Gerhardsson, Birger. *The Reliability of the Gospel Tradition*. Peabody, MA: Hendrickson, 2001.

Millard, Allan. *Reading and Writing in the Time of Jesus*. BibSem 69. Sheffield, UK: Sheffield Academic Press, 2000.

Stein, Robert H. *The Method and Message of Jesus' Teachings*. 2nd ed. Louisville: Westminster John Knox, 1994.

Advanced

Burkett, Delbert. *Rethinking the Gospel Sources*. Vol. 1, *From Proto-Mark to Mark*. London: T&T Clark International, 2004.

Byrskog, Samuel. *Story as History—History as Story: The Gospel Tradition in the Context of Ancient Oral History*. WUNT 123. Tübingen: Mohr Siebeck, 2000.

Gerhardsson, Birger. *Memory and Manuscript: Oral Tradition and Written Transmission in Rabbinic Judaism and Early Christianity* [1961]; *with, Tradition and Transmission in Early Christianity* [1964]. Translated by Eric J. Sharp. BRS. Grand Rapids: Eerdmans, 1998.

Hultgren, Stephen. *Narrative Elements in the Double Tradition: A Study of Their Place within the Framework of the Gospel Narrative*. BZNW 113. Berlin: de Gruyter, 2002.

Riesner, Rainer. "From the Messianic Teacher to the Gospels of Jesus Christ." In *Handbook for the Study of the Historical Jesus*. Vol. 1, *How to Study the Historical Jesus*, edited by Tom Holmén and Stanley E. Porter, 405–46. Leiden: Brill, 2011.

6

Two Source Hypothesis Response

Craig A. Evans

I begin my response with a word of appreciation for the excellent essays that my colleagues have produced. What we have in these essays are carefully considered arguments that explore the strengths and weaknesses of the main contenders in the attempt to solve the Synoptic Problem. The essays by Rainer Riesner, David Peabody, and Mark Goodacre have enriched this important discussion.

Comments on Rainer Riesner's Essay

Rainer Riesner very helpfully underscores the importance of orality in the time of Jesus and the first generations of his movement.[1] With approval he references studies that have probed the role of memory and pedagogy in Judaism and the rabbinic tradition of late antiquity. Moreover, Riesner rightly

---

1. Riesner is correct to say that general scholarly debate concerned with the Synoptic Problem tends to downplay or ignore altogether the role of memory and orality. He rightly notes the helpful exceptions to this observation in the very useful work of Samuel Byrskog and Armin Baum, who in their own ways have built on the earlier work of Birger Gerhardsson and Harald Riesenfeld.

notes that once written Gospels began to circulate, the oral tradition did not cease but continued and thereby influenced the way the written copies were edited and copied.

Riesner goes on to argue that there is good evidence to believe that the oral and written traditions are based on reliable, early tradition,[2] concluding, "Of the two pillars of the Two Source Hypothesis, Markan priority is the stronger one" (p. 108). Nevertheless, he wisely urges us to recognize that in all probability the Synoptic Gospels developed in stages, that therefore the Mark known to Matthew probably was not the Mark known to Luke, and that neither one of these versions of Mark was the version that was eventually received into the canon of Scripture.

I believe that Riesner is on the whole correct. The solution to the Synoptic Problem is more complex than simply arguing that Matthew and Luke made use of Mark independently of each other. The likelihood that the Synoptic Gospels were produced in stages and under the influence of the oral tradition throughout the first century is a factor that must be taken into account as we consider the strengths and weaknesses of the various solutions to the Synoptic Problem that have been put forward.

Comments on David Peabody's Essay

I appreciate David Peabody's careful and succinct statement in support of the priority of Matthew. In my opinion, he has emerged as the ablest proponent of this view. His irenic and respectful tone is also deeply appreciated and will encourage others to take his views seriously and engage him in constructive debate.

As one would expect, Peabody draws attention to the agreements between Matthew and Luke over against Mark as evidence that Matthew and Luke did not work independently of each other. Peabody argues that Luke made use of Matthew, and that Mark, writing last, not only conflates material he has drawn from Matthew and Luke but also has added new material and in places added his own distinctive editorial touches (such as adding *palin* [again] to passages also found in Matthew and Luke).[3] Peabody also underscores the importance of the patristic testimony, which often assumes or argues explicitly

2. Riesner states, "A cultivated Jesus tradition was apparently handed down from very early on, but for the dates of its beginnings, one must look back into pre-Easter times" (p. 99).

3. *Palin* occurs sixteen times in Matthew, three times in Luke, and twenty-six times in Mark. The appearance of *palin* several times (some fifteen) in Markan passages and its nonappearance in the parallel passages in Matthew and Luke work against Markan priority, for it would have been highly unlikely for Matthew and Luke to omit this word every time. This would be true

that Matthew was written first and that Mark was written either second or third. His work with the patristic evidence is far more detailed than what one usually finds in scholarly discussion of the Synoptic Problem. For this alone we owe Peabody our thanks.

Aspects of Peabody's arguments have already been treated in my earlier chapter. Here I will respond to only a couple of points. In making his case that the patristic tradition supports Matthean priority, Peabody cites quotations from Papias's lost work *The Sayings of the Lord* (an early second-century CE work, mostly preserved in Eusebius), in which this early father discusses the Gospels, the evangelists, and the dominical tradition. What I find interesting is that Peabody cites first what Papias says about Matthew (from Eusebius, *Church History* 3.39.16), then what Papias says about Mark (3.39.15). But as one will notice from the references enclosed in the parentheses, Peabody has cited the excerpted material in reverse order.

The Papian/Eusebian recounting of the evangelists and their respective Gospels in fact *begins with Mark*, who is described as "Peter's interpreter." Papias discusses how Mark arranged Peter's reminiscences, which were in the form of *chreiai* (anecdotes), though "not in order" (Eusebius, *Church History* 3.39.15). Quoted next is the very brief tradition that the evangelist Matthew "set in order the logia [of Jesus] in the Hebrew dialect [Hebraic style],[4] and each recorded them as he was able" (3.39.16). Because Eusebius provides only brief quotations, we cannot be certain that the single sentence relating to Matthew actually followed the longer discussion of Mark. If we had the full text of Papias before us, perhaps we would find that the discussion of Matthew appears first. But what Eusebius provides—both the excerpts from Papias and the narrative and commentary that Eusebius himself provides—makes perfectly good sense in the order that we find: the dominical tradition in its written form began with the reminiscences of Peter, which Mark wrote down (but not "in order" [*taxei*]), and continued with Matthew, who "set in order" (*synetaxato*) the logia (or sayings) of Jesus in a different style. Clearly, the implied sequence is (disordered) Mark first, (ordered) Matthew second.[5]

The Papian tradition of Mark-then-Matthew is not the only one we have. A generation or so after the time of Papias, the *Gospel of Thomas* began to

---

if the version of Mark that we now have was the version that Matthew and Luke had before them. But such an assumption is precarious. See the discussion on pp. 106–10.

4. Peabody plausibly translates *hebraidi dialekto* as "in a Hebraic style."

5. See Francis Watson, *Gospel Writing: A Canonical Perspective* (Grand Rapids: Eerdmans, 2013), 123–29. Writing a half-century later, Irenaeus, who depends on Papias, reverses the Mark-then-Matthew order. See *Against Heresies* 3.1.1.

circulate in eastern Syria.[6] In a tradition that scholars think was intended to exalt Thomas the apostle over the apostles Peter and Matthew, we read,

> Jesus said to his disciples: "Compare me to someone and tell me whom I am like." Simon Peter said to him, "You are like a righteous angel." Matthew said to him, "You are a like a wise philosopher." Thomas said to him, "Master, my mouth is wholly incapable of saying whom you are like." (*Gospel of Thomas* 13a)[7]

The passage goes on to say that Jesus took Thomas aside and shared with him secret truths that simply could not be communicated with the other apostles (13b).

This passage in the *Gospel of Thomas* recalls Jesus's question and Peter's confession in the vicinity of Caesarea Philippi, particularly in its fuller Matthean form (Matt. 16:13–19). But in the *Gospel of Thomas* it is not Peter who utters the inspired words and is blessed; it is Thomas. The *Gospel of Thomas* lionizes the apostle Thomas and the Gospel linked to his name and at the same time subordinates the apostles Peter and Matthew and the respective Gospels linked to their names (i.e., Mark and Matthew).[8] What we probably have here in *Gospel of Thomas* 13 is a reflection of regional ecclesiastical rivalry between the East (whose apostolic hero was Thomas) and the West (whose apostolic heroes, at least as far as Gospels were concerned, were Peter and Matthew).

In the *Gospel of Thomas*, the appearance of Peter first, followed by Matthew, corresponds to what we observe in the Papian tradition quoted by Eusebius. The significance of this feature should not be overlooked: our two earliest discussions of Matthew and Mark—one explicit (Papias) and one implicit (*Gospel of Thomas*)—place Mark in first position and Matthew in

---

6. I realize that some scholars date the *Gospel of Thomas* to the latter part of the first century. But this early date flies in the face of too much contrary evidence. *Thomas* was composed in the second half of the second century. For recent studies that rightly date *Thomas* to the second century and view this work as dependent on the Synoptic Gospels, see Mark S. Goodacre, *Thomas and the Gospels: The Case for Thomas's Familiarity with the Synoptics* (Grand Rapids: Eerdmans, 2012); Simon J. Gathercole, *The Composition of the Gospel of Thomas: Original Language and Influences*, SNTSMS 151 (Cambridge: Cambridge University Press, 2012).

7. J. M. Robinson, ed., *The Nag Hammadi Library* (San Francisco: Harper & Row, 1977), 119.

8. A. F. Walls, "The References to Apostles in the *Gospel of Thomas*," *NTS* 7 (1960–61): 266–70; Terence V. Smith, *Petrine Controversies in Early Christianity: Attitudes towards Peter in Christian Writings of the First Two Centuries*, WUNT 2.15 (Tübingen: Mohr Siebeck, 1985), 115–16; Thomas A. Wayment, "Christian Teachers in Matthew and Thomas: The Possibility of Becoming a 'Master,'" *JECS* 12 (2004): 289–311; Richard Bauckham, *Jesus and the Eyewitnesses: The Gospels as Eyewitness Testimony* (Grand Rapids: Eerdmans, 2006), 236–37.

second position. Nevertheless, the Gospel of Matthew does emerge in the second century (and beyond) as the dominant Gospel.[9]

Peabody also argues for Markan posteriority on the basis of Mark's alternating agreements with Matthew and Luke (see the parallel columns on pp. 73–78). But this argument is reversible, for it is just as easy (and I think easier) to conclude this from the data: "Where there is no Mark to follow, Matthew and Luke go their separate ways." For example, Mark provides no infancy narrative or genealogy. Matthew and Luke do, but with many differences. Mark provides a very brief account of Easter (just how brief depends on one's position regarding whether Mark 16:8 was the original, intended ending). Matthew and Luke provide longer accounts, but again with noticeable differences. The bulk of teaching material not found in Mark (i.e., Q) is arranged in different patterns and sequences in Matthew and Luke. All of this is what one expects if Mark was written first and Matthew and Luke were written later, having made use of Mark and a body of dominical tradition not derived from Mark.

Advocates of Matthean priority and Markan posteriority have difficulty in providing a convincing explanation for the addition of material found only in Mark. This material consists of Mark 1:1; 2:27; 3:20–21; 4:26–29; 7:2–4, 32–37; 8:22–26; 9:29, 48–49; 13:33–37; 14:51–52. The first two items (1:1; 2:27) pose no difficulty, but the remaining items do. In my chapter above, I asked which explanation seems most probable: that Mark added this material or that Matthew and Luke found it in Mark and chose to omit it? Given the nature of this material, surely the latter alternative makes better sense. I am not convinced that Peabody and other supporters of the Two Gospel Hypothesis have explained why Mark would add these materials and at the same time omit many excellent traditions found in both Matthew and Luke.

Peabody thinks that if it can be shown that Luke made use of Matthew, then the need for Q has been eliminated. But this does not follow. Luke contains a number of units of tradition not drawn from Matthew or Mark. One immediately thinks of the parable of the good Samaritan (Luke 10:30–35), the parable of the friend at midnight (11:5–8), the parable of the rich fool (12:16–21), the parable of the fig tree (13:6–9), the teaching on humility (14:7–10, 12–14), the parable of the builder (14:28–30), the parable of the king considering battle (14:31–32), the parable of the lost coin (15:8–10), the parable of the prodigal son (15:11–32), the parable of the dishonest steward (16:1–9), the parable of

9. As is ably documented in Édouard Massaux, *The Influence of the Gospel of Saint Matthew on Christian Literature before Saint Irenaeus*, trans. Norman J. Belval and Suzanne Hecht, ed. Arthur J. Bellinzoni, 3 vols., NGS 5.1–3 (Leuven: Peeters; Macon, GA: Mercer University Press, 1990–93).

the rich man and the poor man (16:19–31), the parable of the worthy servant (17:7–10), the parable of the persistent widow (18:1–8), and the parable of the Pharisee and the tax collector (18:9–14). Where did this material come from? Surely it was not all created by the evangelist Luke. Q scholars are uncertain how much of this material, if any, derives from Q, as such, but its existence shows that there was dominical tradition independent of Mark and Matthew. Luke's hypothesized knowledge of Matthew does not eliminate the existence of a substantial body of non-Matthean material.

Patristic testimony itself knows of tradition outside the New Testament Gospels. According to Eusebius, Papias speaks of "certain marvels and other details which apparently reached him by tradition" (*Church History* 3.39.8). Moreover, he "adduces other accounts," Eusebius says, "as though they came to him from unwritten [*agraphos*] tradition" (3.39.11). All of this is vague, to be sure, but it does suggest that in very early times extra–Synoptic Gospel stories and teaching linked to Jesus circulated. The material that Matthew and Luke drew heavily upon, in order to supplement the dominical tradition that they derived from Mark, included what scholars call Q.

Comments on Mark Goodacre's Essay

Mark Goodacre deserves special praise, not least for his clarity and well-chosen examples that he believes support his view of Markan priority without Q.[10] I also appreciate the courage with which he stands up for this minority position. Goodacre's skillful and well-articulated defense will no doubt draw new adherents.[11]

Before discussing the most important examples that Goodacre believes support the hypothesis that Luke made use of Mark and Matthew, I want to take up where I left off in my engagement with David Peabody and say a bit more about the probability of the existence of Q.

If we agree with Goodacre that the Gospel of Mark was written first and that Matthew used Mark, then the need for postulating the existence of a body of dominical tradition becomes even more pressing than it is in the case

10. Goodacre's essay in the present book is all the more welcome in light of the fact that the Farrer-Goulder-Goodacre hypothesis has been confused with the hypothesis of Matthean priority. For a concise and recent articulation of his view, see Mark Goodacre, *The Case against Q: Studies in Markan Priority and the Synoptic Problem* (Harrisburg PA: Trinity Press International, 2002). The book is subjected to trenchant but very fair criticism in John S. Kloppenborg, "On Dispensing with Q? Goodacre on the Relation of Luke to Matthew," *NTS* 49 (2003): 210–36.

11. For a recent presentation of Luke as an interpreter of Matthew, see Watson, *Gospel Writing*, 117–216.

of those who argue that the Gospel of Matthew was written and circulated first. If Matthew was written first and Luke made use of Matthew, we need to account for the dominical tradition (which I list above) that is special to Luke. But if Mark was written first, we need to account for an even greater amount of dominical tradition.

If Mark was written first (and I think it was), then from where did Matthew derive his distinctive dominical traditions? These traditions include the teaching on alms and fasting (Matt. 6:2–4, 16–18), the parable of the wheat and weeds (13:24–30), the parable of the pearl (13:45–46), the parable of the fish net (13:47–50), the parable of the unforgiving servant (18:23–35), teaching on celibacy (19:10–12), the parable of the laborers in the vineyard (20:1–16), the parable of the two sons (21:28–32), the parable of the wise and foolish maidens (25:1–13), and the parable of the last judgment (25:31–46). And, of course, we still must ask: If Luke made use of Matthew (there being no Q to draw upon), from where did Luke derive his distinctive dominical tradition? My point is simply this: whether one argues for Matthean priority (as does Peabody) or Markan priority (as does Goodacre), there is no escaping Q. Non-Markan material appears in Matthew and Luke, most of it appears in different locations, and much of it has been edited in distinctive ways.

To avoid concluding, as most Markan prioritists do, that Matthew and Luke made use of Mark and a large body of dominical tradition not derived from Mark, Goodacre draws attention to what might be called "not-so-minor agreements" of Matthew and Luke against Mark. Seven or eight such agreements have been identified that are felt to be especially problematic for the Two Source Hypothesis. In his essay, Goodacre cites one example (addressed below), but it is important to show that in several of these cases the evidence does not point to Luke's use of Matthew. I will highlight three common examples of "minor agreements" and show that even in these cases the implications of the data do not require us to conclude that Luke drew on Matthew.[12]

A first example of agreement between Matthew and Luke against Mark is found in the question about the resurrection (Matt. 22:23–33//Mark 12:18–27//Luke 20:27–40). Mark reads, "Last of all the woman also died" (Mark 12:22). Mark uses the adverb *eschaton* (last), but both Matthew and Luke use *hysteron* (later, after, afterward): "After them all, the woman died" (Matt. 22:27); "Afterward the woman also died" (Luke 20:32). It is sometimes noted that the word *hysteron* occurs seven times in Matthew but only once in Luke, in

---

12. These three examples were selected because they are used by Goodacre in his work *The Case against Q* (152–69) in support of Luke's use of Matthew as a part of his solution to the Synoptic Problem.

the passage under consideration. In his book *The Case against Q*, Goodacre describes the appearance of *hysteron* in Luke as "idiosyncratic," especially in light of its rareness in New Testament literature.[13] (Outside the Synoptic Gospels the word occurs only in John 13:36; 1 Tim. 4:1; Heb. 12:11.) The implication, Goodacre supposes, is that Luke used the rare word *hysteron* because he saw it in Matthew.

But is the adverb *hysteron* really that rare? It occurs twenty times in the Septuagint (and the evangelist Luke was quite familiar with the Septuagint). It occurs three times in the body of literature known as the Apostolic Fathers; thirty times in the second-century fathers Irenaeus, Justin Martyr, and Theophilus; and another thirty-nine times in Eusebius. More to the point, *hysteron* occurs many times in the first-century writers Philo and Josephus: 131 times in Philo and 122 times in Josephus. It seems that *hysteron* is not a rare word in Greek writers of the eastern Mediterranean. Given the rareness of Mark's use of *eschaton pantōn* (elsewhere in the New Testament it occurs only in 1 Cor. 15:8), perhaps the coincidence of Matthew's and Luke's choice of the more widely used *hysteron* is not especially striking.

A second example of agreement between Matthew and Luke against Mark is found in the story about the healing of the paralyzed man, whose friends bring him to Jesus (Matt. 9:1–8//Mark 2:1–12//Luke 5:17–26). Mark says, "And they came, bringing to him a paralytic carried by four men" (Mark 2:3). There is no mention of the manner by which the sick man is conveyed until the end of verse 4, after readers are told that they removed some of the roof and made an opening: "They let down the pallet [*krabattos*] on which the paralytic lay." We are not told that the sick man has been brought to the crowded house on a pallet. (Perhaps a makeshift pallet was fashioned from some poles and roofing materials?) I suspect that most readers would have assumed that the man had in fact been carried to the house on the pallet. In any case, when the man is healed, Jesus says to him, "I say to you, rise, take up your pallet and go home" (v. 11).

The evangelists Matthew and Luke remove the ambiguity of Mark's story by making it clear at the outset that the sick man was brought to the house "on a bed" (*epi klinēs*).[14] Matthew puts it this way: "And behold, they brought to him a paralytic, lying on his bed" (Matt. 9:2); Luke puts it this way: "And behold, men were bringing on a bed a man who was paralyzed" (Luke 5:18).

---

13. Goodacre, *Case against Q*, 155.

14. Some copyists of Mark sense the same problem. For example, we find in Codex W: "And behold, men come to him bearing a paralytic on a pallet." Reference is again made to the pallet at the end of v. 4. In v. 3 a number of Latin manuscripts add *in grabatto* (on a pallet) either before or after mention of the paralytic.

The appearance of "on a bed" in both Matthew and Luke, instead of Mark's "pallet" (*krabattos*), has been emphasized by Goodacre and others, especially in light of the fact that the evangelist Luke uses the word *krabattos* elsewhere (e.g., Acts 5:15; 9:33).[15] It is reasoned that if Luke had Mark before him (and not Matthew), then how is this coincidence to be explained? Surely if Luke had only Mark as his source, he would have used Mark's word *krabattos*. The appearance of *klinē* in Luke's version of the story suggests, then, that Luke had Matthew before him as well as Mark.

So why does *klinē*, instead of *krabattos*, appear in Luke? The question is a good one. We might ask it of Matthew as well. After all, in using Mark, the evangelist Matthew would have had the word *krabattos* in the passage before him. He chose *klinē* instead. Both *krabattos* and *klinē* can be translated "bed." In some contexts the words seem to be interchangeable. So why did Matthew choose *klinē*? Why did Luke also, who had before him both Mark and Matthew (on Goodacre's hypothesis)?

As it turns out, the two words are sometimes used differently. Mark's *krabattos*, translated "pallet" in the RSV, sometimes is used as a "poor man's bed" (cf. BAG ad loc.). The Latin cognate, *grabatus* (or *grabattus*), means the same thing. But more importantly, the word *klinē* is often used in reference to the "sickbed" (e.g., Gen. 48:2; 49:33; 1 Kings 17:19; 20:4 [21:4 ET]; 2 Kings 1:4, 6, 16; 4:10, 21, 32; Ps. 40:4 LXX [41:3 ET]; Jdt. 8:3; Tob. 14:11; *T. Abr.* A 20:7; *Jos. Asen.* 10:8; Josephus, *Ant.* 6.217; 8.326, 369; Rev. 2:22: "Behold, I will throw her on a sickbed"). Indeed, sometimes *klinē* is used for "bier," on which the corpse is placed (2 Sam. 3:31; 2 Chron. 16:14; Josephus, *J.W.* 1.671–72; *Ant.* 7.40; 17.197–98; 19.237; *Life* 323).

I suspect that Matthew and Luke both chose *klinē*, instead of *krabattos*, for the same reason, and that it is not necessary to think that Luke had to see Matthew's version of the story of the paralyzed man to think of the word *klinē*, which he uses elsewhere (Luke 8:16; 17:34) and so is not averse to it.

In *The Case against Q*, Goodacre also observes the presence of the word *idou*, "behold," in the versions of the story found in Matthew and Luke (Matt. 9:2; Luke 5:18) but not in Mark's version of the story. Is this agreement against Mark evidence that Luke knew and used Matthew? It could be, but I suspect that it is an example of the kind of minor agreements we should expect when two writers edit a document independently of each other. Of the thousands of changes that they make, many of which are quite minor, surely they make dozens, if not hundreds, of the same changes. Included in these changes will be common omissions and common additions.

15. Goodacre, *Case against Q*, 156–57.

The word *idou*, "behold," occurs only seven times in the Gospel of Mark. It occurs sixty-two times in Matthew and fifty-seven times in Luke. This means that the evangelists Matthew and Luke have each added *idou* to the Markan text fifty times or more. It is not surprising that sometimes they add it to the same passage. When they do, they create a minor agreement. Of course, we must be cautious in cases like this, for it would be very easy for a copyist to add a simple word like *idou* to a Gospel story, thus expanding the number of minor agreements in the manuscript tradition. (Indeed, *idou* appears in Codex W's version of Mark's story, thus eliminating a minor agreement against Mark!)

I might also add that Matthew makes a number of changes to Mark's story of the paralyzed man that are not reflected in Luke's version of the story. For example, Matthew frames the story with reference to Jesus crossing the lake in a boat. He omits reference to the crowd and to removing the roof and lowering the paralyzed man through the opening. Matthew replaces Mark's reference to amazement with reference to being afraid. Matthew adds the comment about God giving "such authority" to men (i.e., to Jesus). None of these Matthean changes, additions, or omissions are reflected in Luke's version of the story.

I note that Luke's failure to capitalize on the reference to "such authority" is a bit odd, not only because Luke likes the word "authority" (*exousia*), but also because it has occurred in the story itself ("the Son of man has authority") and has been used in reference to Jesus in very positive ways earlier in Luke's narrative (e.g., Luke 4:32, 36). Why not adapt Matthew's comment, if Luke in fact had Matthew in front of him? Apart from the two minor agreements just considered, Luke's changes to Mark's version of the story do not seem to be inspired by Matthew's changes.

A third example of agreement between Matthew and Luke against Mark is found in the story of the officers' brutal treatment of Jesus following his hearing before the high priest and his colleagues (Matt. 26:67–68//Mark 14:65// Luke 22:63–64).[16] In Matthew and Luke, the officers who mock the blindfolded Jesus demand that he prophesy by telling them who strikes him. The two evangelists have the identical question: "Who is it that struck you?" (Matt. 26:68; Luke 22:64). The question does not appear in Mark (see Mark 14:65). This could certainly be seen as a difficult passage to explain, but it is not as damaging to the Two Source Hypothesis as Goodacre may want us to believe.

If there were many examples such as these, and if the Two Source Hypothesis lacked robust explanatory power (in this case, in explaining Matthew's and

16. Goodacre cites this example in his essay (p. 56). See also Goodacre, *Case against Q*, 158–60.

Luke's independent use of the non-Markan material that they have in common), I would have to agree with Goodacre. But such troublesome agreements of Matthew and Luke against Mark are rare. Goodacre has challenged his skeptics with the best he has. One would think that if the Farrer-Goulder-Goodacre Hypothesis of Luke directly and heavily depending on Matthew were correct, we would have many more examples and far more difficult ones.

But how difficult is this third example? There are many variants, including harmonizing glosses, in the manuscript tradition concerned with Jesus's hearing before the high priest and his colleagues. For example, at Mark 14:62 Jesus replies to the high priest's question, "I am." But in several manuscripts Jesus says, "You have said that I am," which is likely a gloss inspired by Matthew 26:64, "You have said so." Another important feature is that Luke has significantly rearranged the material, placing the challenge to prophesy (Luke 22:63–64) after Peter's denials (Luke 22:54–62), which is not the order found in Matthew and Mark. In Luke it is the next day when Jesus appears before the assembly of priests and elders and then is asked about his identity. Even here Luke has broken up the high priest's question into two parts: "If you are the Christ, tell us" (Luke 22:67); "Are you the Son of God, then?" (22:70). On the Farrer-Goulder-Goodacre Hypothesis of Luke making use of Matthew, we would have to believe that Luke not only has taken some remarkable liberties with Mark but also has taken liberties with Matthew, whose narrative on the whole follows Mark's narrative very closely. In important ways we have even more agreement of Mark and Matthew against Luke.

There are also oddities in both the Markan and the Matthean versions of the challenge put to Jesus to prophesy. In Mark's version Jesus's face is covered, he is struck, and his tormentors demand that he prophesy (Mark 14:65). But we are not told what it is that he is to prophesy. Because his face is covered (so that he cannot see who strikes him), we assume that Jesus, possessed with prophetic insight (which includes clairvoyance), would be able to identify which officer has struck him. This seems to be the point of the mockery. It is clear that Matthew and Luke understand it that way, as indicated by the question found in their respective narratives, "Who is it that struck you?" (Matt. 26:68; Luke 22:64).

What is curious is that Matthew omits reference to the covering of Jesus's face (he instead says the officers spat in Jesus's face). Without his face covered, Jesus would be able to see who strikes him, so the demand that he prophesy loses its force. Luke retains this detail and, like Matthew, has the longer reading. But Luke lacks a number of elements that Matthew added to Mark's narrative. These include the question "What is your judgment?" (in Mark it is "What is your decision?"), spitting in Jesus's face, slapping

Jesus, and addressing him, "You Christ!" Luke retains Mark's comment that Jesus's face was covered (though Luke uses different wording). In retaining this detail, Luke does not follow Matthew, who has omitted it. Luke does not reflect Matthew's distinctive beginning of the high priest's question "I adjure you by the living God . . ." (Matt. 26:63).

Let us return to Matthew and Luke's agreement against Mark. Mark's "Prophesy!" (Mark 14:65) expects some sort of clarification of what is meant. A number of Markan copyists agree, penning the text to read just as we find it in Matthew and Luke, "Who is it that struck you?"[17] Goodacre and others will, of course, reply that this is a scribal harmonization. And it may well be. But it makes good sense of the data that we actually have. If Mark's text originally read, "Prophesy! Who is it that struck you?," the meaning of Mark's passage is clear: Jesus's face has been covered (so that he cannot see), he is struck, and he is asked to act as a prophet who can identify the one who strikes him, even though he cannot see the striker. Mark's version is then followed by Luke (though in a new location) and by Matthew, who preserves the location but expands the words spoken to Jesus: "Prophesy *to us, you Christ*! Who is it that struck you?" (Matt. 26:68 [expansion in italics]).

Even in these three examples of not-so-minor agreements between Matthew and Luke against Mark, the developments and directions of the data are not unambiguous. The raw data in these limited cases, by themselves, do lend support to advocates of Luke's direct use of Matthew, but are they sufficient to overthrow the evidence in support of viewing Matthew and Luke as independent compositions? Most scholars do not think so.

Conclusion

Given the evidence of scribal harmonization, given the probability that all three Synoptic Gospels were "published" in two or more recensions, and given the ongoing influence of the oral tradition,[18] no theory of Synoptic origins and relationships should rely heavily on the appearance of minor

17. For manuscript data, see NA[28] ad loc.; B. H. Streeter, *The Four Gospels: A Study of Origins, Treating of the Manuscript Tradition, Sources, Authorship, and Dates* (London: Macmillan, 1924), 325–26; S. C. E. Legg, *Novum Testamentum Graece secundum Textum Westcotto-Hortianum: Euangelium secundum Marcum* (Oxford: Clarendon, 1935), ad loc.

18. It is easy for us moderns to fail to appreciate how influential the oral tradition was, even after the publication and circulation of the written Gospels. I remind readers again of Papias's remarkable declaration that he preferred the "living and abiding voice" over written material (in Eusebius, *Church History* 3.39.4). When he said this, the Synoptic Gospels had been in circulation forty to fifty years.

agreements or the appearance of this or that word. If we were in possession of the autographs, or had certain knowledge of the form and wording of the texts that the respective evangelists had before them, evidence of this nature would have a great deal more weight.

Rather, priority must be given to analysis of the larger units of double and triple tradition and consideration of what the differences and similarities suggest. Of this tradition we must ask, which theory possesses the most exegetical and critical explanatory power? Most Gospel scholars and commentators continue to believe that the Two Source Hypothesis is that theory.

7

Farrer Hypothesis Response

Mark Goodacre

Introduction

Like many areas in the study of the New Testament, arguments about the Synoptic Problem can be polarizing. The value of a book like this is that it helps not only to clarify the points of divergence between differing theories but also to illustrate where the points of contact lie. I am grateful to my colleagues in this project for arguing so clearly and forcefully for their theories while at the same time bringing perspectives that complement one another. David Peabody's essay, for example, focuses helpfully on the external evidence, making up a lack in the essays by the rest of us. Craig Evans's essay provides a strong statement of the status quo in Synoptic scholarship, helpfully orienting the newcomer to the normal starting point for the current discussion. And Rainer Riesner's essay provides a welcome reminder of the important role played by oral tradition and memory in all Synoptic theories.

Moreover, in spite of the differences between us, there is a degree of similarity between our approaches to the issue; and for the student learning about the Synoptic Problem, there are key points here to be grasped. We are agreed on the following important points:

1. *The Synoptic Problem is essentially a literary problem.* The degree of verbatim agreement between Matthew, Mark, and Luke is so striking that it

is impossible that they are not linked in some way, either directly or indirectly, at the literary level. It is a point that is sometimes not grasped by introductory students because they have not spent time looking at a Gospel synopsis. Both Peabody and I draw attention to Matthew 3:7–10//Luke 3:7–9 (John the Baptist's preaching) as a good example of agreement that is so close that it points to a literary link of some kind. Examples like this could be multiplied.

2. *Literary solutions to the Synoptic Problem take us only so far.* While the Synoptic Problem is a question about the literary relationships between related works, a comprehensive perspective on the origin and development of the Synoptic Gospels requires understanding of a range of factors, including the role played by oral tradition. Although Riesner is the essayist specifically tasked with exploring the topic, it is clear that each of us recognizes its importance, even though much of the discussion of oral tradition takes place outside of disputes about the literary relationship between the Synoptics.

3. *Discussion of the ordering of Synoptic passages is a key part of the problem.* For Peabody, Matthew's and Luke's alternating agreement with Mark provides evidence that Mark conflated Matthew and Luke. For Evans, Luke's order provides evidence that Luke used Q rather than Matthew. For me, careful attention to Luke's ordering of Markan material provides clues for his ordering of Matthew's material.

4. *Detailed comparison between texts is essential.* The Synoptic Problem will not be solved in the abstract. All solutions build their case by careful comparisons between parallel texts. Much Synoptic discussion revolves around the plausibility of specific changes that a given evangelist makes to his source texts.

If we are all broadly agreed on these key points, there are also specific points of contact between individual essayists. In particular, I find much to agree with in Evans's case for Markan Priority, while also lining up alongside Peabody in finding the case for Luke's use of Matthew to be strong. Moreover, in spite of the fact that—unlike the evangelists—we all wrote independently of one another, it is striking that the same examples come up several times: Matthew 3:7–10//Luke 3:7–9 (John the Baptist's preaching) for Peabody and me; the minor agreement at Mark 14:65 for Evans, Peabody, and me; and Mark's use of the Greek word *palin* (again) for Peabody and Riesner. Nevertheless, there are key differences in our approaches and conclusions. I will focus on several of the most important.

Markan Posteriority

David Peabody's essay helpfully sets out the case that Mark's Gospel was written third, conflating Matthew and Luke. He generally configures his case as an argument against Matthew's and Luke's independent use of Mark (the Two Source Hypothesis), and his arguments tend to express wonder at the idea that both Matthew and Luke could have edited Mark in the way they did. The case has a little less force against the Farrer Hypothesis, according to which Luke will often be influenced by Matthew's modification of Mark. Nevertheless, there are still major points of difference between our perspectives on the evidence.

Peabody's table of parallels in order between the Synoptics (pp. 73–76), for example, attempts to illustrate "Mark's alternating agreement" (p. 72) with Matthew and Luke in order to suggest that Mark was conflating Matthew and Luke. However, the table simply illustrates that Mark is the "middle term" among the three Synoptics when it comes to the order of passages. In other words, there is usually agreement in order between Matthew and Mark alone, between Mark and Luke alone, or between all three. It is Mark that is the mediating factor, the common denominator when it comes to order. But this does not mean that Mark is the third Gospel to have been written. The fact that Mark is usually the middle term simply means that Matthew and Luke both valued Mark's order. Sometimes Matthew followed Mark, sometimes Luke followed Mark, and sometimes both did. There is nothing unexpected or remarkable about this.

Peabody's argument also emphasizes the so-called Markan Overlay, the idea that there are certain linguistic features that make sense as Mark's editorial additions to his conflation of Matthew and Luke. The idea here is that it is more likely that Mark added these distinctive expressions in his editing of Matthew and Luke than that Matthew and Luke omitted them in their editing of Mark. The choice example is Mark's distinctive use of the Greek word *palin* (again) to link two passages. Peabody lists fifteen usages of this phenomenon, none of which are found in Matthew and Luke, something that he regards as quite implausible on the theory that they used Mark.[1]

Phenomena like these are nothing like as remarkable as Peabody claims. Many of the examples of this usage in Mark occur in passages that are absent altogether from Luke,[2] and several others occur in passages where Matthew lacks the linking passage.[3] Moreover, literary style is a personal thing, and it

---

1. See further David L. Peabody, Lamar Cope, and Allan J. McNicol, eds., *One Gospel from Two: Mark's Use of Matthew and Luke; A Demonstration by the Research Team of the International Institute for Renewal of Gospel Studies* (Harrisburg, PA: Trinity Press International, 2002), 37, 383–84; and the endorsement in Delbert Burkett, *Rethinking the Gospel Sources*, vol. 1, *From Proto-Mark to Mark* (London: T&T Clark International, 2004), 17–18.

2. For example, four of the occurrences (Mark 7:14, 31; 8:1, 13) are found in passages that are part of Luke's "great omission."

3. The first example, Mark 2:1, refers back to Mark 1:21, a passage that is absent from Matthew. Matthew is hardly going to include a link with "again" to a passage that he has omitted.

is never surprising when given writers choose not to use their source's literary idiosyncrasies. It is unreasonable, therefore, to expect either Matthew or Luke to have carried over every piece of Mark's literary narration. As writers, we are all familiar with avoiding certain terminology in the way we structure our prose. I am not keen on the use of "precisely because," an emphatic conjunction common in contemporary academic writing, and you will never find it in my prose, in spite of the fact that I may use the words "precisely" and "because" in other contexts. There is nothing theological or ideological about my dislike of the expression; it is simply a question of personal taste. It would be surprising if the evangelists were not also guided by personal taste in the way that they constructed their narratives.

Markan Priority

Craig Evans rightly emphasizes that the Two Source Hypothesis is currently the dominant Synoptic theory. He appeals to what "most scholars" or "most interpreters" say several times in the essay. While this provides a useful barometer of opinion for those unfamiliar with the field, it is always possible that today's consensus will be tomorrow's memory. For much of the nineteenth century it was the Griesbach Hypothesis, not the Two Source Hypothesis, that held sway, and the study of changing trends in New Testament scholarship often gives us reasons to be cautious.

I agree with Evans's stress on the plausibility of Markan priority, and his own reflections complement my distinct but overlapping arguments for the same thing.[4] We differ, though, on an important issue. Evans thinks that Matthew and Luke accessed Mark independently of each other, while I think that Luke knew both Mark and Matthew. Evans's own examples tend to support my view rather than his. His first example is the wording of the opening of the temptation story:[5]

Matthew 4:1	Mark 1:12	Luke 4:1
Then Jesus	And the Spirit immediately	Jesus, full of the Holy Spirit, returned from the
was <u>led up</u> by the	<u>drove him out</u>	Jordan and was <u>led</u> by the
Spirit into the wilderness . . .	into the wilderness.	Spirit in the wilderness . . .

4. However, I am not convinced of the value of arguing with C. S. Mann, *Mark*, AB 27 (Garden City, NY: Doubleday, 1986), which is a weak exposition of the Griesbach Hypothesis. Evans refers to Peabody, Cope, and McNicol, *One Gospel from Two*, as a "more recent and better effort," in which case one should focus on this stronger work instead.

5. Translations are from the NRSV.

Evans points out that Mark's choice of verb *ekballō* (to drive out) is somewhat less appropriate than Matthew's *anagō* (to lead up) and Luke's *agō* (to lead), effectively making the point that it is more likely that Matthew and Luke were editing Mark than that Mark was conflating Matthew and Luke. But while this example helpfully illustrates the plausibility of Matthew's and Luke's use of Mark, it also illustrates the implausibility that Matthew and Luke used Mark independently of each other. As so often, Matthew and Luke here agree in their rewording of the Markan narrative, and it is this regular agreement that places a question mark over the idea that they were independent.

Indeed, the extensive agreement between Matthew and Luke in much of the rest of this passage (Matt. 4:1–11//Mark 1:12–13//Luke 4:1–13) makes it impossible that Matthew and Luke are solely dependent on Mark here. Thus, whereas the Farrer Hypothesis simply suggests that Luke revised Mark in light of Matthew, Two Source theorists appeal to the theory of "Mark-Q overlap." As we saw above, this is a serious weakness for the Two Source Hypothesis, according to which Matthew and Luke are not supposed to show such extensive agreement with each other when they rewrite Mark.[6]

Evans's second example is similar. As he rightly points out, Matthew and Luke revise Mark's verb in the incident of the high priest's servant's ear (Matt. 26:51//Mark 14:47//Luke 22:50), from *paiō* to *patassō*, synonyms meaning "to strike," but what Evans does not underline is the fact that Matthew and Luke once again make the same change to Mark. This is a repeated pattern in the Synoptics. There are hundreds of such agreements between Matthew and Luke against Mark. Evans inadvertently draws attention to another in the same context: Matthew's and Luke's use of *paiō* (Matt. 26:68//Mark 14:65//Luke 22:64) in a complete sentence that is absent from Mark. Agreements like these provide evidence that Matthew and Luke did not access Mark independently. Luke revised Mark with an eye also on Matthew.[7]

Q and Pre-Gospel Traditions

The focus of our disagreement is, of course, on the question of the existence of Q. As Evans rightly points out, Q is postulated "out of logical necessity"

6. In this respect, Evans's example is also unhelpful from the perspective of the Two Source Hypothesis. For most Two Source theorists, Matthew and Luke here choose their wording from Q and not from Mark, so it oversimplifies the theory to say that "the evangelists Matthew and Luke, having read Mark and having decided to use Mark as their principal narrative source, both chose to use some other verb" (p. 31).

7. Evans's next example of triple-tradition material, Matt. 8:23–27//Mark 4:35–41//Luke 8:22–25 (the stilling of the storm), is again a passage replete with minor agreements between Matthew and Luke against Mark. His other examples in this section are only in Matthew and Mark.

(p. 36). If Matthew and Luke used Mark independently of each other, the double-tradition material must have come from another source, and this is where adherents of the Farrer Hypothesis draw attention to the links that are found between Matthew and Luke not only in the double-tradition (Q) material but also in the triple-tradition (Markan) material. In other words, the Farrer Hypothesis is able to make good sense of all the data. Luke borrows directly from Matthew in the double tradition, and from both Mark and Matthew in the triple tradition. There is no need to postulate an extra hypothetical document in this scenario.

It is important to make clear, though, that arguing against the existence of a hypothetical document does not entail the viewpoint that Matthew and Luke had no sources for their non-Markan material, still less that they invented new material from nowhere. The notion that there were traditions that predate the Gospels is a given in all but the most extreme Synoptic hypotheses.

The perceived advantage with the Two Source Hypothesis is that it attempts to identify and name one of these pre-Synoptic sources by isolating one particular data set, the double tradition, and aligning it with a hypothetical document, Q. This helps one to conceptualize at least one element from the misty period of Christian origins about which we would so like to know more. Q offers us an apparently tangible witness to Jesus traditions from the 40s or 50s of the first century, and it is not surprising that it has become so popular. But our desire to have a concrete witness to which we can assign some kind of identity is not sufficient reason to invest in the existence of Q. Q exists as a discrete entity only if Matthew and Luke are demonstrably independent of each other, the very thing that is in question here.

I agree with Evans, therefore, that "a solid case can be made for the existence of a body of Jesus's teachings, along with stories about him" (pp. 36–37), but I see no reason to link this with one homogeneous body of data that is artificially extracted from Matthew's and Luke's double-tradition material. Traditions about Jesus were likely much more rich, dynamic, and expansive than the restrictive focus on Q leads us to imagine. In addition to Mark and Q, Evans himself draws attention to stories and sayings that are "quoted or alluded to in Paul's Letters and the Letter of James" (p. 38), and we might add that there are huge numbers of traditions that are found in Matthew alone and Luke alone.

Rainer Riesner's contribution here provides a useful reminder about the extent and importance of pre-Gospel traditions. His examples of parables that are "memorable mainly through their vivid narrative and impressive images" (p. 101) include passages found in Luke's special material (Luke 18:10–14, the

Pharisee and the tax collector; 15:11–32, the prodigal son) and Matthew's special material (Matt. 25:1–12, the ten bridesmaids), as well as in Mark and Q. In other words, the pre-Gospel traditions are not the special preserve of a hypothetical collection that we call "Q." They are spread far and wide across every stream of Gospel data, whether triple tradition, double tradition, Special Matthew, or Special Luke.

Moreover, as Riesner points out, Paul provides a key witness to the early existence of traditions about Jesus, including Eucharist (1 Cor. 11:23–26); death, burial, and resurrection (1 Cor. 15:3–7); and teaching about Jesus's return (1 Thess. 4:15–17; 5:2). The Pauline witness is striking in that it testifies to the breadth and dynamism of the early Jesus tradition, with parallels to material later found in several of the different strands in the Gospels. Thus some traditions found in Paul find parallels in the double-tradition (Q) material, such as the saying about mission (1 Cor. 9:14, cf. Matt. 10:10// Luke 10:7), but there are also traditions that find parallels in other material, especially the triple tradition (Eucharist, death, burial, resurrection). Indeed, Paul's closest parallels can be to the particular ways in which triple-tradition material is configured in Matthew and Luke, so that 1 Thessalonians 4:15–17 is closer to Matthew's version of the eschatological discourse than it is to Mark's or Luke's (especially Matt. 24:30), and 1 Corinthians 11:23–26 is closer to Luke's version of the Last Supper than it is to Matthew's or Mark's (Luke 22:14–23).

In short, we are all agreed on the existence of oral traditions that predate the Gospels, and there is nothing to be gained in trying to draw artificial lines between the different theories on this point. The issue that the Q theory spotlights is solely the question about identifying and naming a particular data set, Matthew's and Luke's double-tradition material, something that requires insistence on the notion that Luke wrote independently of Matthew. It is this proposition, the independence of Matthew and Luke, that therefore remains key.

Arguments for the Existence of Q

Evans puts forward "two major arguments for the existence of Q that grow out of the Gospel data themselves" (p. 39). The first is effectively a continuation of his discussion about pre-Gospel traditions, further focusing the issue by asking, "Where did the evangelist Matthew derive the several hundred verses of non-Markan material that we observe in his Gospel?" (p. 39). If Matthew did not invent this material, the best explanation is "a substantial

non-Markan source" (p. 39). The difficulty, however, is that there is no reason to identify all of Matthew's non-Markan material with a single, static,
documentary source, in a move that diminishes the dynamism and variety
of the pre-Matthean traditions, limiting them by privileging those that are
paralleled in Luke. Although Evans suggests that there was Q material that
Matthew included and Luke omitted, he is surprisingly reticent about drawing
attention to the extensive body of tradition that is found solely in Matthew,
the so-called Special Matthew or M material. But the existence of this body
of data is crucial. Unless Matthew invented all the M material, which Evans
does not believe, then for Evans too there is a substantial body of material
that is derived from neither Mark nor Q. In other words, both of us believe
that Matthew drew on traditional material outside of his written source(s).
The only difference between us is that he thinks he can identify two hundred
verses or so of this material by looking at parallels in Luke, whereas I am
not so optimistic.

Evans's second major argument is that Luke's use of a non-Markan
source is more plausible than Luke's use of Matthew. He focuses the argument by asking two questions, the first of which is "Why would Luke have
disassembled Matthew's well-structured discourses?" (p. 39). This is an old
chestnut that becomes no more persuasive for its frequent repetition. I have
sketched an answer to the question in my essay above, itself a summary of
other discussions of the topic,[8] but it is worth reiterating that the question
stems in large part from a failure to appreciate how important Mark's Gospel is to Luke. Luke values Mark and makes his narrative structure key to
the body of his Gospel. Mark's narrative thrust, with its lively, ever-present
journeying forward toward Jerusalem, in which "the Way of the Lord" is a
key concern, provides Luke with his own theological center, the idea of the
Christian story as "the Way" (Acts 9:2; 19:9, 23; 22:4; 24:14, 22), in which
Jesus first journeys toward Jerusalem, from where the gospel goes out to
the ends of the earth in the journeys of the apostles, especially Paul. It is
hardly surprising that Luke chooses to integrate the material from Matthew's large, static discourses into his own, new journey structure, echoing
Mark's sense of movement rather than following Matthew's tableau-style
approach.

Evans's second question is "If Luke drew heavily upon Matthew, would we
not find many examples of distinctive Matthean redaction and materials in

---

8. See especially Mark Goodacre, *The Case against Q: Studies in Markan Priority and the
Synoptic Problem* (Harrisburg, PA: Trinity Press International, 2002), 81–132; Goodacre, *The
Synoptic Problem: A Way through the Maze*, BibSem 80 (London: Sheffield Academic Press,
2001), 123–28.

Luke?" (p. 39). Given that advocates of the Farrer Hypothesis argue that Luke is full of distinctive Matthean redaction, the question is a curious one. One clear example appears in Evans's own essay. The phrase "O you of little faith!" is found five times in Matthew (Matt. 6:30; 8:26; 14:31; 16:8; 17:20), never in Mark, and only once in Luke (Luke 12:28). Evans explains the phenomenon in terms of the Two Source Hypothesis, by suggesting that Matthew saw the phrase in Q, liked it, and repeated it on another four occasions. Whatever the explanation, it is clear that we do, in fact, have distinctive Matthean expressions appearing in Luke. The same phenomenon is so widespread in the parallels between Matthew and Luke that advocates of the Farrer Hypothesis treat these as strong evidence in favor of Luke's familiarity with Matthew.[9]

Exegetical Test Case: The Centurion's Boy

As Evans points out, the proof of a theory is in its exegetical effectiveness. His chosen example is the centurion's boy (Matt. 8:5–13//Luke 7:1–10), and his particular concern relates to Matthew 8:11–12, the saying about people coming "from east and west" to dine in the kingdom, and the sons cast out "where there shall be weeping and gnashing of teeth." The saying is in a different context in Luke, at 13:28–30, where it appears with other sayings about election and judgment. Evans suggests that in Luke's context the saying does not work well, so it would be surprising if he removed it from its more fitting Matthean context.

However, it is straightforward to see why Luke has relocated the saying, and the idea that it comes from Q has its own problems. In Luke, unlike in Matthew, the centurion himself is not present. Instead, there is a delegation of sympathetic "Jewish elders" who implore Jesus on behalf of the centurion, whom they praise as the man responsible for building their synagogue (Luke 7:4–5); it is these men, alongside others of the centurion's "friends," who are with Jesus as he journeys (7:6). While praising the centurion to his friends for his remarkable faith (7:9), it would hardly be appropriate, given this new Lukan audience, for Jesus to launch into a tirade about Jews who will be cast into the outer darkness, where there will be weeping and gnashing of teeth. This is a saying that will work better elsewhere, and in Luke's new context, in 13:22–30, it effectively joins other material that focuses on judgment, the narrow door, and those who are shut out, where a tirade about

9. For a sophisticated version of the argument as it relates to the reconstruction of Q, see especially Michael Goulder, "Self-Contradiction in the IQP," *JBL* 118 (1999): 506–17.

hell is narratively and thematically appropriate. It is often important to pay attention to the audience of particular passages. Moreover, if Evans is right to detect a seam in Luke's construction of the passage, this is because Luke has removed the saying from its Matthean context and relocated it to a new one—it is just what we would expect.[10]

Test cases like this are useful, and Evans's chosen passage helpfully illustrates the plausibility of Luke's familiarity with Matthew. As always, it is important to pay attention to the context of Luke 7:1–10, which provides a clue that he is working with Matthew. Matthew locates the healing of the centurion's boy soon after the Sermon on the Mount (Matt. 5–7), with only the healing of the leper (8:1–4) intervening. Luke locates the passage at almost exactly the same point, straight after the Sermon on the Plain (Luke 6:20–49), having already told the story of the leper in its Markan context (Mark 1:40–45//Luke 5:12–16). It is striking that Luke here echoes the characteristically Matthean closing to the sermon:

Matthew 7:28–29; 8:5	Luke 7:1–2
Now when Jesus had finished saying these things, the crowds were astounded at his teaching, for he taught them as one having authority, and not as their scribes. . . .	After Jesus had finished all his sayings in the hearing of the people,
When he entered Capernaum, a centurion came to him. . . .	he entered Capernaum. A centurion there had a slave whom he valued highly. . . .

Matthew has closing formulas like this, "When Jesus had finished saying these things . . . ," after each of his five major discourses (Matt. 7:28–29; 11:1; 13:53; 19:1; 26:1), and Luke here echoes the first of these. It is another good example of a distinctive Matthean feature appearing in Luke, and a problem for the Q hypothesis.[11]

Furthermore, there is verbatim agreement in this passage of the kind that points to Luke's direct use of Matthew:

10. Nevertheless, Evans is here at odds with other Q scholars who see the Lukan context for this Q saying as original to Q, in which Q 13:28–29 is nested in a section comprising judgment sayings, Q 13:24, 25, 26–27, 28–29, 30, 34–35 (e.g., John S. Kloppenborg, *Excavating Q: The History and Setting of the Sayings Gospel* (Minneapolis: Fortress, 2000), 70, 118; James M. Robinson, Paul Hoffmann, and John S. Kloppenborg, *The Critical Edition of Q: Synopsis Including the Gospels of Matthew and Luke, Mark and Thomas with English, German, and French Translations of Q and Thomas*, HermSup (Minneapolis: Fortress; Leuven: Peeters, 2000), 414–17.

11. The Greek of Matt. 7:28 and Luke 7:1 differs, but the parallel is unmistakable, so much so that many Q theorists concede that this Matthean formula also appears in Q. See Robinson, Hoffmann, and Kloppenborg, *Critical Edition of Q*, 102–3.

Matthew 8:9–10	Luke 7:8–9
"For I also am a man under authority, with soldiers under me; and I say to one, 'Go,' and he goes, and to another, 'Come,' and he comes, and to my slave, 'Do this,' and the slave does it." When Jesus heard him, he was amazed and said to those who followed him, "Truly I tell you, in no one in Israel have I found such faith."	"For I also am a man set under authority, with soldiers under me; and I say to one, 'Go,' and he goes, and to another, 'Come,' and he comes, and to my slave, 'Do this,' and the slave does it." When Jesus heard this he was amazed at him, and turning to the crowd that followed him, he said, "I tell you, not even in Israel have I found such faith."

This example of high verbatim agreement features an uninterrupted string of twenty-five words in Greek (from the words translated "under authority" to the words translated "When Jesus heard . . ."). This kind of verbatim agreement is far more likely to occur when one author is copying directly from a source, here Luke copying Matthew, than when both are independently copying from a hypothetical source. In other words, this is another case of agreement that is too good to be Q.

Conclusion: How Do We Decide?

For some readers, there are good reasons to ignore a book like this, which presents differing views on a topic that can seem tedious and technical. The discussion of issues such as "minor agreements" and "middle terms" or the ordering of passages can appear to be the worst excesses of New Testament studies, solely for those who are stuck in an old-fashioned way of looking at the evidence—appropriate, perhaps, for those who like doing crossword puzzles or playing Scrabble. It would be a disappointment, though, if readers were to emerge from this project without a sense of the thrill of studying the Synoptic Gospels and comparing them with one another, for this is fundamental to the open, critical, historical study of the Gospels. It is in embracing the study of both the similarities and the differences between the Synoptics that we begin to understand what it means to explore these books as distinctive literary works, each with its own perspective, its own theology, its own style, its own character. Far from being a question of minutiae, this is the beating heart of academic study of the New Testament.

It is of course the case that there are technical and detailed elements to the study of the Synoptic Problem, and that without grasping these, one cannot hope to gain a full understanding of the problem. But those who make the effort generally find it hugely rewarding. Not only does it lead to a greater appreciation of the Gospels, the historical Jesus, and Christian origins, it also hones the student's critical skills in this and related fields. The very act of constructing and coloring Gospel synopses is itself an exciting means of representing the key evidence graphically, thereby facilitating the kind of rigorous critical analysis that gets to the heart of the issue in a way more dynamic than great wedges of prose.

Each of us in this volume has argued strongly for his particular solution to the Synoptic Problem. While I am passionate about the solution to the problem that I advocate, I am still more passionate about this more fundamental issue, on which I am sure I agree with my colleagues, that studying the Synoptic Gospels is one of the most intriguing issues in the study of ancient Christianity. If we have achieved anything here, I hope that it is to invite the reader to explore this fascinating world.

8

Two Gospel
Hypothesis Response

David Barrett Peabody

In Response to Rainer Riesner

The hypothesis here advocated by Rainer Riesner combines the importance of ongoing oral tradition with a multiple-stage hypothesis, by which it is hypothesized that the similarities and identities found in the Synoptic Gospels of Matthew, Mark, and Luke resulted from their mutual use of quite a number of now-nonextant prior sources.[1] This includes both ongoing and relatively fixed oral tradition, combined with a mutual use by all the Synoptic evangelists of a variety of stages of other developing written sources that, like Q, are not extant and therefore must be reconstructed from the content of the canonical Gospels.

I do not think that any of the hypotheses presented and defended in this volume would argue that there was no continuing influence of oral tradition on the development of the three Synoptic Gospels. However, since oral tradition by definition preserves no written record, and the content of the

1. As in my initial essay, the full names "Matthew," "Luke," and "Mark" are used here to indicate the authors of the Gospels that now carry their names, even though these Gospels remain, strictly speaking, anonymous compositions.

oral record must be reconstructed from written records influenced by it, it is difficult to be certain where oral sources may have left off and written ones taken over, assuming Riesner's hypothesis. However, the combination of the mutual dependence of Matthew, Mark, and Luke upon both this ongoing oral tradition and on *multiple earlier and equally hypothetical written stages of these Gospels*, as reconstructed from the texts of the extant written Gospels in the canon, is solely advocated here by Riesner. He, however, does not stand alone in advocating this type of source hypothesis for the eventually canonized Gospels, which he has ably advocated and defended, both now and certainly as early as, and perhaps earlier than, the Jerusalem Conference on the Synoptic Problem in April 1984. This can be demonstrated in some of the published works by the French scholars Marie-Émile Boismard and Pierre Benoit, who were also in attendance at Jerusalem, along with works by Philippe Rolland and, more recently in the United States, by Delbert Burkett and perhaps others whose work may yet be unfamiliar to me.[2]

What advocates of the Two Gospel Hypothesis, the Two Source Hypothesis, and the Farrer Hypothesis find most problematic about the source hypothesis of Riesner and these other scholars who share some of his views is not so much the continuing import of ongoing oral tradition on the Synoptic Gospels, which seems most probable and is taken quite seriously by advocates of all the hypotheses reviewed in this volume. Rather, the issue concerns the likelihood of the many interim hypothetical sources that are postulated and necessarily reconstructed from the texts of the extant, canonical Gospels— sources projected as parts of their comparatively complex theories outlining the development of the four canonized Gospels.

To the advocates of other source theories presented and defended in this book, direct literary dependence among the now-canonical Gospels of Matthew, Mark, and Luke seems quite sufficient to explain the clear literary relationships. However, both Evans and Goodacre disagree with advocates of the Two Gospel Hypothesis by affirming the priority of Mark's Gospel, while advocates of the Two Gospel Hypothesis affirm the priority of both Matthew's and Luke's Gospels to Mark's Gospel.

The three advocates of the primarily literary source hypotheses outlined and advocated in this volume (the Two Source, the Two Gospel, and the

---

2. Delbert Burkett's work on the multiple-stage hypothesis is probably the best source in English for reading about this kind of source theory of the development of the Synoptic Gospels. His published works on the Synoptic Problem include *Rethinking the Gospel Sources*, vol. 1, *From Proto-Mark to Mark* (London: T&T Clark International, 2004); and *Rethinking Gospel Sources*, vol. 2, *The Unity or Plurality of Q*, SBLECL 1 (Atlanta: Society of Biblical Literature, 2009).

Farrer Hypotheses), by way of contrast, share a common interest in Occam's razor—that is, the minimizing of the number of hypothetical sources needed to advance and defend a source theory of the Synoptic Gospels. The multistage aspect of Riesner's hypothesis is somewhat speculative and certainly more cumbersome than are the three other theories of Gospel development discussed here.

In Response to Mark Goodacre and Craig Evans

Professor Goodacre denies the literary dependence of either Matthew's or Luke's Gospel on the Sayings Gospel, Q, because advocates of the Farrer Hypothesis doubt the very existence of Q, as do advocates of the Two Gospel Hypothesis. It is unnecessary to posit that source if one affirms that there is sufficient evidence of direct literary relationships among the Gospels of Matthew, Luke, and Mark. In the cases of both the Farrer Hypothesis and the Two Gospel Hypothesis, agreements between Matthew's Gospel and Luke's Gospel are believed to be the result of the direct literary dependence of Luke on the Gospel of Matthew, although the Farrer Hypothesis advocates the priority of Mark's Gospel to both Matthew's and Luke's Gospels, and the direct literary dependence of Matthew upon Mark's Gospel, and Luke's direct literary dependence upon both Matthew's and Mark's Gospels. The advocates of the Two Gospel Hypothesis posit the priority of Matthew's Gospel, with Luke first utilizing it and Mark then making use of both Matthew's and Luke's Gospels. By way of contrast, proponents of the Farrer Hypothesis, which advocates the priority of Mark's Gospel to the Gospels of Matthew and Luke, unite with the Two Source Hypothesis on this point and distinguish themselves from proponents of the Two Gospel Hypothesis, which advocates the priority of the Gospels of Matthew and Luke to Mark's Gospel.

A major weakness of both the Two Source Hypothesis and the Farrer Hypothesis is their advocates' seeming unwillingness or, perhaps, inability to explain the alternating agreements of Mark, now with Matthew's Gospel and now with Luke's, in terms of both the sequence of pericopae and the order of the actual words within pericopae. One suspects that these facts are avoided precisely because they are anomalous for both of these source hypotheses. Specifically, how would Mark, if that author wrote first, manage to alternately agree now with Matthew's Gospel and now with Luke's, both in a macrocosmic manner (the alternating order and content of pericopae) and in a microcosmic manner (the alternating order of words within pericopae)? German scholar Hans-Herbert Stoldt once described this alleged process

of Matthew's and Luke's mutual and complementary yet independent ac-
companiment of Mark's Gospel on the Two Source Hypothesis as "scarcely
believable." Stoldt's critique of Markan priority and the mutual, but allegedly
independent, use of Mark's Gospel by Matthew and Luke is worth a careful
read in the authorized English translation.[3]

The advocates of the Two Source Hypothesis and the Farrer Hypothesis
also typically avoid calling any attention to the patristic evidence about
Gospel relationships that is unanimously in favor of the temporal priority of
Matthew's Gospel to all of the other canonical Gospels and the secondary
nature of the Gospels of Mark and Luke to Matthew's Gospel. By way of
contrast, it is posited by advocates of both the Two Source and the Farrer
Hypotheses that the order of composition of the canonical Gospels was
first, Mark; second, Matthew; third, Luke; and fourth, John. The former
sequence of composition—Matthew first; Luke second; and Mark third,
as a combination of the Gospels of Matthew and Luke—was advocated by
Clement of Alexandria (ca. 150–215 CE) and was also the "more probable
view" of the relations of the canonical Gospels advocated by Augustine of
Hippo (354–430 CE), as he lays out that view in his *Harmony of the Gospels*
(4.10.11). However, Augustine does pass on other, differing views on the
question of the sequence and interrelationships among the Gospels in the
course of this work, particularly in part 1 of his *Harmony of the Gospels*.
After completing his work with all of the material that has a parallel in
any of the other three Gospels and turning, in conclusion, to the material
unique to John, Augustine affirms what he says is his "more probable" view
of Mark—namely, that Mark combined the contents and themes of Matthew's and Luke's Gospels, which, if intentional, would require that Mark's
Gospel be composed after and dependent upon the other two Synoptic
Gospels.

As a first and general principle, I prefer, if possible, to explain the relationships among the Synoptic Gospels on the basis of direct literary dependence
among them, rather than by postulating in the first place a number of sources
that are nonextant or must be reconstructed from extant texts to explain those
relationships. That is, I prefer to advocate source hypotheses that do not posit
nonextant sources, as advocates of the Farrer and the Two Source Hypotheses
do, as advocates of Q do, or especially as Rainer Riesner champions with an
array of alleged intermediate sources.

3. Hans-Herbert Stoldt, *History and Criticism of the Marcan Hypothesis*, trans. and ed.
Donald L. Niewyk, SNTW (Macon, GA: Mercer University Press; Edinburgh: T&T Clark,
1980), esp. 142.

These generalities can be said about the work of all the contributors to this volume, but I would like to conclude my response by focusing on a number of issues raised by Craig Evans in his advocacy of the Two Source Hypothesis. The following comments are responses to specific issues raised by Evans in his essay outlining the Two Source Hypothesis, and they appear in the same order in which he introduced them there.

1. While it is true that the Two Source Hypothesis remains the dominant view among generalists in New Testament studies, the degree of that dominance is diminished if one limits the poll to the approximately forty or fifty current international experts on various aspects of the Synoptic Problem who attended the Oxford Conference on the Synoptic Problem in 2008.

2. The alternating character of Matthew's and Luke's allegedly independent use of Mark's Gospel and Q on the Two Source Hypothesis, both in terms of pericope order and in terms of wording within pericopae, is much more difficult to explain than it is on the Two Gospel Hypothesis.

3. What are the criteria for detecting "improvement" from one Gospel to another? Even if some criteria could be provided for isolating "improvement," how would this be a relevant question for solving the Synoptic Problem, which is a matter not of literary taste but rather of sequence and interrelationships among the Synoptic Gospels? We simply do not know what each of the later Synoptic evangelists would have liked or disliked in the text of a previous evangelist that was utilized by a later evangelist. Incorporation of texts of a previous evangelist into the text of a later evangelist may be taken as a sign of approval, but there may be other reasons for such incorporation into a later work, perhaps to alter it, for example. We can only guess at these matters of how each later Synoptic evangelist has made use of his source or sources. It is inappropriate to impose our own tastes and views, as twenty-first-century scholars, on texts most likely composed in the late first and early second centuries CE. The destruction of the Jewish temple in Jerusalem (70 CE) probably was a watershed moment for the early Jewish Christians in shifting from oral to written records of the life of Jesus.

4. The most defensible answer to the Synoptic Problem should be a necessary presupposition of exegesis and theological interpretation, not the result of it.

5. Certainly, commentators who have presupposed the Two Source Hypothesis may manage to do creditable exegesis, but that is not an argument for Markan priority. In fact, if Mark's Gospel was written last, some conclusions about Markan theology might be demonstrated as even more likely than they might be claimed to be on the Two Source Hypothesis.

6. The Anchor Bible commentary on Mark's Gospel by the late C. S. Mann is not the best representative of scholarship done by advocates of the Two Gospel

Hypothesis. Rather, the volumes by the Two Gospel Hypothesis Research Team,[4] *One Gospel from Two*[5] and *Beyond the Q Impasse*, are better representatives of the strengths of that hypothesis. In particular, one would not find a number of C. S. Mann's statements about the import of the witness of Peter on the Gospel of Mark in works by the Two Gospel Hypothesis Research Team.

7. The so-called linguistic argument as a contribution to solving the Synoptic Problem has been in place at least since the mid-nineteenth century and was best clarified and applied by Eduard Zeller, who concluded that, on balance, Matthew's Gospel was prior to the Gospel of Luke, and that Mark's Gospel was secondary to both Matthew's and Luke's Gospels. Therefore, Evans's linguistic argument for the priority of Mark's Gospel based upon the few literary characteristics that he has chosen to discuss, given space constraints in this volume (e.g., his discussion of the Synoptic uses of *ekballō* versus *anagō* and *agō*), carries little weight because it is not a large-enough sampling of the relevant literary evidence to be representative. The linguistic evidence in fact weighs in every possible direction, but there is actually much more linguistic evidence in favor of the Gospel of Matthew's priority to Mark's Gospel than the reverse, and more evidence of the Gospel of Luke's priority to Mark's Gospel than the reverse.

8. Evans's novel argument from "dignity" seems to be, at the very least, debatable, if not anachronistic. It presupposes that scholars can know what

4. In addition to David B. Peabody, Lamar Cope, and Allan J. McNicol, who edited *One Gospel from Two: Mark's Use of Matthew and Luke*, other members of the Two Gospel Hypothesis research and writing team that produced that volume included William R. Farmer, longtime Professor of New Testament at the Perkins School of Theology; David L. Dungan, longtime Professor of Religion at the University of Tennessee, Knoxville; Thomas R. W. Longstaff, longtime Professor of Religion at Colby College in Waterville, Maine; and Philip L. Shuler, longtime Professor of Religion at McMurry University in Abilene, Texas. Peabody is Professor of Religion at Nebraska Wesleyan University in Lincoln; Cope was Professor of Religion at Carroll College (now University) in Waukesha, Wisconsin; and Allan J. McNicol is Professor of New Testament Theology at the Austin Graduate School of Theology in Texas. With the exception of Longstaff, each of these scholars also served on the research and writing team that produced *Beyond the Q Impasse: Luke's Use of Matthew*. More recently than the times when these two volumes were produced, this Two Gospel Hypothesis Research Team now includes Professor J. Samuel Subramanian, recently appointed Assistant Professor of New Testament Theology at the United Theological Seminary of the Twin Cities in Minnesota.

5. David B. Peabody, Lamar Cope, and Allan J. McNicol, eds., *One Gospel from Two: Mark's Use of Matthew and Luke; A Demonstration by the Research Team of the International Institute for Renewal of Gospel Studies* (Harrisburg, PA: Trinity Press International, 2002); Allan J. McNicol, David L. Dungan, and David B. Peabody, eds., *Beyond the Q Impasse: Luke's Use of Matthew; A Demonstration by the Research Team of the International Institute for Gospel Studies* (Valley Forge, PA: Trinity Press International, 1996). For charts and a brief discussion related to the so-called linguistic argument for contributing to a solution to the Synoptic Problem, see Peabody, Cope, and McNicol, *One Gospel from Two*, 354–82.

people reading the Gospels in the first and second centuries might have found "undignified." It probably was not until the first Council of Nicaea in 325 CE that the church began intentionally and systematically to separate acceptable from unacceptable views of Christian faith and practice. However, in the estimate of some scholars, the majority of Christians in the fourth century CE included Apollinarians, Arians, Docetics, Gnostics, Ebionites, Eutychians, Nestorians, and probably others less numerous or well known, who were declared heretics by the church fathers assembled at Nicaea I and subsequent ecumenical councils of the ancient church. Would those who officially defined the contents of the Christian Bible allow the Synoptic Gospels to be published in the fifty copies of the newly approved Christian canon, sponsored by the Roman emperor, Constantine the Great, if elements of those Gospels were considered by the attendees at Nicaea I to include "undignified" statements?

9. Even assuming that "Q" existed and was a source for Matthew and Luke, the term *oligopistoi*, "those of little faith," is much more likely to have been a favorite literary expression of Matthew (four times), which Luke chose to utilize only once in parallel to a usage in Matthew's Gospel. Mark never utilizes this vocabulary item. Given the scarcity of this term in Luke's Gospel, there is a very low to zero probability that this expression appeared in Q, if such a document ever existed. We have Matthew 6:30//Luke 12:28 as the only possible usage in Q. How, therefore, could one say from this single usage that this term was characteristic of Q? It is much more likely that this was something of a favorite expression of Matthew, and that Luke chose to utilize it only once in a parallel while Matthew utilized it three more times without parallel in either Luke's Gospel or Mark's Gospel. This is a good example of the so-called linguistic argument for distinguishing the source of a literary usage from a usage in a secondary and dependent document. In this example, the weight of the scales favors Matthew's four usages as an indicator that this is a favorite expression of Matthew, and that Luke utilizes this term not independently but rather in dependence upon Luke's source material. In this case, on the Two Gospel Hypothesis, that source was the Gospel of Matthew.

10. Mark 6:51–52. Here Mark may be retrospectively emphasizing and interpreting the two feeding stories, the feeding of the five thousand (Mark 6:34–44//Matt. 14:13–21//Luke 9:10–17) and the feeding of the four thousand (Mark 8:1–10//Matt. 15:32–39), which both Matthew's and Mark's Gospels contain in parallel. Furthermore, in these same literary contexts a typically Markan manner of expression is found: "hardened hearts."[6] On the Two

6. See David B. Peabody, *Mark as Composer*, NGS 1 (Macon, GA: Mercer University Press; Leuven: Peeters, 1987), table 61 (pp. 88–89), table 166 (p. 91).

Gospel Hypothesis, these are both features of the typically Markan overlay—that is, a layer of material in Mark's Gospel that he imposed upon his conflation of the Gospels of Matthew and Luke.

Here we have a very clear Markan expansion of the other two Synoptics. Matthew's Gospel has two feedings, as does Mark's. For Mark, these two feedings may well have represented for him the initial Pauline mission to Jews (the Twelve), but also to the Gentiles (the Seven), an idea also present in Luke-Acts, where Mark may well have first encountered the language and its metaphorical numerical significance, while utilizing both Matthew's Gospel and Luke-Acts in composing his Gospel. Compare Acts 4:4 on "the five thousand" and the feeding described in Acts 6:1–7, in which the Hellenists, probably Gentile Christians (the Seven), are contrasted with the Hebrews / Jewish Christians (the Twelve) in this same context. The latter were to focus on preaching, while the former were to focus on a ministry of feeding. "Hardened hearts" is certainly a linguistic characteristic of the text of Mark's Gospel.[7] "Hardened heart" (*sklērokardia*) appears twice in Mark's Gospel, once with a parallel in Matthew's Gospel (Mark 10:5//Matt. 19:8) and once independently, in the longer ending (Mark 16:14). This word never appears in Luke-Acts. In addition, "heart" (*kardia*) in combination with "hardened" (the perfect middle/passive participle, *pepōrōmenē*) or "hardness" (the noun, *pōrōsis*) appears three times in Mark's Gospel (3:5; 6:52; 8:17), but nowhere else in the Synoptic Gospels (but see John 12:40 and Eph. 4:18 for similar expressions outside of the Synoptics). The image of "hardened hearts" would, therefore, seem to be a typical Markan literary feature with which Mark painted his own perspective on the traditions that he was borrowing, from Matthew's Gospel in this case.

11. There is no literary-critical principle that affirms the priority of either "heightened Christology" or "lower Christology." I would agree that Paul has a relatively "low Christology" in Romans 1:1–4, when he affirms that Jesus was "made Son of God" by virtue of God's having raised Jesus from the dead—that is, *after* Jesus's life and death was over. Matthew and Luke have Jesus declared "Son of God" no later than during his baptism by John, when a voice from the heavens affirms of Jesus, "This is my beloved son, with whom I am well pleased!" (Matt. 3:17; cf. Luke 3:22). Mark has the same comment, but only on the Mount of Transfiguration, where he is in agreement with Matthew's Gospel (Matt. 17:5//Mark 9:7). This is potential evidence of Mark utilizing a theme that Matthew introduces in two literary contexts.

---

7. Mark 6:52; 8:17; cf. 3:5; 10:5 (and 16:14, in the longer ending). For data, see Peabody, *Mark as Composer*, table 166 (p. 91).

That is, Mark partially utilized a theme contained in Matthew's Gospel and thus demonstrates his literary dependence on that Gospel.

Nevertheless, Mark does affirm Jesus as "Son of God" in the very first verse of his Gospel ("The beginning of the good news [i.e., the gospel] of Jesus Christ, the Son of God"), which is the earliest affirmation of Jesus as "Son of God" within the texts of the Synoptic Gospels. As just noted, Matthew and Luke agree with each other in affirming Jesus as "Son of God" at Jesus's baptism, and Matthew follows that with a second and identical affirmation on the Mount of Transfiguration. Because Matthew has this pronouncement in two separate literary contexts, but Luke has only one of these (the one on the Mount of Transfiguration), Luke presumably is dependent upon Matthew's Gospel for Luke's shared scene in this second Matthean context in which this affirmation appears.

12. "Herodians" is a Markan literary characteristic.[8]

13. Matthew's pairing of Pharisees and Sadducees is one indication that his Gospel is the most Jewish of the Synoptic Gospels and therefore probably the earliest to have been composed. On the assumption that Mark replaced Matthew's "Sadducees" with "Herodians," this brings a balance of both Jews and Gentiles to the group of opponents of Jesus in Mark's version of the Gospel. Clearly, Matthew is more knowledgeable about Jews and Judaism than either Mark or Luke. On the presupposition that the church began as a Jewish sect and, primarily through the efforts of Paul, extended its membership to the Gentiles, this piece of evidence argues for Matthew's Gospel representing an earlier and more Jewish proclamation of the gospel, which would have better appealed to a Jewish audience than that preserved in either Mark's Gospel or Luke's.

Matthew knows the sects of Judaism better than either Luke or Mark, and he does not confuse the Herodians (supporters of Herod Antipas or, perhaps, others in the Herodian line, past and present) with the Jewish religious sects, as Mark may be doing in the two contexts where Herodians appear (Mark 3:6; 12:13). This is a clear indication of a later date and more Gentile-oriented focus for Mark's Gospel when compared to the Gospel of Matthew.

Luke's interpretation of "leaven" as "hypocrisy" (Luke 12:1) could easily have been based upon Matthew 23, where the Pharisees are repeatedly and mercilessly referred to as "hypocrites." In contrast to the two appearances of "Herodians" in Mark 3:6 and 12:13, only one of these has a parallel in Matthew's Gospel (Matt. 22:16//Mark 12:13). Mark has twice as much interest

---

8. See ibid., table 92 (p. 65), which contains a chart of the identities and similarities in Greek between Mark 3:6 and 12:13.

in "Herodians" as does Matthew. In this case, Matthew demonstrates his better understanding of first-century Judaism than that observable in the Gospels of Luke or Mark. Luke reveals his lack of understanding of Jewish sects, as does Mark. Matthew does not have this problem. A more Jewish text is intrinsically more likely to have been written earlier or even first than would more Gentile-oriented Gospels, like the Gospels of Luke and Mark.

14. A Canaanite was not necessarily a Jew and therefore hardly stands in tension with Matthew's repeated admonition on the lips of Jesus that he and his disciples were to "enter no town of the Samaritans." Neither were the disciples to go on a mission to the Gentiles because, in Matthew's Gospel, Jesus's mission was to go rather "to the lost sheep of the house of Israel," a term that only Matthew utilizes (Matt. 10:6; 15:24). Matthew presumes that his Jewish readers will understand what this means.

15. What is meant by "holy land" in Evans's analysis of the Gospels? This term is anachronistic and probably should be avoided in historical work. In Jesus's day, Jews would have called the primary regions in which Jesus did his ministry either "Galilee" in the north or "Judah" in the south. By the time of Roman occupation of the region, the northern kingdom of Israel had long been dismantled by the Assyrians. The Romans called the remainder of Jewish territory in the southern region "Judea," in reference to the former Jewish kingdom of Judah.

16. The only argument that Jesus loses in any of the canonical Gospels is in Matthew 15:22–28 (and its parallel in Mark 7:24–30), where Jesus is depicted as confronted by a "Canaanite" woman, according to Matthew, who asks for healing for her daughter. In the Markan parallel she is identified as "Greek," from "Syrophoenicia," perhaps to identify her clearly as a "Gentile," since Syrophoenicia was outside of Jewish territory in Galilee. It is unclear whether this story implies that the woman considered herself one of the puppies ("a dog," metaphorically) or, perhaps, compares her to a "Cynic" philosopher, which is spelled similarly in Greek. However, her self-identification with "the puppies who eat the crumbs that fall from the master's table," in her plea for the healing of her daughter, leads to Jesus ultimately conceding to her request for that healing.

"Lost sheep of the house of Israel" is a much more Jewish and positive epithet for those whom Jesus invites to table fellowship with him than is "tax collectors and sinners," which Jesus's opponents use to label a similar grouping of people. The former expression is distinctively Matthean, appearing only in Matthew 10:6 and 15:24 and nowhere else in the New Testament, including, of course, nowhere in Mark's Gospel. What theological interests are presupposed here, according to Evans's reading of the story of the Canaanite woman?

17. Addressing the limited amount of material within the Gospel of Mark that does not find a parallel in either Matthew's Gospel or Luke's, advocates of the Two Gospel Hypothesis would respond that, on any hypothesis of direct literary dependence among the Synoptic Gospels, there is a "problem" of omissions of material from whatever Gospel is viewed as first from the later and, *ex hypothesi*, literarily dependent evangelists. This "problem" is minimized, of course, when Mark's Gospel is assumed to be the first of the Gospels composed, since it is the shortest of the Synoptic Gospels in overall length, even though Mark's Gospel is most often the longest of the three Synoptic Gospels within the individual pericopae that it shares with the other two. The alleged "problem of omissions" is more serious if Matthew's Gospel or Luke's Gospel is taken as the first Gospel composed, but Luke's prologue (Luke 1:1–4) would seem to make it clear that this evangelist had a number of earlier sources of which he made use, so it is unlikely that his was the first canonical Gospel to be written.

Advocates of the Two Gospel Hypothesis would respond to this "problem of omissions" in a number of ways.

(a) The "problem of omissions" may have been raised by those who presuppose that the Gospel tradition always grew by incremental gain (perhaps under the influence of Darwin's theory of evolution, once it appeared), and placing Mark's Gospel third in the order of composition of the Synoptic Gospels clearly does not conform with Darwin's theory, which never should have been applied in the field of literary criticism in any case.

(b) This problem of omissions can also be addressed if one assumes not that Mark's intention, in writing third, was to replace the Gospels of Matthew and Luke, but rather that Mark sought to introduce them. As Mark's Gospel is comparatively brief, his purpose in writing could well have been to provide a brief introduction to the Christian gospel that could be utilized as an evangelistic tool in attracting people to this relatively new religion in the Greco-Roman world. Mark's Gospel can be read aloud in about an hour. I have seen it done, even while the reader was also dramatically acting out the text.

(c) Another purpose in Mark writing a comparatively short Gospel may have been apologetic. In antiquity, ancient philosophies were criticized if the philosophy was inconsistent. On the Two Gospel Hypothesis, when only Matthew's Gospel existed, the new Christian philosophy was in little danger of being criticized for inconsistency, but once Luke's Gospel appeared, there was ample evidence that these two Gospels were at odds with each other in a number of ways. For example, compare the differing genealogies of Jesus (Matt. 1:1–17; Luke 3:23–38), or contrast the birth and infancy stories in these two Gospels. Was Jesus's birth attended by magi (Matt. 2:1–2) in a house

(2:11), or by shepherds at a manger (Luke 2:16)? Did Joseph receive messages from God related to the nativity of Jesus (Matt. 1:20–23), or was Mary the recipient of these (Luke 1:28–38)?

There are several long speeches by Jesus in Matthew's Gospel that interrupt the flow of the narrative (Matt. 5–7; 10; 13; 18; 23–25), each ending with the phrase "when Jesus had finished" (7:28; 11:1; 13:53; 19:1; 26:1). There is no long "travel narrative" in Matthew's Gospel, as there is in the Gospel of Luke (beginning at Luke 9:51 and ending somewhere in chap. 18 or 19). By eliminating such differences between the Gospels of Matthew and Luke from Mark's version of "the gospel," Mark helped to defend the new faith against attacks of inconsistency.

A shorter version of the gospel also might have been helpful. Once someone heard Mark's relatively brief version of the gospel, that person could then be directed to the longer versions of the gospel contained in the Gospels of Matthew and Luke for more details, particularly about the teachings of Jesus, which are not very prominent in Mark's Gospel, which describes one of the exorcisms accomplished by Jesus as "new teaching" (Mark 1:27).

In short, on the view of Mark's Gospel as the third of the Synoptic Gospels to have been composed on the basis of a conflation of the Gospels of Matthew and Luke, there are a number of very good ways in which Mark might have been more serviceable than the longer versions of the gospel, including serving as an introduction to them.

9

Orality and Memory Hypothesis Response

Rainer Riesner

The Necessity of a Complex Solution

The Two Source Hypothesis, the Farrer Hypothesis, and the Two Gospel Hypothesis are very ably defended by Craig Evans, Mark Goodacre, and David Peabody.[1] All three hypotheses have the charm of apparent simplicity. But, as will be shown, they are not as simple as they appear at a first glance. The fact that serious scholars hold to different hypotheses that at least partially exclude one another demands an explanation. Every hypothesis offers elucidation of some of the Synoptic phenomena and not so good or no solutions to others. Depending, for example, on what one considers the most important phenomena, one of the three hypotheses seems more appealing than the others. But if every hypothesis has some strengths and some weaknesses, it seems reasonable to look for a solution that can integrate the strengths and avoid the weaknesses as far as possible. In other words, the state of the discussion points to a complex solution of the Synoptic Problem. In the following response, the strengths and the weaknesses of the three proposed hypotheses

1. In the following, the four initial essays (including my own) are referred to only by name of author and page number.

will be briefly examined, and a complex solution will be defended with some additional arguments for further discussion.

Absolute Markan Priority?

If one had only to decide between the alternatives of Markan or Matthean priority, I would choose the former. The omission of so much Matthean material by Mark is hard to understand, and on many occasions the Matthean version could reasonably be explained as the redaction of a more primitive Markan form (Evans 28–34; Goodacre 49–51). But sometimes this explanation is not as self-evident as it seems. Some aspects of the Matthean version of the healing of the daughter of a Canaanite woman (Matt. 15:21–28) are readily understandable as a redaction of Mark 7:24–30 (Evans 34). But it is a fact that except for the rebuking word of Jesus and the answer of the woman (Matt. 15:26–27//Mark 7:27–28), there are nearly no verbal agreements. From this observation James Dunn concludes that Matthew also knew the story in an oral parallel version.[2] Dunn's conclusion would be strengthened by reverting one of the arguments for Matthean redaction of Mark. Matthew "identifies the woman as a 'Canaanite' (15:22), which links her to the holy land and increases her eligibility for messianic blessing" (Evans 34). But in the Old Testament and in early Judaism (see *Jub.* 22:20–22), the relation of the Canaanites to the promised land is seen only in a negative way. The designation of the woman as a "Canaanite," and so as a paradigmatic pagan, is understandable within a Jewish Christian milieu. According to Burnett Hillman Streeter, the Matthean version belonged to the overlaps of Mark and the Matthean special source M.[3] For a modern commentator like Craig Keener, a Matthean special version seems to be at least possible.[4] Marie-Émile Boismard also thinks that Matthew was directly dependent not upon canonical Mark but rather upon a more archaic form.[5]

According to Luke 9:10, the feeding of the five thousand took place in the vicinity of "a city called Bethsaida." Indeed, it might be a sign of "editorial

2. James D. G. Dunn, *The Oral Gospel Tradition* (Grand Rapids: Eerdmans, 2013), 128–31, 296–97.

3. B. H. Streeter, *The Four Gospels: A Study of Origins, Treating of the Manuscript Tradition, Sources, Authorship, and Dates* (London: Macmillan, 1924), 260.

4. Craig S. Keener, *A Commentary on the Gospel of Matthew* (Grand Rapids: Eerdmans, 1999), 415.

5. M.-É. Boismard, A. Lamouille, and P. Sandevoir, *Synopse des quatre Évangiles en français: Avec parallèles des Apocryphes et des Pères*, vol. 2, *Commentaire*, 2nd ed. (Paris: Cerf, 1980), 235–36.

fatigue" that the evangelist "subsequently appears to drift into the Markan wording" that locates the feeding "'in a desert place' (Luke 9:12; cf. Mark 6:35–36)" (Goodacre 51). But in the opinion of John Nolland, "No really satisfactory [redactional] explanation has yet been offered for Luke's relocation of the feeding to Bethsaida."[6] The Lukan version not only shows strong minor agreements (see especially Matt. 14:13//Luke 9:10–11) but also, as is often to be observed, displays contact with the Johannine tradition (see John 6:2).[7] Apparently Luke knew the feeding story also in a non-Markan version, and the name of the location could have been part of it. An explanation of the minor agreements prominent in some German-speaking exegetical circles is the so-called Deutero-Mark. That is, Matthew and Luke could have used a revised form of canonical Mark. But then one has to explain why the version known and cherished by two evangelists vanished and the older, apparently deficient, form survived.

"Supporters of the Two Source Hypothesis agree that this [the minor agreements] is the most vulnerable point in their hypothesis" (Evans 40).[8] However, two other sets of observations present difficult obstacles to absolute Markan priority as well. (1) Evidence of conflation in individual Markan pericopae, as proponents of the Two Gospel Hypothesis rightly point out (Matt. 8:16–17// Mark 1:32–34//Luke 4:40–41 being a classic example) (Peabody 72).[9] Adherents of the Two Source Hypothesis rarely discuss this evidence. However, this phenomenon is explained not only by canonical Mark conflating Matthew and Luke but also by Mark combining two versions of Proto-Mark (Riesner 106–7). This solution has the advantage of not needing to explain the great omissions of material common to Matthew and Luke. This absence of the double tradition in Mark is one of the greatest problems for the Two Gospel Hypothesis (Evans 34–35; Goodacre 50). (2) The total or nearly total absence of clear Markan redactional features in Matthew and Luke (Riesner 108–10) is seldom addressed in the context of the Two Source Hypothesis. This evidence strongly speaks against a direct dependence of the two Gospels upon canonical Mark. That canonical Mark often (or sometimes) seems to present

---

6. John Nolland, *Luke 1–9:20*, WBC 35A (Dallas: Word, 1989), 440.

7. See Tim Schramm, *Der Markus-Stoff bei Lukas: Eine literarkritische und redaktionsgeschichtliche Untersuchung*, SNTSMS 14 (Cambridge: Cambridge University Press, 1971), 129–30. For a Jesus tradition in John independent of the Synoptics, see Paul N. Anderson, *The Riddles of the Fourth Gospel: An Introduction to John* (Minneapolis: Fortress, 2011).

8. See Richard Vinson, "How Minor? Assessing the Significance of the Minor Agreements as an Argument against the Two-Source-Hypothesis," in *Questioning Q: A Multidimensional Critique*, ed. Mark Goodacre and Nicholas Perrin (Downers Grove, IL: InterVarsity, 2004), 151–64.

9. See also Philippe Rolland, *Les premiers évangiles: Un nouveau regard sur le problème synoptique*, LD 116 (Paris: Cerf, 1984), 109–22.

a more primitive form of the tradition may be explained by his closer following of a version (or versions) of Proto-Mark. Understood this way, we do, so to speak, have a form of relative Markan priority.

Matthew as a Source of Luke?

The Farrer Hypothesis has the charm of dispensing with the hypothetically reconstructed source Q by postulating Luke's use of Matthew. A general argument reads: The closer the degree of agreement between two works, the more likely it becomes that the two are directly related. And it is further argued: When the essays of two students show verbal agreements, then "our first instinct would be to imagine that one had copied from the other, not that both had copied from a hypothetical, unseen third source" (Goodacre 53). This might be so, but it is not necessarily so. Today students can download exemplary exegeses of New Testament texts from the internet, so it's possible for two students to copy from the same document. According to the prologue of Luke's Gospel, before him "many [had] undertaken to set down an orderly account of the events that have been fulfilled among us" (Luke 1:1). Thus one cannot exclude a priori the possibility that Matthew and Luke used another common written source besides Mark.

A further argument for direct literary dependence is presented: in "the triple tradition [material common to all three Synoptics], Matthew and Luke are never as close to each other as they are in the double tradition [the so-called Q-material], and this is true for sayings material as well as narrative" (Goodacre 53). One of the problems with this statement is that we have very little narrative material in the double tradition to make comparisons with the triple tradition. It is hard to see that the verbal agreements in the main section of the temptation of Jesus (Matt. 4:3–10//Luke 4:3–12) are greater than in the main section of the healing of the leper (Matt. 8:2–4//Mark 1:40–44//Luke 5:12b–14) or the call of Levi (Matt. 9:9–13//Mark 2:14–17//Luke 5:27–32). Besides that, about half of the agreements between Matthew and Luke in the temptation narrative consist of Old Testament citations. The story about the centurion of Capernaum in Matthew 8:5–13 is told in about 165 words, the version in Luke 7:1–10 in about 187 words. They have about 68 words in common, which is not a very impressive ratio. All verbal agreements, except four at the beginning, are concentrated in the very picturesque question of the centurion and the short answer of Jesus (Matt. 8:8–10//Luke 7:6b–9). We see the same phenomenon in the triple tradition, where memorable sayings are retained in greater agreement than the surrounding narrative. This phenomenon has its origin in the phase of oral tradition. It is not even true that the sayings in the Q material are always in closer verbal agreement than sayings in the triple tradition (see below).

To make the Farrer Hypothesis probable, it must be shown that Luke derived the material held in common with Matthew directly from this Gospel (Goodacre 51–58). In this way it is possible to give some explanation for the minor agreements (Goodacre 54–56; Peabody 80–82). But is it so obvious that Luke used Matthew and not vice versa, as Martin Hengel has claimed?[10] Let us look at the story of the centurion of Capernaum. The Farrer Hypothesis and the Two Gospel Hypothesis must assume that about half of the Lukan version was created by the evangelist construing a double delegation of friendly Jews pleading for the pagan officer (Luke 7:3–6). But we also have here another agreement between Luke and the Johannine tradition in that the healing is from a distance (see John 4:46–53). Apparently there existed at least one other non-Matthean version of the story. Furthermore, it is hard to explain why Luke, who was so interested in the Gentile mission, would have omitted the logion about those "coming from east and west" in Matthew 8:11–12 (Evans 41–42). On the other hand, it would be understandable that Matthew, who was so critical of the Jewish leaders of his time (see Matt. 23), abbreviated the story by leaving out the double delegation but inserted the warning logion.

The parable of the talents (Matt. 25:14–30) or pounds (Luke 19:11–27) is presented as one of the best examples for Luke using and revising Matthew (Goodacre 57). The Matthean version has 301 words, and Luke's version has 281. They have only about 60 words in common, and this is not untypical. As Klyne R. Snodgrass remarks, "Much greater similarity exists in parables of the triple tradition than in parables common to Matthew and Luke. Whereas the former tend to be very close, the dissimilarity in some of the double tradition parables is sufficient to question whether one is dealing with the same account."[11] One need not go so far as Snodgrass and opt for two different parables of the talents/pounds. The development of an original parable into two different directions in the early tradition seems an easier explanation than an elaborate Lukan redaction of Matthew.[12]

Two other observations speak strongly against the assumption that Luke used Matthew. (1) Some omissions of Matthean material—like the parable

10. Martin Hengel, *The Four Gospels and the One Gospel of Jesus Christ: An Investigation of the Collection and Origin of the Canonical Gospels*, trans. John Bowden (Harrisburg, PA: Trinity Press International, 2000), 169–207.

11. Klyne R. Snodgrass, *Stories with Intent: A Comprehensive Guide to the Parables of Jesus* (Grand Rapids: Eerdmans, 2008), 523.

12. See Dunn, *Oral Gospel Tradition*, 281.

of the laborers in the field (Matt. 20:1–16) and the story of the healing of the daughter of a Canaanite woman (Matt. 15:21–28//Mark 7:24–30)—by Luke pose a severe problem (Evans 44; Riesner 109). The last omission is also problematic within the Two Source Hypothesis. (2) Clear Matthean redactional features are absent in Luke (Riesner 109). Far more attention should be given to this phenomenon, amply demonstrated by Delbert Burkett.[13] Sometimes the belief in the discerning literary-critical capacities of Luke (and Matthew) seems to be so strong that other explanations are ignored.

"One key issue is that the very shape of Luke's Gospel resembles Matthew's in a way that may be too much to be coincidence"; but later on this is rightly relativized: "It is quite possible, of course, that Matthew and Luke independently hit on the idea of reworking Mark's Gospel in parallel fashion, structuring their Gospels by adding a prologue dealing with Jesus's birth and an epilogue dealing with his resurrection, and filling in the ministry with lots of extra teaching and other material" (Goodacre 53–54). But is there any concrete evidence that Luke took notice of Matthew 1–2? Bethlehem as Jesus's birthplace, the virginal conception, and Joseph were all known traditions outside of Matthew (see John 1:14, 45; 6:42; 7:42; 8:41). Luke did not need to know Matthew's Gospel to gain this knowledge. Is Luke 1:31, the only remarkable verbal agreement in the birth narratives, proof that the evangelist had read Matthew 1:21 (Goodacre 60–61)?

Matthew 1:21	Luke 1:31
She *will give birth to a son, and you shall call his name Jesus.*	You *will give birth to a son, and you shall call his name Jesus.*

The words in italics are a near citation of the Septuagint form of the messianic promise in Isaiah 7:14. This is very clear in Matthew, since he says explicitly that this name giving was the fulfillment of the Isaianic prophecy (Matt. 1:22–23). It is in no way astonishing that the Lukan birth narrative is also colored by this important Old Testament prophecy.

Some inner consistency appears when Michael Goulder, as a proponent of the Farrer Hypothesis and aiming to avoid hypothetical sources, sees Luke as the creative inventor of his special material.[14] Mark Goodacre does not go so far but allows for Lukan knowledge of oral traditions. This is also his explanation for when Luke sometimes seems to be more original than Mat-

13. Delbert Burkett, *Rethinking the Gospel Sources*, vol. 1, *From Proto-Mark to Mark* (London: T&T Clark International, 2004), 43–59.

14. Michael Goulder, *Luke: A New Paradigm*, 2 vols., JSNTSup 20 (Sheffield: JSOT Press, 1989).

thew. He cites as examples the Lord's Prayer (Matt. 6:9–13//Luke 11:2–4) and Jesus's words during the Last Supper (Matt. 26:26–29//Mark 14:22–25//Luke 22:14–20) (Goodacre 64–65). However, far more examples than these two liturgical texts show Lukan originality as greater than Matthew's (Evans 43–44). The Lukan special tradition, comprising about half of his Gospel, has some characteristic linguistic features,[15] including Hebraisms,[16] and a Judean local coloring that provides coherence from the birth narrative to the passion and resurrection story.[17] These characteristics distinguish this special tradition from Luke's own style as it can be seen especially in the second half of the Acts of the Apostles. The sheer size of the Lukan special tradition makes a written Proto-Luke probable, as does Luke's compositional technique. He inserted Markan-like materials in blocks into his special tradition.[18] This shows that canonical Mark was not the first to create a historical framework for the Jesus tradition. The similarity between these two frameworks can be explained in two ways: (1) by a historical framework already in the oral tradition, or (2) by influence of a Proto-Mark. Neither of these explanations excludes the other. The characteristic features of the Lukan special tradition can also be detected in Luke's triple and double tradition. Apparently there were many overlaps between the different streams of the Jesus tradition (Riesner 110).

The Q Hypothesis

If the material common to Matthew and Luke cannot be satisfactorily explained by Luke's use of Matthew, then is the Q hypothesis in its conventional form the only explanation? Its problems include the strong variations in verbal agreement between Matthew and Luke in the double tradition.[19] This evidence goes against a uniform written source, and so, even for some supporters of

---

15. See Joachim Jeremias, *Die Sprache des Lukasevangeliums: Redaktion und Tradition im Nicht-Markusstoff des dritten Evangeliums*, KEK (Göttingen: Vandenhoeck & Ruprecht, 1980).

16. See James R. Edwards, *The Hebrew Gospel and the Development of the Synoptic Tradition* (Grand Rapids: Eerdmans, 2009). See also R. Steven Notley, Marc Turnage, and Brian Becker, *Jesus' Last Week: Jerusalem Studies in the Synoptic Gospels*, vol. 1 (Leiden: Brill, 2006), esp. 7–11, 257–317.

17. See Rainer Riesner, "Luke's Special Tradition and the Question of a Hebrew Gospel Source," *Mishkan* 20, no. 1 (1994): 44–52.

18. See D. A. Carson and Douglas J. Moo, *An Introduction to the New Testament* (Grand Rapids: Zondervan, 2005), 212–14.

19. See the statistics in Armin D. Baum, *Der mündliche Faktor und seine Bedeutung für die synoptische Frage: Analogien aus der antiken Literatur, der Experimentalpsychologie, der Oral Poetry-Forschung und dem rabbinischen Traditionswesen*, TANZ 49 (Tübingen: Francke, 2008), 428–30.

Q, it is understood as only a relatively fixed stratum of oral tradition. In the double tradition of Matthew and Luke, a series of pericopae with a unified order, shared stylistic features, and strong verbal agreements is seen to speak for an underlying written source.[20] Yet variations of wording in the double tradition may be explained by the overlapping with other traditions or sources.

It is another question whether Q was purely a source of sayings of Jesus, as most proponents believe. The *Gospel of Thomas* should not be adduced as a parallel because it uses the Synoptics in a gnosticizing way (Goodacre 58n13; Riesner 108). Stephen Hultgren has made two relevant observations: there are narrative elements in the double tradition, and it is likely "that Matthew and Luke had access to common, non-Markan narrative material in their passion narratives."[21] These observations strengthen the possibility that Q should be expanded as a source containing traditions beginning from John the Baptist and Jesus's temptation through a Galilean ministry to his passion in Jerusalem.[22] To this source could belong not only the widely accepted Mark-Q overlaps but also other texts of the triple tradition with strong minor agreements (Riesner 110).

Matthew and Luke as Sources of Mark?

As noted above, the absence in Mark of most of the words of Jesus contained in Matthew and Luke is an Achilles' heel of the Two Gospel Hypothesis. Could the fact that in Matthew the Sermon on the Mount is Jesus's first great sermon (Matt. 5:1–7:27), whereas in Luke the Sermon on the Plain (Luke 6:20–7:1) is preceded by a synagogue sermon in Nazareth (Luke 4:16–30), really explain why Mark left out even the logia common to both other evangelists (Peabody 73)? Is it possible to find a plausible historical scenario for such a redactional process? The existence of two Gospels, Matthew and Luke, with a large amount of logia material shows the great interest in the verbal teaching of Jesus. Do we know of a later situation when such an interest vanished? Also the exclusion of some narrative material common to Matthew and Luke seems to be erratic. The versions of the temptation of Jesus in Matthew 4:1–11 and Luke 4:1–13 have the same content and show some verbal agreements. But

20. See Delbert Burkett, *Rethinking the Gospel Sources*, vol. 2, *The Unity and Plurality of Q*, SBLECL 1 (Atlanta: Society of Biblical Literature, 2009).

21. Stephen Hultgren, *Narrative Elements in the Double Tradition: A Study of Their Place within the Framework of the Gospel Narrative*, BZNW 113 (Berlin: de Gruyter, 2002), 309.

22. See Eric Franklin, "A Passion Narrative for Q?," in *Understanding, Studying and Reading: New Testament Essays in Honour of John Ashton*, ed. Christopher Rowland and Crispin H. T. Fletcher-Louis, JSNTSup 153 (Sheffield: Sheffield Academic Press, 1998), 30–47.

according to a commentator, who is presupposing the Two Gospel Hypothesis, it "is certainly correct in considering the brief temptation account in Mark [1:12–13] as not derived from Matthew and Luke."[23] If it were, then Mark would have replaced the clearly understandable versions of Matthew and Luke by a short account full of enigmatic apocalyptic symbolism. It seems fair to remark, "To the extent that this commentator's analysis of the tradition is on target, his results are more compatible not with Markan posteriority but with Markan priority" (Evans 29). Also hard to explain is why Mark excluded the story of the centurion of Capernaum (Matt. 8:5–13//Luke 7:1–10). It is a Roman centurion who pronounces in Mark's Roman Gospel the concluding christological confession: "Truly this man was God's Son!" (Mark 15:39).

One may also ask whether Mark always "chose to make alternating agreements with the Gospels of Matthew and Luke in terms of the order of the pericopae that Mark chose to include within his Gospel" (Peabody 72). For example, the following sequence is given as proof (here in a shortened form):

Matthew	Mark	Luke
22:41–46	12:35–37a	20:41–44
23:1–36		
	12:37b–44	21:1–4
24:1–25:30	13:1–37	21:5–36

The gray overlay indicates how Mark's order of blocks of pericopae alternates between Matthew and Luke. Upon a closer look, this alternation might be a little bit less impressive:

Matthew	Mark	Luke
22:14–46	12:35–37	20:41–44
23:6–7	12:37–40	20:45–47
	12:41–44	21:1–4
24:1–22	13:1–20	21:5–24
24:23–25	13:21–23	
24:26–28		
24:29–36	13:24–32	21:25–33

Nevertheless, there are two alternations on the level of individual pericopae: the widow's mite (Mark 12:41–44//Luke 21:1–4) and the warning against pseudoprophets (Matt. 24:23–25//Mark 13:21–23). But in the latter

23. C. S. Mann, *Mark*, AB 27 (Garden City, NY: Doubleday, 1986), 202.

case, the exclusion of the following verses Matthew 24:26–28 is astonishing. The parallels in Luke 17:23–24 and 17:37 could show that Matthew
24:26–28 combined two originally isolated logia and inserted them into a
preexisting eschatological sermon. Then one does not need to presuppose
that Mark consciously left out Matthean redaction; rather, Mark followed
a more primitive form of the apocalyptic sermon that was written down
before the Gospels, around the time of the crisis under the emperor Caligula
in 40/41 CE, as an informal tract.[24] Matthew 24:24 has inserted the adjective
"great" in the citation of Deuteronomy 13:2 that "pseudoprophets" will do
"signs and omens." Matthew had a predilection for forms of the adjective
"great," *megas* in Greek. Should we think that the parallel Mark 13:22 left
out this adjective to be closer to the Septuagint version? This lack of possible Matthean redactional features in Mark speaks against the Two Gospel
Hypothesis, and there are other striking examples of Matthean redaction
absent from Mark (Riesner 109).

The little pericope about the widow's mite is also very interesting (Mark
12:41–44//Luke 21:1–4). Marie-Émile Boismard has shown that the Markan
version is characterized by Lukan vocabulary that is astonishingly absent
in the Lukan parallel.[25] And this Lukan coloring of Mark seems not to be
by mere chance. Epiphanius of Salamis cites a version that is close to Luke
but not dependent on him (*Panarion* 60.81). Apparently there existed a version of the story that was close to but not integrated into the Lukan special
tradition. All this seems to be rather complicated, but if one pays attention
to the philological subtleties, one is led to see complex relations between the
Synoptic traditions that call for a complex overall solution.

It is argued that the Two Gospel Hypothesis is the only solution to the
Synoptic Problem that has some support in the tradition of the ancient church
(Peabody 82–87).[26] According to Eusebius, around 200 CE Clement of Al-
exandria "said that those of the Gospels comprising the genealogies were

24. See Gerd Theissen, *The Gospels in Context: Social and Political History in the Synoptic
Tradition*, trans. Linda M. Maloney (Minneapolis: Fortress, 1991), 280.

25. M.-É. Boismard, *L'Évangile de Marc: Sa préhistoire*, ÉB 26 (Paris: Gabalda, 1994), 25–28.

26. The problems of freeing oneself from the external witness of the ancient church are
shown by two new proposals regarding the Synoptic Problem that make Marcion's gospel the
source of all the canonical Gospels (contra Tertullian, *Adversus Marcionem* 4.4.3). According to
Matthias Klinghardt, *Das älteste Evangelium und die Entstehung der kanonischen Evangelien*,
2 vols., TANZ 60.1–2 (Tübingen: Francke, 2015), Marcion has preserved a proto-gospel; according to Markus Vinzent, *Marcion and the Dating of the Synoptic Gospels* (Leuven: Peeters,
2014), he was himself the creator of the first gospel. For a critique, see Otto Zwierlein, *Die
antihäretischen Evangelienprologe und die Entstehung des Neuen Testaments* (Stuttgart: Franz
Steiner Verlag, 2015), 77–83.

written before" (*Church History* 6.14.5). The Greek verb *prographō* has two possible meanings: "to write before," in a temporal sense, or "to write before (a public)." In this case, the latter sense must be preferred because the former would bring Origen in contradiction with his revered teacher Clement.[27] According to Origen, the chronological sequence of the four canonical Gospels was Matthew, Mark, Luke, and John (Eusebius, *Church History* 6.25.4–6). At the beginning of his treatise *Harmony of the Gospels*, Augustine also had this sequence (1.2.3–4), yet later he says, "Although he [Mark] agrees with Matthew in many things, he nevertheless agrees more with Luke in others. By this may be demonstrated his relating to the lion [Matthew] and the calf [Luke]" (4.10.11). It is unclear whether for Augustine this was a literary relationship or only an agreement in content. Even if he was thinking of the former possibility, this would have been only a literary-critical guess and not the handing down of an earlier tradition. Indeed, the most ancient testimony from Papias of Hierapolis (Eusebius, *Church History* 3.39.15), reaching back to the turn of the first to the second century CE, connects Mark with Peter (Riesner 106), and this "tradition of authentic Petrine material lying behind Mark fits better with an early Mark" (Evans 35).

The Founding and Ongoing Oral Tradition

All three other Synoptic theories acknowledge the existence of an oral tradition. But in one case this appears to be a mere concession (Peabody 67), and in another it seems mainly to function as an additional relief action (Goodacre 64–65). Only in the third case does the oral tradition seem to be foundational, starting from Jesus the teacher, next being mediated through the memories of the apostles and teachers, and then being incorporated into the written Gospels (Evans 36–39). The decisive role of Jesus as the teacher of his disciples, encapsulating his message in carefully formulated memorable sayings, cannot be overestimated (Riesner 99–102).[28] Furthermore, the formation and handing down of the Gospel tradition should be studied against the background of Hellenistic-Roman and Jewish education (Riesner 94–97). Many of the isolated traditions in the Synoptic Gospels would match the definition of the ancient *chreia*, "(i.e., 'useful anecdote'), in which the student memorizes small units of a master's teaching and learns how to adapt and apply them

---

27. See Stephen C. Carlson, "Clement of Alexandria on the 'Order' of the Gospels," *NTS* 47 (2001): 118–25.

28. See Rainer Riesner, "Teacher, Teaching Forms, and Styles," in *Encyclopedia of the Historical Jesus*, ed. Craig A. Evans (New York: Routledge, 2008), 624–30.

in various settings" (Evans 37).[29] The oldest extra–New Testament notice, by
Papias of Hierapolis, about the prehistory of a Gospel shows Peter himself
teaching his memories of Jesus in the form of *chreiai* (Eusebius, *Church His-tory* 3.39.15) (Riesner 104).

When writing his Gospel, Luke relied on the oral tradition as it was "handed
on to us by those who from the beginning were eyewitnesses and servants of
the word" (Luke 1:2). The use of the technical term "handing on," in Greek
paradidōmi (see 1 Cor. 11:23; 15:1–3), points to the delivering of a cultivated
tradition (Riesner 97–98). Luke's phrase shows also that this evangelist did not
belong to the third Christian generation but was nonetheless in direct contact
with members of the first generation and their memories.[30] At the beginning
of the second century CE, when all four canonical Gospels had already been
written and were known by him, Papias of Hierapolis interrogated the last
witnesses of apostolic times for oral traditions (Eusebius, *Church History*
3.39.3–4). The so-called Apostolic Fathers prior to *2 Clement* seem to cite
logia of Jesus often from oral tradition.[31] James Dunn rightly underlines that
all three Synoptics also knew Jesus traditions in oral form,[32] although he tends
to underestimate the importance of literacy and the role of writing for the
preservation of the Synoptic tradition in the first decades after Easter.[33]

Note Taking and Informal Pre-Synoptic Sources

A majority of scholars believe that Jesus traditions were first written down
in the form of Q around 50 CE. But should one postulate a phase of early
Christian abstinence from writing for the first two decades after Easter?
As Loveday Alexander remarks, "Once memory has achieved the relatively
stable form of anecdote ('reminiscence'), the initial transfer to writing can
be managed with relative ease."[34] The early and wide geographical spread
of the Jesus movement and its rapid growth were factors that promoted the

29. See Samuel Byrskog, "The Early Church as a Narrative Fellowship: An Exploratory
Study of the Performance of the *Chreia*," *TTKi* 78 (2007): 207–26.

30. See Darrell L. Bock, *Luke 1:1–9:50*, BECNT 3A (Grand Rapids: Baker, 1994), 58–59.

31. See Stephen E. Young, *Jesus Tradition in the Apostolic Fathers: Their Explicit Appeals to
the Words of Jesus in Light of Orality Studies*, WUNT 2.311 (Tübingen: Mohr Siebeck, 2011).

32. James D. G. Dunn, "Altering the Default Setting: Re-envisaging the Early Transmission
of the Jesus Tradition," in Dunn, *Oral Gospel Tradition*, 41–79.

33. See Mark Goodacre, *Thomas and the Gospels: The Case for Thomas's Familiarity with
the Synoptics* (Grand Rapids: Eerdmans, 2012), 139–42.

34. Loveday Alexander, "Memory and Tradition in the Hellenistic Schools," in *Jesus in Mem-ory: Traditions in Oral and Scribal Perspectives*, ed. Werner H. Kelber and Samuel Byrskog
(Waco: Baylor University Press, 2009), 148–49.

note taking of Jesus traditions either as personal memory aids or for use by teachers (Riesner 104–5). The proposed intermediary sources are related to known Christian personalities, groups, and community centers: Proto-Mark to John Mark and Peter; a revision of Proto-Mark for Pauline communities; another version supplemented by Galilean material for Jewish Christians in Galilee and southern Syria; a third version supplemented by the double tradition for Hellenist Jewish Christians in Phoenicia and Antioch; the special Lukan source from circles of Jesus's extended family in Jerusalem and Judea (Riesner 106–8). Also for this reconstruction, it is true "that Synoptic diagrams, like the Synoptic theories that they are modeling, are necessarily simpler than the reality that they are attempting to represent" (Goodacre 48). But a complex solution, as proposed here, might be closer to the past reality than simpler ones are.

A Necessary Methodological Demand

If the main lines of the proposed reconstruction of the transmission process and the redaction of the Synoptic Gospels are true, they demand a necessary methodological consequence. Then none of the Synoptic Gospels can be claimed as the sole or even primary source of original Jesus traditions. Every evangelist had access to several oral traditions, as is conceded at least theoretically by proponents of hypotheses of direct literary dependence between the Synoptics (Evans 44–45; Goodacre 48; Peabody 67–68), and also access to informal written sources. In one and the same pericope, all three Synoptics can be both original and secondary. A deeper analysis of individual texts confirms this rather complex situation.[35] Scholars holding to different Synoptic theories should at least agree with the methodological principle that the late John A. T. Robinson cast in the following words: "We must seek . . . to establish what is the basic form of the *synoptic* tradition, again without prejudging the priority of any particular gospel."[36]

---

35. See Guido Baltes, *Hebräisches Evangelium und synoptische Überlieferung*, WUNT 2.312 (Tübingen: Mohr Siebeck, 2012); Rainer Riesner, "The Question of the Baptist's Disciples on Fasting (Matt. 9:14–17; Mark 2:18–22; Luke 5:33–39)," in *Handbook for the Study of the Historical Jesus*, vol. 4, *Individual Studies*, ed. Tom Holmén and Stanley E. Porter (Leiden: Brill, 2011), 3305–47.

36. John A. T. Robinson, "The Parable of the Wicked Husbandmen: A Test of Synoptic Relationships," in *Twelve More New Testament Studies* (London: SCM, 1984), 22.

10

What Have We Learned regarding the Synoptic Problem, and What Do We Still Need to Learn?

Stanley E. Porter and Bryan R. Dyer

In 1961 Stephen Neill noted that in 1850 the notion of Markan priority in study of the Synoptic Problem was "little known even as a hypothesis," but that by the end of the nineteenth century it had become "one of the assured results of the critical study of the New Testament."[1] As a result, when he concluded his volume on New Testament scholarship, he could claim that "Mark is almost certainly the earliest written Gospel," and that it "is almost certain that Matthew and Luke both used Mark's Gospel," along with a "collection of the 'Sayings of Jesus,'" now usually called Q.[2] In his revised second edition of this volume, published in 1988, Tom Wright begins the chapter that he contributed to the book (and that replaced Neill's original

1. Stephen Neill, *The Interpretation of the New Testament, 1861–1961* (London: Oxford University Press, 1964), 108.
2. Ibid., 339. These statements come from the sixth and seventh positive achievements of twelve that Neill notes.

conclusion) by noting that the "first edition" of Neill's book "was scarcely off the press when there appeared a solid work, by an already distinguished American scholar, in which one of the most 'assured results' of a century of research was painstakingly dismantled, leaving (so it appeared) scarcely one stone upon another." Wright is referring to the work of William Farmer, who "argued that Mark was the last of the three synoptic Gospels to be written, that Matthew was the first, and that the consensus of opinion in favour of Marcan priority had been established as much by sophisticated theological power politics as by the actual weight of the arguments adduced."[3] Wright then goes on to trace some of the intervening discussion against and in defense of Markan priority and the view that had gained ascendance in the late nineteenth century. Twenty-five years later, we are again in a suitable place to assess where we stand in discussion of the Synoptic Problem, this time in light of four presentations of various positions held by scholars on this important issue. By way of conclusion, we will offer three types of comments: first, a brief statement of an overall perspective on the topic; second, a summary of the major points of dispute that have emerged in the course of these proposals and responses; and third, some speculative thought regarding elements for further discussion.

Overall Perspective on the Topic of the Synoptic Problem

Four major positions on the Synoptic Problem are represented in the four proposals offered in this volume. There are, however, other positions not represented in the proposals here that might have merited inclusion in another volume. Nevertheless, we believe that these four proposals probably (though one must be cautious in using such language in discussion of this issue) represent the positions held by the vast majority of scholars who have studied the issues. One of the points of disagreement within the essays—and rightly so—is what constitutes an informed opinion on these issues. Evans believes that "most New Testament scholars" hold to his position of Markan priority and Q. However, Peabody disputes this by wanting to narrow the number to those who participated in the Oxford Conference on the Synoptic Problem held in 2008. Regardless of the number considered—and the number for examination probably rests somewhere between the two, including scholars who

3. Stephen Neill and Tom Wright, *The Interpretation of the New Testament, 1861–1986*, 2nd ed. (Oxford: Oxford University Press, 1988), 360, with assessment of positive achievements 6 and 7 on pp. 362–63. He refers to William R. Farmer, *The Synoptic Problem: A Critical Analysis* (New York: Macmillan, 1964).

have considered the issues and written on the topic—there now is a legitimate diversity of opinion, with the four represented in this volume probably being the most viable and important to consider.

Even though the proponents of the respective positions sometimes seem to find it hard to understand why their position is not obvious to others, the discussion in this volume makes clear why the diversity exists. There are numerous issues where legitimate and debatable differences of opinion remain. As a result, the four positions can be further analyzed in several ways. Three of the four opinions promoted in this volume are based upon some type of Markan priority. Evans takes the now well-established view of Markan priority with Q, the so-called Two Source/Document Hypothesis. Goodacre takes the much more recently developed view of Markan priority without Q, but with Matthew using Mark and Luke using both. This is sometimes referred to as the Farrer (or Farrer-Goulder-Goodacre) Hypothesis. Both believe that the material common to Mark, Matthew, and Luke (the triple tradition) is best explained with Mark being used in some way by the others. Evans further believes that the Two Source Hypothesis is more elegant with a second definable source, Q, to answer most of the questions regarding common material between Matthew and Luke (the double tradition), while Goodacre believes that a more elegant hypothesis is not to posit a hypothetical source but rather to posit dependence among the three Gospels. Riesner's Orality and Memory Hypothesis embraces multiple independent sources and hence moves in the opposite direction, away from elegance and simplicity to complexity. He contends that memory and orality, as well as shorter written documents, must be given their rightful place, and the complex nature of the interrelationships of the sources must be taken into account, to the point that no single simplified theory can suffice (and thus leaving him open to a version of Q, as well as a type of Markan priority). The singular viewpoint in this discussion is Peabody's Two Gospel Hypothesis, which argues that Mark is not the first but rather the last Gospel, and that Mark used both Matthew, which was first, and Luke, which used Matthew. Peabody—in finding a dependency relationship between Matthew and Luke (the minor agreements), which he shares with Goodacre—also finds no need for Q. He contends that this is the only position that has widespread support from the early church, although both Evans and Riesner challenge his interpretation of some of the early sources.

As a result of this brief summary, we already see that there are larger issues at stake in discussing the Synoptic Problem than simply the priority of the Gospels known to us. The discussion also involves issues such as (1) the nature of hypothesis building—for instance, whether it is appropriate to posit and even define the parameters of a nonextant document (such as Q); (2) whether more elegant or more complex solutions are to be preferred and are more or less defensible; (3) determination of degrees of plausibility in explaining given occurrences of textual phenomena; and (4) the role of tradition in examining such a historical issue. And surely there are other issues.

Major Points of Dispute

In the course of articulating the proposals and their responses, we have seen that on some occasions similar issues have been raised by several of the proponents, while on other occasions certain issues are not addressed by all the positions.

The Historical Evidence

Peabody contends that even though Augustine at one time listed the Gospels in the order of Matthew, Mark, Luke, and John, his later considered opinion was that Mark used both Matthew and Luke (*Harmony of the Gospels* 4.10). In either case, Matthew was thought to be the first Gospel, which was the view of the church until the nineteenth century. Riesner, however, is not certain whether, even in his later view, Augustine is discussing a literary or a content relationship. Evans goes further and challenges Peabody's interpretation of the evidence from Papias, in which Peabody defends Mark's omissions or errors in relation to a posited Matthean Gospel as his source. Evans contends that taking the passages in Eusebius in their textual order (*Church History* 3.39.15, then 3.39.16) results in Mark before Matthew.

There are two questions regarding the historical evidence. The first is whether this evidence is sufficient to answer the kind of question of textual origins that we are asking, and the second is whether and to what degree the position of the early church is determinative for contemporary scholarly discussion.

Triple Tradition

The so-called triple tradition—substantive material found in all three Synoptic Gospels (not called this by Peabody, because it appears to imply a particular view of Gospel origins)—is important for all four positions. For both the Two Source and the Farrer Hypotheses, the triple tradition indicates both Markan priority and the dependence of the other two Gospels on Mark. This argument is made on the basis of the three Synoptics sharing the same ordering of material and having often identical wording in all three sources.

For both Riesner and Peabody, the triple tradition is not convincing, but for different reasons. Riesner finds it implausible that on numerous occasions both Matthew and Luke deleted Markan features, unless they used a Proto-Mark. Peabody sees an alternating pattern whereby Mark has conflated material in Matthew and Luke.

The questions concerning the triple tradition must address how one determines whether Mark is the source or the result and not simply the "middle term" between Mathew and Luke, how one best accounts for unique Markan features (such as the use of the word *palin*, "again," and whether this is deleted by the other Gospel authors or was a later Markan stylistic overlay or points to a Proto-Mark), and how one accounts for other similarities and differences among the three accounts (e.g., between Matthew and Luke if one assumes Markan priority).

Double Tradition

The so-called double tradition—substantive material found in Matthew and Luke but not in Mark (again, not referred to in this way by Peabody)—is also important for all four positions. The Farrer Hypothesis and the Two Gospel Hypothesis believe that the kinds of substantive similarities, as well as relatively minor disagreements, found in the double tradition can best be accounted for on the basis of either Luke using Matthew or Matthew using Luke, respectively. The Two Source Hypothesis attributes the double tradition to a source that Matthew and Luke used in common, the so-called Q source. Riesner believes that if one wishes to use the Q source to account for the double tradition, it must be redefined to include some narrative elements and to have contained some overlap with features of the triple tradition.

The use of the double tradition also raises a number of questions. These include the most plausible explanation of material common to Matthew and Luke in light of their own authorial tendencies, and how to account for major divergences within a similar episode for Matthew and Luke.

Minor or Major Agreements

The question for the minor agreements—those places where Matthew and Luke agree against Mark where they share material—is how major such agreements are to the discussion. Synoptic Gospel criticism has long recognized what have been called "minor agreements" where Matthew and Luke agree against Mark, and these have posed a problem for the Two Source Hypothesis. As a result, Peabody treats these—whether they include positive

changes or omissions—as major agreements, or at least as major problems
for theories of Markan priority, because for him it seems implausible that
Matthew and Luke arrived at similar changes, whether addition or omission,
without some form of dependence between them. Evans, while recognizing
the point of vulnerability for the Two Source Hypothesis, claims that they
can be accounted for on the basis of oral tradition and multiple recensions
of the Gospels.

The minor agreements raise a number of further questions for theories
addressing the Synoptic Problem. These questions touch on the extent and
nature of these minor agreements and whether they can thereby assume the
status of major problems difficult to explain, and whether explanations of
documentary relations that must then introduce theories of multiple sources
or oral tradition have provided assessable means of answering these questions.

Oral Tradition

Only one of the theories advocated in this volume makes oral tradition
a mainstay of its proposal. Riesner argues that memory and orality were
essential features of the educational environment of the ancient world. He
further contends that these features must be taken into account in examining
the Synoptic Problem, since the rest of the New Testament also indicates the
importance of an oral gospel tradition, in which Jesus was a teacher whose
sayings were retained by his followers. All the other contributors to the volume
also agree on the existence and importance of oral tradition, at least in the
pre–written Gospels stage, with Evans and Goodacre affirming its continuing relevance. Peabody is more skeptical about what can be made of such a
theory since it is difficult to assess oral tradition, and the discussion of the
Synoptic Problem is predominantly a literary or written-document problem.

In considering the role of oral tradition in solutions to the Synoptic Problem, the several questions here concern how one might quantify the role and
influence of oral tradition, and whether invoking such a category mitigates
the distinctiveness or even essence of any of the hypotheses. If the role of oral
tradition is recognized in the Two Source and Orality and Memory Hypotheses, as indicated in the essays and their responses, there may be little left to
differentiate them, as Q may end up being a predominantly oral source. These
theories then may also in some ways begin to resemble the Farrer Hypothesis,
in which the interaction of the written Gospels includes their interaction with
various oral materials, which may account for significant differences. Even
the Two Gospel Hypothesis loses some of its distinctiveness if the influence
of oral tradition grows larger.

Determining Textual Movement

All four theories regarding the Synoptic Problem are formulated around an idea of what it means that texts have relationships to other texts. The Two Source Hypothesis, as well as presumably the Farrer Hypothesis, appears to follow a developmental model in all regards, including both literary elements and theology. The Orality and Memory Hypothesis is less rigid in its use of this model, as it attempts to account for relations on the basis of the continuous influence of oral tradition. The major issue is whether such a pattern of development is justifiable in light of what we know about the use of Greek at the time and the nature of New Testament Christology. If either, or both, are not pertinent to the discussion—that is, that there is no way necessarily to determine literary dependence upon the basis of stylistic changes and that Christology was sufficiently fluid so as to have both "high" and "low" elements concurrently—then this raises a further question about how to chart lines of development between the two. The Two Gospel Hypothesis raises such questions, although it too has its own theories regarding how texts relate to one another, such as Mark drawing in alternating fashion from Matthew and then Luke.

In response, there are a number of questions to raise. These include the question of what kinds of textual features indicate borrowing, how many features are necessary and of what type to determine a clear pattern of dependence, and how other issues, such as Christology, play a role in such determinations in light of the evidence of early Christianity (e.g., Paul's high Christology, the arguably high Christology of the beginning of Mark's Gospel).

Explanations for Mark

One of the abiding issues in the discussion regarding the Synoptic Problem is how to explain Mark. On one side of the equation, the Two Source Hypothesis contends that Mark's Gospel is the most primitive, and that the other Gospels show signs of improving Mark in language, style, and even content. This perspective encompasses Evans's argument from dignity, in which undignified elements of Mark's Gospel have been reworded in the other Gospels. Even though this is not a major plank of the Farrer Hypothesis, a similar set of assumptions seems to be in place. The other two theories question elements of this assumption on the basis of features of Mark's Gospel that are said to evidence Markan redaction not present in the other two Gospels. On the other side of the equation, the Two Gospel Hypothesis contends that Mark's Gospel can be explained as the last of the Gospels written, designed as an introduction, apology, or explanation of the other Gospels.

A number of questions are raised by the attempt to examine Mark in the various perspectives represented in this volume. In some ways, the major contention revolves around how to conceive of Mark, around which the other Gospels arrange themselves. If one conceives of Mark's Gospel as only possible as an early example of early Christian writing, or if one conceives of Mark's Gospel to be explainable as the result of adapting earlier Christian Gospel material, then one's conclusions will vary widely in relation to the hypotheses presented in this volume.

These are at least some of the issues that have been raised, and raised again, within the proposals and responses within this volume. On the one hand, there is significant agreement at a number of points among the various proponents. The Two Source Hypothesis and the Farrer Hypothesis have several points in common regarding the place of Mark's Gospel within any framework for discussing the Synoptic Problem, as both of them are concerned to assert and begin with Markan priority. However, the Farrer Hypothesis and the Two Gospel Hypothesis have much in common regarding the relationship of Matthew and Luke, as both of them believe that Luke used Matthew (whether Mark was also a source or not). The Orality and Memory Hypothesis sees fluidity in all regards, as this perspective wishes to work with three independent, yet interrelated, sources, including pre-Gospel sources.

Elements for Further Discussion

In light of the foregoing discussion, we have seen that, regardless of the numbers of scholars who may or may not hold to particular viewpoints, there are at least four positions worth considering and weighing seriously. There may be reasons why various scholars and their students adopt particular viewpoints. Some of these reasons may involve evaluation of particular pieces of evidence that seem, when all is said and done, to be overwhelmingly convincing for one position or the other. Some of these reasons, however, may involve less tangible influences upon the decision-making process and be much harder to quantify or even to defend. Our hope for this volume is that it will arouse further discussion of the strengths and weaknesses of these various positions, in light of the robust defenses that each position has received from its respective proponent. We do not believe that there is a weak presentation among the four, which makes it much more difficult to decide the correctness of any given position—if only a single position is the correct answer to the Synoptic Problem.

As a result, in view of the perspectives presented, we believe that there are a number of further issues—apart from the ones raised in the section above regarding some of the major planks of the arguments presented—that merit continuing discussion.

Q

The first of these items for further discussion is the hypothetical document called "Q." There is no way to determine for certain, but it appears to be the case that the majority of New Testament scholars, whether they have studied the issues or not, believe in some form of existence of the hypothetical document Q. They may consider it as a minimal source that comprises the material common to Matthew and Luke, a sayings source, a written document, a source that contained more than just sayings but also some narrative material, a document that was more like Luke's material than Matthew's, a full-fledged written document that had gone through various recensions and could be identified with a particular community, or even a Sayings Gospel (similar in some ways to the *Gospel of Thomas*). The various views of Q attest to the status of the Two Source Hypothesis, which requires that there be such a source as Q.[4]

Within the framework of our discussion in this volume, however, there is only one theory that relies upon Q, and that is the Two Source Hypothesis. The Orality and Memory Hypothesis is willing to entertain the notion of such a thing as Q, but it would be a Q that is different from the usual conception and more open to the kinds of variances to be found within a more complex and fluid situation with multiple sources.

In other words, from what we have seen in these proposals and their responses, Markan priority and Q may have firmly established themselves as two fundamental components for solving the Synoptic Problem in the later nineteenth century and endured in some ways relatively unhindered into the mid-twentieth century. Since that time, however, other theories have tended to move away from the necessity of Q. As a result, even the Orality and Memory Hypothesis is not wedded to the necessity of Q and seems to indicate that one could explain the Synoptic Problem without having to posit a Q. The Farrer Hypothesis and the Two Gospel Hypothesis are fundamentally against Q and do everything that they can to explain Synoptic relations without it. All of

4. Major works on Q include John S. Kloppenborg, *Q, the Earliest Gospel: An Introduction to the Original Stories and Sayings of Jesus* (Louisville: Westminster John Knox, 1998); Kloppenborg, *The Formation of Q: Trajectories in Ancient Wisdom Collections*, SAC (Philadelphia: Fortress, 1987); Christopher M. Tuckett, *Q and the History of Early Christianity: Studies on Q* (Edinburgh: T&T Clark, 1996); Ronald A. Piper, ed., *The Gospel behind the Gospels: Current Studies on Q*, NovTSup 75 (Leiden: Brill, 1995).

this is occurring while development of views regarding Q and its surrounding environment continues apace.

The importance of Q for the Synoptic Problem is found in the need to explain the similarities between Matthew and Luke. The Two Source Hypothesis requires such a theory to explain the double tradition—that is, the material that Matthew and Luke have in common against Mark. As we have seen, this is not the only conceivable way to explain these similarities. Both the Farrer Hypothesis and the Two Gospel Hypothesis explain these similarities on the basis of Luke using Matthew. Both theories also are able to explain unique features of Mark, though by different means. The Farrer Hypothesis believes that these features originated in Mark and were retained either by Matthew or Luke, whereas the Two Gospel Hypothesis believes that these features were added by Mark (Markan Overlay) to either Matthew and/or Luke.

The theory of Q, regardless of the final shape that it ends up taking, probably will continue to develop, so long as some scholars believe that having a relatively independent source separate from Mark, Matthew, and Luke best accounts for the material shared by Matthew and Luke. This is opposed to a theory that shows that Matthew and Luke, or one of them alone, whether using Mark or being used by Mark, can sufficiently account for the same materials.

Oral Tradition and Its Possibilities

The wild card in the discussion at the heart of this book, as several of the contributors have pointed out and as we have already mentioned, is the role of oral tradition. In the proposals within this volume, oral tradition has a primary role to play in the Orality and Memory Hypothesis, but it is only belatedly or reluctantly included by some of the other proposals. All the contributors except for Riesner believe that the Synoptic Problem is a matter of literary dependence, although Riesner does too, to the extent that he believes that the solution rests in recognizing multiple sources in a complex relationship, even if oral tradition was involved in some way. In his history of discussion Riesner mentions the Tradition Hypothesis, essentially an oral theory hypothesis regarding the origins of the Gospels, which he attributes to Brooke Foss Westcott and traces through a number of more recent scholars.[5] To date within the contemporary environment of Synoptic studies, their theories have not garnered significant adoption. In other words, the nature of the Synoptic Problem has remained a literary problem rather than becoming a problem of oral tradition and oral transmission.

---

5. Brooke Foss Westcott, *An Introduction to the Study of the Gospels*, 8th ed. (London: Macmillan, 1895), 165–212.

If there were to come a time when scholars became convinced that the usual literary hypotheses were untenable, or even that they could offer nothing further to the discussion, there may be an increase in attention to the Tradition Hypothesis or oral theory. We already see this, at least to some degree, in the proposal of Riesner, with his drawing upon the work of the Scandinavian school (Harald Riesenfeld, Birger Gerhardsson, and Samuel Byrskog).[6] One of the strengths of the three other hypotheses that we have seen, however, is that they are theories of literary dependence and thus involve the examination of written sources, so far as we have them. The examination of oral traditions, by definition, is far more difficult—some might even say impossible for the ancient world. Nevertheless, if, as most of the contributors recognize, oral tradition was an integral part of the equation from the start, then it appears that more needs to be done to consider what role oral tradition might play in attempting to answer the question of the origins of the Synoptic Gospels.

There are several different ways forward that might merit attention. One way is to pay more attention to modern oral cultures and attempt to interpret how their demonstrable orality may relate to the ancients and their practices. A second way is to explore more fully the relationship between orality and literacy, in both modern and ancient contexts. The growing interest in the relationship between orality and literacy in modern scholarship has tended to dissolve the traditional divide between the two and has shown that they may have more in common than separates them. One of the areas of further exploration might include the notion of secondary orality, in which written texts become oral texts again. There is growing thought that this scenario, originally devised for discussion of modern literacy, is true of the ancient world as well. A third way is to attempt to define legitimate means of determining signs of orality within written documents. This would require development of more sophisticated linguistic tools than have traditionally been used to examine the question of the Synoptic relationships.[7] There are other possibilities as

6. Harald Riesenfeld, *The Gospel Tradition: Essays*, trans. E. Margaret Rowley and Robert A. Kraft (Oxford: Blackwell, 1970); Birger Gerhardsson, *Memory and Manuscript: Oral Tradition and Written Transmission in Rabbinic Judaism and Early Christianity* [1961]; *with, Tradition and Transmission in Early Christianity* [1964], trans. Eric J. Sharp, BRS (Grand Rapids: Eerdmans, 1998); Gerhardsson, *The Reliability of the Gospel Tradition* (Peabody, MA: Hendrickson, 2001); Samuel Byrskog, *Story as History—History as Story: The Gospel Tradition in the Context of Ancient Oral History*, WUNT 123 (Tübingen: Mohr Siebeck, 2000).

7. Major sources that address some of these issues include Douglas Biber, *Variation across Speech and Writing* (Cambridge: Cambridge University Press, 1988); Ruth Finnegan, *Oral Poetry: Its Nature, Significance, and Social Context* (Cambridge: Cambridge University Press, 1977); Finnegan, *Literacy and Orality: Studies in the Technology of Communication* (Oxford:

well that might lead to transcending both the perceived disjunction between orality and literacy and, perhaps more importantly, the inherent encumbrance that we do not have oral sources from the ancient world for examination, but have only written sources that themselves must provide our access to an oral tradition.

Has a Stalemate Been Reached?

At the beginning of this concluding essay, as well as in conjunction with Riesner's survey of the history of discussion of orality in Synoptic research, we noted that the Two Source Hypothesis emerged in the late nineteenth century as the predominant theory of Gospel origins. That position is ably and forcefully propounded by Evans in this volume, with some noteworthy personal arguments developed by him to divert standard criticisms of this position (e.g., discussion of Markan dignity). Nevertheless, this position has come under attack on several fronts. In some ways, the oldest attack is by the Orality and Memory Hypothesis, which also dates back to the nineteenth century and has continued to be promoted up to the present, even if it has not commanded nearly as much widespread assent as the now-standard theory of Markan priority and Q. Although in a revived form, the Two Gospel Hypothesis dates back at least to Johann Griesbach, if not earlier to Augustine (a debated point, as the essays and responses make clear), and has had a renewal in more recent work by William Farmer (the scholar mentioned at the outset of this essay) and a number of his students (including Peabody) and his followers. The Farrer Hypothesis, though perhaps argued in an earlier form by others (e.g., E. W. Lummis), is dated to the 1955 essay about dispensing with Q by Austin Farrer, even if developed much more rigorously by Michael Goulder and then Goodacre himself, as Goodacre's essay makes clear.[8] By any reckoning, there have been at least these four theories of the Synoptic Problem on the table for consideration for a minimum of fifty years and quite possibly a minimum of one hundred years, if not far

---

Blackwell, 1988); John Miles Foley, *The Theory of Oral Composition: History and Methodology*, Folkloristics (Bloomington: Indiana University Press, 1988); Jack Goody, *The Logic of Writing and the Organization of Society*, SLFCS (Cambridge: Cambridge University Press, 1986); Albert Bates Lord, *The Singer of Tales*, HSCL 24 (Cambridge, MA: Harvard University Press, 1960); Lord, *Epic Singers and Oral Tradition*, MP (Ithaca, NY: Cornell University Press, 1991); Walter J. Ong, *Orality and Literacy: The Technologizing of the Word*, NA (London: Methuen, 1982); Rosalind Thomas, *Literacy and Orality in Ancient Greece*, KTAH (Cambridge: Cambridge University Press, 1992).

8. See Austin Farrer, "On Dispensing with Q," in *Studies in the Gospels: Essays in Memory of R. H. Lightfoot*, ed. D. E. Nineham (Oxford: Blackwell, 1955), 55–88; Michael Goulder, *Luke: A New Paradigm*, 2 vols., JSNTSup 20 (Sheffield: JSOT Press, 1989).

longer for at least some of them. And yet we are still seriously debating the fundamental plausibility of the various proposals, with most of the essential arguments being the same ones that have been used over and over during this same period of time.

This situation raises the question of whether we have reached a stalemate in the study of the Synoptic Problem. In other words, after using the same arguments that have been used over the last fifty or more years regarding these issues, what are the results of such debate? One or more of the positions may claim to be making progress in relation to the other, and no doubt there are strong advocates of each position who perceive that their arguments are beginning to have an effect and to convince others to join their ranks. Those of the other positions are no doubt less inclined to see such positive results from others' apologetic efforts. This situation brings us back to the question of whether we have reached a stalemate in the study of the Synoptic Problem.

Our answer to this question is both yes and no. On the one hand, we indeed do observe that many of the same arguments are repeatedly made on behalf of the positions represented in this volume. We believe that this volume contains exemplary presentations of the arguments for each of the positions represented, with the added feature of direct response by the various participants to the arguments of the others. Nevertheless, the arguments have been made before, even if not made as cogently as found here. The lines are still starkly and strongly drawn. On the other hand, we are optimistic that the impasse is not unbreachable. We believe that there is still potential for further developments in the discussion of the Synoptic Problem. We are encouraged to think that this volume may play a role in such discussion by offering some new insights to those familiar with the discussion and inciting new ideas in those perhaps fresh to the topic. In any case, we are convinced that the way forward involves the development of new means of presenting the arguments, assessing the evidence both old and new, and creating scenarios that account for the ways in which the Gospels are related to one another. Some recent scholarship has hinted that discussion of John's Gospel (usually excluded from treatment of the Synoptic Problem) in relation to the other Gospels may offer a next stage in any continuing examination of the issues, in an attempt to provide an inclusive view of the relations among all the Gospels. We do not know what form any new developments will take, but we are firm in our belief that such progressive discussions are necessary—not merely to provide convincing arguments for others but also to provide more sophisticated and developed arguments that will push the discussion forward.

Conclusion

We thus conclude this volume, not with a conclusion in the sense of a final word, but with a conclusion in the sense of having reached a point in the ongoing discussion in which the major positions have been articulated, and it is now time to pause and take stock of the situation. The major positions have been articulated and responded to, in each case by a major proponent of the positions represented. The issues represented are not easily assessed and decided, and any attempt to establish or assert a consensus probably is misguided at this stage in the history of scholarship. We thank our contributors not only for their individual essays and responses but also for raising once more, and in such clear fashion, the fundamental issues in treatment of the relations among the Synoptic Gospels. As editors of this volume, we will be content if its essays, including the introduction and the conclusion as attempts to frame the issues, make a useful contribution to a continuing discussion in what remains one of the central issues in New Testament studies: the Synoptic Problem.

Glossary

double tradition: Material that is found in both Matthew's and Luke's Gospels but is absent from Mark's.

external evidence: Data found outside of the Gospel texts used for an argument regarding the Synoptic Problem.

Farrer Hypothesis: Proposed solution to the Synoptic Problem that maintains that Mark's Gospel was written first, that Matthew used Mark's Gospel when writing second, and that Luke had access to both previous Gospels when writing third. Named after its major proposer, Austin Farrer.

form criticism: A type of biblical criticism that identifies units of texts by literary pattern and attempts to tie them to oral conventions and contexts.

Griesbach Hypothesis: Proposed solution to the Synoptic Problem that maintains that Matthew's Gospel was written first, followed by Luke, and then Mark (who had access to both earlier Gospels). Named after its major proposer, J. J. Griesbach.

harmonization: The attempt to reconcile seeming contradictions in the Gospels by arguing that the Gospel writers are describing separate events or different aspects of a single event.

harmony: A document or interpretation that compiles multiple Gospel material into a single account.

internal evidence: Data found within the texts of the Gospels used for an argument regarding the Synoptic Problem.

literary dependence: The argument that the relationship between material found in two or more Gospels is on a written or literary level, as opposed to dependence upon oral or eyewitness accounts.

Markan Overlay: Used by proponents of the Two Gospel Hypothesis to refer to literarily unifying material found in Mark's Gospel that, after conflating material found in the previous Gospel accounts, ties the third Gospel together.

Markan priority: Shorthand term for the argument that Mark's Gospel was the first to be written.

Matthean priority: Shorthand term for the argument that Matthew's Gospel was the first to be written.

minor agreements: Places in Matthew's and Luke's Gospels in which material is similar or in agreement against Mark's Gospel.

oral tradition: Tradition that is passed on orally as opposed to being put into writing.

pericope: A collection of verses that form a contained unit in a text.

Q: Used by proponents of the Two Source Hypothesis to refer to material common to Matthew and Luke, possibly indicating a common source (now lost) used by both Matthew and Luke in composing their Gospels. Taken from the German word for "source" (*Quelle*).

Special Luke (L): Material that is found only in Luke's Gospel.

Special Matthew (M): Material that is found only in Matthew's Gospel.

synopsis: The presentation of parallel Gospel texts side by side in vertical columns in order to compare and contrast the individual accounts.

Synoptic Gospels: The first three Gospels in the New Testament, which are noted for their similarities in content, narrative sequence, and wording, and as such stand apart from the Gospel of John.

Synoptic Problem: The inquiry into the relationship among the Synoptic Gospels, usually on a literary level.

Tradition Hypothesis: Proposed solution to the Synoptic Problem that maintains that the relationship among the Synoptic Gospels can be explained purely by their incorporation of oral traditions or sources.

triple tradition: Material or stories that appear in all three Synoptic Gospels.

Two Gospel Hypothesis: Proposed solution to the Synoptic Problem that builds upon the Griesbach Hypothesis, arguing that Matthew used several sources to write the earliest Gospel, that Luke used Matthew's Gospel, and that Mark used both of the previous Gospels in his composition.

Two Source Hypothesis: Proposed solution to the Synoptic Problem that maintains that Mark's Gospel was the first written and was used alongside another source (Q) by both Matthew and Luke.

Contributors

Bryan R. Dyer (PhD, McMaster Divinity College) is the New Testament acquisitions editor at Baker Academic in Grand Rapids, Michigan.

Craig A. Evans (PhD, Claremont Graduate University) is the John Bisagno Distinguished Professor of Christian Origins and Dean of the School of Christian Thought at Houston Baptist University in Houston, Texas.

Mark Goodacre (DPhil, University of Oxford) is Professor of New Testament and Christian Origins in the Department of Religious Studies at Duke University in Durham, North Carolina.

David Barrett Peabody (PhD, Southern Methodist University) is Professor of Religion at Nebraska Wesleyan University in Lincoln, Nebraska.

Stanley E. Porter (PhD, University of Sheffield) is President, Dean, and Professor of New Testament and holds the Roy A. Hope Chair in Christian Worldview at McMaster Divinity College in Hamilton, Ontario.

Rainer Riesner (PhD, University of Tübingen) is Professor Emeritus at Dortmund University in Germany.

Index of Authors
and Subjects

Index of Scripture
and Other Ancient Sources